CRINGEWORTHY

CRINGEWORTHY

A THEORY OF AWKWARDNESS

Melissa Dahl

PORTFOLIO/PENGUIN

Portfolio/Penguin
An imprint of Penguin Random House LLC
375 Hudson Street
New York, New York 10014

Most Portfolio books are available at a discount when purchased in quantity
for sales promotions or corporate use. Special editions, which include personalized covers, excerpts, and corporate imprints, can be created when purchased in large quantities. For more information, please call (212) 572-2232
or e-mail specialmarkets@penguinrandomhouse.com. Your local bookstore
can also assist with discounted bulk purchases using the Penguin Random
House corporate Business-to-Business program. For assistance in locating a
participating retailer, e-mail B2B@penguinrandomhouse.com.

ISBN: 9780735211636 (hardcover)
ISBN: 9780735211643 (e-book)
ISBN: 9780525536420 (international edition)

Printed in the United States of America
10 9 8 7 6 5 4 3 2 1

Book design by Daniel Lagin

For Dodie Potthoff

How embarrassing to be human.

—Kurt Vonnegut, *Hocus Pocus*

CONTENTS

CONTENTS

CRINGEWORTHY

CHAPTER 1

The Awkward Age, Part 1

How come no one here likes Hanson?!!" I exclaim weakly. I'm reading aloud from a small spiral-bound notebook—dark neon purple with multicolored swirls and stars—purchased for $6.99 at a Claire's in 1997. It is my seventh-grade journal, and I'm reading it now, twenty years later, to three people I only met this morning. "I've been getting pictures of them off the Internet almost all day today and they're *so cute!* How could anyone *not* like them?"

I stop and look up from the journal. "I feel like I should note that every time I write 'to,' it's the number and not the word," I say to my audience. All four of us are seated in armchairs near the bar at Littlefield, a performance venue in Brooklyn. Before today, I've only been here at night, and it's a little disorienting to see it in the muted light of a sunny January afternoon, though this is by far the least surreal aspect of what's happening right now.

The three strangers listening to me read are Stephen Chupaska, a bespectacled man with floppy brown hair and a skinny scarf, both of which he has a habit of tossing back with a flourish; Christina Galante, a woman with a wry smile and animated eyes who is taking notes on a laptop as I speak; and John Dorcic, an affable, extroverted guy with a neatly groomed goatee. They are producers for the New York City branch of *Mortified*, a live show in which performers read from their teenage diaries. Onstage. In front of hundreds of people. I think I've had a version of that nightmare before, but in it I was only physically naked, not emotionally so.

This is my "audition" for a spot in the show later this year, and I feel like I'm maybe blowing it. The word "audition" is in quotes because I've been instructed by Dave Nadelberg, the creator of *Mortified*, not to call it that. It isn't one, not really, because anyone brave enough to volunteer to be in this show is welcome to participate, provided they have enough material they created during their teenage years for a ten-minute piece. But I'm skeptical about my chances. I've spent the last two hours sitting in on a "curating session," to use Nadelberg's preferred term, and I'm in awe of the people I've seen already today. True, a lot of it's been silly. One guy ended every journal entry with a detailed description of everything he wore and everything he ate that day, plus a signature daily sign-off: "PEACE, one love." But most of what I've heard today has suggested the beginnings of some real artistic talent. Earlier this morning, a woman read poetry she wrote in high school, which Galante, the show's lead producer, rejected *because it was too good*. I do not expect to encounter that problem.

At my " '2,' not 'to' " explanation, the three producers nod politely, then indicate that I should keep going. I take a shaky breath and continue reading the March 7, 1998, entry, cringing harder with every word. "What am I gonna do? I have to call long distance if I want to talk about Hanson!"

I pause again. It's an unseasonably warm day, but somehow I don't think that's why I'm sweating. "This is so ridiculous," I say. "None of this seems usable. Is any of this usable? I just—I don't want to waste your time, and I really respect the show and what you guys do—"

Galante cuts me off. "We won't know if it's usable unless you keep going," she says, raising her eyebrows at me over her laptop.

Later all three of them will swear I'm the most tense, tight-lipped participant they've ever had. I start reading an entry and then decide it's too stupid to keep going, so I flip ahead and try another, only to abandon that one just as quickly. I stammer, I blush, I start sweating so much I have to remove the olive-green jacket I'm wearing, though it's too late—there are telltale wet spots under the arms, two large circles now colored a slightly darker olive green. *You idiot*, I think. *Wearing dark colors to hide nervous underarm sweat was something you came up with* in middle school. *The kid who wrote this diary is smarter than you.*

But in my own defense, it makes sense that I'm more hesitant than a typical *Mortified* performer. I'm *not* a performer. It's not like I'm auditioning because I'm dying to read my middle-school journal in front of hundreds of strangers; even just these three are a little much for me. I'm only doing this for research.

BY THE TIME I AUDITION FOR *MORTIFIED*, I'VE BEEN OFFI-cially studying awkwardness for the better part of two years; unofficially, for the better part of three decades. (They do say to write what you know.) Most of us went through an awkward stage, and I am no exception. I had a somewhat unique experience growing up in that my family moved every two years or so, which meant the second I got the hang of *cool* at one school, we'd leave for another town, and usually another state. Awkward moments inevitably ensued every time I had to play the new kid, and I quickly learned that what is acceptable at one school will be roundly mocked at another. You could love Hanson in Nashville in 1998, but in Chicago you'd better learn to like the Backstreet Boys. You could wear *Clueless*-style kneesocks in southern Louisiana in the early 2000s, but in northern California you'd be side-eyed for clinging to a passé trend. Every young person is hyperaware of social rules, but learning different ones over and over as I grew up made me even more sensitive to moments that deviate from the norm. And perhaps more prone to causing them.

Anybody who writes for a living ends up writing what they know, whether they mean to or not, but the truism tends to be rather literal when your subject is psychology, a field I've reported on for the last ten years. "The best thing about this job," an old boss used to say to me, "is that we don't just get to ask interesting questions. We get to find the answers too." She and I shared a predilection for oddball queries about the human experience: Why do so many of us hate the sound of our own voices? Why does remembering something stupid I said or did *years* ago still make me blush today? And what could possibly be the point of feeling embarrassed on behalf of people I'll never meet—like the cast and crew of *La La Land* when they accepted the Best Picture Academy Award (which actually belonged to *Moonlight*)? In these cases, my former manager's words turn out to be only half true. They are interesting questions, but I couldn't find a satisfying answer to explain why each of these things made me cringe; nothing like a Unified Theory of Awkwardness appeared to exist in the scientific literature. And so I set out to create my own.

But here's a journalism tip for you: Don't just trust your own instincts. Consult the experts. In this case, I've taken care to interview the people who know the subject best. Some scientists and philosophers, for example, have devoted their daily lives to the study of emotions like happiness, or envy, or guilt, or boredom. For my research I needed to talk to the people who spend their days investigating what it means—indeed, how it *feels*—to cringe, to experience the physical, visceral tightening in your gut and the flush in your cheeks and the sweat on your palms and the panic in your heart when you've totally, utterly embarrassed yourself.

Which means, obviously, that I consulted middle schoolers.

A handful of twelve- and thirteen-year-olds from northern California and central Minnesota were nice enough to answer what increasingly felt to me, as I spoke with them, like cringeworthy questions from a weird adult. One of the things I asked them was to define what "awkward" meant to them. Here are a few of my favorites, taken from conversations, e-mails, or texts:

Awkwardness is when no one is talking.

It's when you don't know what to do.

Awkwardness is a feeling of being uncomfortable. Where you are often left speechless or unable to speak. You are going to want to get out of that place as quick as you can.

Their definitions highlighted their unease when navigating ambiguous situations, and the discomfort that results when someone deviates from the norm. And they're right, of course; no one knows awkward like a middle schooler. But I'm not sure that entirely captures the feeling.

We expect a lot out of "awkward" these days; the word has become a catchall term for any situation that makes us uneasy, whether trivial or serious. Not long ago I was at a small gathering at a friend's apartment when one woman started telling the rest of us that her fiancé's brother had recently come out—but only to her. No one else in the family knew he was gay, including her fiancé. "It's just so *awkward*," she kept saying. "I just feel so awkward around them now." But things can also be "adorably awkward," a phrase *BuzzFeed* has used to headline stories describing puppies, first-kiss stories, and childhood photos of Miley Cyrus. Sex can be awkward. Work can be too, but you knew that if you've had either a job or a television in the last decade or so. Recently I came across a board game called Awkward Moment at Work, which offers a welcome reverse from reality in that the most socially inept employee *wins*.

But I've been struck lately by how often the feeling is asked to shoulder considerably more weight. Some disability rights advo-cates have argued in a long-running ad campaign called "End the Awkward" that able-bodied people feel so uncomfortable around disabled people that many of them choose to simply avoid disabled people whenever possible. In late 2016 the *New York Times* pub-lished a short video titled "Why We're Awkward," which turns out to be because of racial bias. The comedian W. Kamau Bell has for years encouraged Americans to have more "awkward conversa-tions," which for him are typically discussions of consequential but sensitive subjects like racism or sexism. Bell's technique is gentler than many typical examples of online "call-out culture," a term for the practice of publicly shaming people on social media for their offensive language or behavior, and yet those advocating for these kinds of intense and sometimes callous confrontations often use the same word that Bell does, encouraging one another to #MakeItAwkward.

Have you ever repeated a word so often that it loses its mean-ing? I wonder sometimes whether we've done that to "awkward." How can this one word be used to describe the way you feel when a relative says something sexist at Thanksgiving, and when nego-tiating a raise at work, *and* when you accidentally "like" an old photo when you're sixteen weeks deep into an acquaintance's Instagram feed? Part of my challenge in studying the emotion was properly defining it.

To me, awkwardness is self-consciousness tinged with uncer-tainty, in moments both trivial and serious. In its Middle English usage, "awkward" meant something like "wrong-ward" or "turned in the wrong direction," which in my college years was frequently represented by the Awkward Turtle: You placed one hand on top of the other and circled your thumbs around, and the whole thing was meant to look like an upside-down turtle who has bumbled his way into an uncomfortable yet inescapable situation. Any mildly uncomfortable event was deemed awkward and an occasion for the Awkward Turtle. Late to class? *Awk-warrrd!* Run into an ex at the bar? *Awk-warrrd!* In retrospect, talk about cringeworthy.

The turtle hand sign was a silly, jokey way to lighten the tension of a mildly tense interaction, something you could do when words failed you. The legacy of this understanding is that awkwardness is mostly characterized as silly and insignificant, and so it can seem inadequate to apply the word to matters of greater consequence. But I think it's a feeling that's worth taking much more seriously than we often do. It's an alert system, letting you know when something's gone wrong. The alarm sounds in those moments when you don't know what to say to a friend whose father has just died; or when you are desperately trying to avoid offending someone when talking about race or class; or when you find yourself in smaller but still emotionally fraught instances—say, when you're trying to work up the nerve to see whether a work friend could possibly become a real friend by asking her to drinks. All of these are moments in which you risk revealing too much of yourself, whether it's your ignorance or your earnestness or your simple lack of basic social graces.

If awkwardness sounds the alarm, *cringing* is what happens when it goes off. It's the intense visceral reaction produced by an awkward moment, an unpleasant kind of self-recognition where you suddenly see yourself through someone else's eyes. It's a forced moment of self-awareness, and it usually makes you cognizant of the disappointing fact that you aren't measuring up to your own self-concept. The alarm sounds, and the cringe tells you to *abort, abort, abort*, and so usually you do. You say nothing to your grieving friend. You don't even try to challenge your own thoughts or beliefs about issues of social consequence. You go home instead of going to happy hour.

That's the meaning that we've assigned to cringing, anyway, but is it true, necessarily? It's so hard to look at yourself from someone else's point of view when it means taking in the ways you're not measuring up to your own sense of self. But if you can stand it, seeing yourself through someone else's eyes can help you move a little closer toward becoming the person you wish you were. "If we are not regularly deeply embarrassed by who we are," the philosopher Alain de Botton has written, "the journey to self-knowledge hasn't begun." Try to see the world every once in a while through the eyes of an upside-down turtle.

***

BACK AT MY *MORTIFIED* AUDITION, DORCIC SEEMS UNABLE to stop himself from laughing at how flustered I've become. I spent the morning in journalist mode; I've always loved the job for the way it gives me a reason—and, as a happy side effect, the confidence—to ask strangers nosy questions. But the minute the producers made me start reading my diary in front of them, all my poise deserted me. "Look at you!" Dorcic says. "You came in here this cool, confident journalist, and now . . ." He shakes his head and laughs again, though he's nice about it.

Chupaska, perhaps sensing that I am moments away from bolting, has a suggestion. "Why don't you just flip to a random page and start reading from there?" he offers.

"Okay," I agree, grateful for direction. I choose a page at random—and then immediately regret this plan when I see the entry I've landed on. I try to keep flipping ahead but Galante catches me. "Just start reading," she says.

I start reading. "Okay, now I'm *really* scared of Ann. She had a book of *witchcraft* today. A book of *spells*. And when I tried to tell Mike B. or Jenna, they thought it was *cool*. They wanted to *see* the book." I knew already that the Latin root of the word "mortify" is "death," but what formerly felt like a fun little linguistic fact now feels a little too real, in that reading this aloud is making me want to die. The journal captures the months after my family moved from Nashville, where I attended a tiny religious school, to the suburbs of Chicago, where I attended a gigantic public school. The wicked ways of these unchurched children terrified thirteen-year-old me. "I am never, ever, *ever* gonna get involved with that stuff. I promise you, Jesus, right now, that I am a Christian, and I plan to stay that way. I promise I will never get mixed up in that stuff. And I am going to *keep* that promise."

It's the strangest thing: *I* wrote these words, but it feels like I'm reading from a script, like I'm playing a part. Erving Goffman, the famed midcentury sociologist, described his "dramaturgical" theory of social life in his classic 1956 book *The Presentation of Self in Everyday Life*. Taking seriously the Shakespearean notion that "all the world's a stage," Goffman theorized that every social interaction functions as if it were part of a play: We present ourselves to be a certain way, in order to fit the expectations of a certain audience. In contrast, the backstage is where you can relax, and be your true self. Awkward moments arise when the stage and the backstage clash, when the audience can see you mid–costume change. It's a metaphor that helps explain why my experience auditioning for *Mortified* is so strange. It's the backstage intentionally brought onstage.

As I read from my diary, I'm cringing because I'm not still the naive, sheltered kid who wrote this, but I'm also cringing because I am *totally* still the naive, sheltered kid who wrote this. I've come to realize that cringing happens when you accidentally let an unscripted, unpolished version of yourself escape. And what could be more unpolished than your teenage self? Middle-school me, for example, is a goody two-shoes who is insecure about friendships, is given to petty enthusiasms, and has a tendency to take everything way too seriously. (A sampling from the April 14, 1998, entry of this diary: "Eighty-six years ago, the *Titanic* sank. That is *so sad*.") I've changed in the two decades since seventh grade, but truthfully, thirtysomething me is all of these things too; it's just that I now work very hard to conceal those aspects of my personality. Any time I do something that reveals me to be overly excited or too eager to follow the rules, it's like middle-school me is back on the scene, staring wide-eyed at my adult life as I desperately try to shove her back into the past before anyone sees. *You get back to 1998. Go on. Get!!*

It's not just me either. In an episode of his podcast *You Made It Weird*, comedian Pete Holmes tells a story about the time he co-hosted a live show with Glen Hansard, the Irish musician most famous for his 2007 Oscar-nominated musical *Once*, in which he starred and sang with Markéta Irglová. At the show, Hansard invited Holmes's girlfriend, Valerie Chaney—who has a nice singing voice—to join them onstage. As he started to play "Falling Slowly," a lovely duet from *Once*, he turned to Holmes and Chaney and said, "Do you want to join in?"

"*Me?*" Holmes mouthed back. Hansard didn't reply, presumably because he was too busy playing, so Holmes rose from his seat and sang the love song with Hansard. "Take this sinking boat, and point it home, we still have tiiiii-iiime." Holmes was elated. The song ended. The crowd clapped.

And then Hansard said, "I meant *Valerie*."

The audience burst into laughter. Holmes tried to take it in stride, but in truth, he later said on his show, he felt humiliated. "Somewhere deep inside, I am the fat kid in eighth grade. I'm the sweaty-hand, weird-haircut, ill-fitting-T-shirt-with-boobs kid who's afraid and keeps tripping when he tries to dance. . . . And I can go out and convince people, for bursts at a time, that I'm solid. But that kid's still in there. And when I do something like that . . . I'm him again."

There's a reason why your teenage years stay with you. Perhaps you've heard of the reminiscence bump, a term psychologists use to describe the way the episodes of our lives that occur between the ages of ten and thirty tend to be recalled more vividly than those that occur earlier or later in life. Researchers have a few theories to explain the phenomenon; maybe, for instance, these memories stand out because of their novelty. It makes sense that you would remember your very first kiss more than your very eleventh kiss. But beyond that, throughout our life span, the moments that take prominence in our memories are those that are linked to our self-concept. During your awkward teenage years, you are laying the foundation for the path you'll follow as an adult—you join the school newspaper and see your name in print for the first time, or you take a volunteer tutoring job after school and realize you want to be an elementary school teacher. You carry your teen self around with you for life in part because these are the years you *become* yourself in the first place.

I've come to think of my inner teen as the unseen instigator of the awkwardness I still feel in my adult life. When I'm embarrassed by something dumb I said in a presentation at work, that's her—it's the same self-conscious feeling of wearing the wrong jeans to school, the extreme social fear of being rejected because you don't belong. When I don't know what to say after saying good-bye to someone only to realize we're headed in the same direction, that's her too—it reminds me of the way I felt those two weeks in eighth grade when I had a "boyfriend" whom I never talked to because I never knew what to say. Ambiguity in social settings is terrifying to teenagers, but the truth is most of us grown-ups are not great at handling this kind of uncertainty either. But underlying both the self-conciousness and the uncertainty is the dread of catching a glimpse of my looking-glass self, a phrase long used in psychology research to describe the way that others' perceptions of us help form our self-concept. We look to others to see reflections of ourselves, in other words, and it's deeply embarrassing when we don't like what we see.

When I've told people I'm researching awkwardness, they've

tended to assume I'm writing about it as if it were a personality trait, like introversion or shyness. I'm not so sure that's accurate. I'm interested in understanding awkwardness as an emotion rather than a trait, though it can be both of these things. Researchers who study emotions like boredom, for example, make this distinction with the terms "trait" and "state." Trait boredom is an individual's tendency to experience the feeling—some people are more easily bored than others, a characteristic that tends to be stable and enduring, regardless of the situation. State boredom, on the other hand, is fleeting and dependent on context. Likewise, there are people who feel awkward more frequently than others, but there are also certain situations that make *most* people cringe.

The philosopher Adam Kotsko has observed that American popular culture envisions the problem of awkwardness most frequently as a personality trait, treating it as if the cause were socially inept individuals. If only Michael Scott or Larry David or *you*, dear awkward person, could simply learn how to follow the rules of polite society, awkwardness would cease to exist. But is that really how awkwardness always works? In a season-two episode of the American version of *The Office*, Michael invites Billy, the building's property manager, to a hastily called meeting about the importance of respecting and not stigmatizing people with disabilities. Billy, who uses a wheelchair, says to the gathered employees of Dunder Mifflin, "I've been in a wheelchair since I was four years old. I don't even notice it anymore." To this Michael replies, "They notice it. Don't you?" He motions to his staff, adopting an accusatory tone. "It was the first thing you saw when he rolled in here, wasn't it?" It's an awkward, cringeworthy moment, but it's clear that Michael himself doesn't feel awkward. It's moments like these that suggest to me that it isn't quite enough to understand awkwardness only in terms of "awkward people."

As I've studied the facets of awkwardness, I've gotten an unexpected sense of common humanity out of it, unlike individual traits like introversion or shyness or neuroticism, which can feel isolating. If it's a feeling, like other good old-fashioned American emotions such as happiness or envy or curiosity, then it's a concept we can all recognize. "There's no such thing as an embarrassing moment," Oprah Winfrey has said, "because I know that there is not a moment that I could possibly experience . . . that somebody else hasn't already experienced." Embarrassment, by the way, is an integral part of awkwardness, in that an awkward moment is an embarrassing one too (or at least it involves the risk of embarrassment). To my mind, awkwardness is the self-conscious aspect of embarrassment *plus* a degree of ambiguity: *Oh god, I have no idea what to say or do now.* Anyway, I don't mean to start a fight with Oprah, but the fact of the apparent universality of embarrassment or awkwardness doesn't mean it doesn't exist. It means exactly the opposite, *and* it underlines the importance of the feeling. The things that make you cringe are usually the things worth sharing, because they can help others feel less alone. You experience this every time you feel secondhand embarrassment for somebody else. I dated a sensitive soul in the mid-2000s who had to leave the room when we watched the *American Idol* auditions together, because he was so uncomfortable for the singers who were embarrassing themselves on national television. He felt their pain as if it were his own. It's an understandable reaction to flee the situation that makes you cringe, but what if you could teach yourself to tolerate it? You could, maybe, learn to use the empathy as a route to compassion, for other people and for yourself. Looked at in a certain light, cringing becomes a worthwhile feeling, an emotion worth exploring, not avoiding. Little humiliations can bring people together, if we let them. The ridiculous in me honors the ridiculous in you.

BACK AT MY *MORTIFIED* AUDITION, I FINALLY HIT ON SOMEthing that makes the producers perk up. "April 26, 1998," I read. "This time last year, me and my friends were just beginning to like Hanson. We were getting ready for our Huntsville trip. I remember we wanted to sing 'MMMBop' on the bus, but we didn't know the words."

Dorcic cracks up, which I take as a welcome invitation to stop reading again. "You wanted to sing 'MMMBop,'" he repeats, "but you didn't know the words—oh my god." He turns to Chupaska and Galante. "That, to me, is classic *Mortified*," he says to them. In casting the show, they look for examples of the sweet, naive, earnest, totally misguided teen who still lives in all of us, and this entry of mine has apparently checked all of those boxes. Even though I knew it wasn't a real audition, I'm still sort of surprised when they add me to their March lineup. I'm paired with Chupaska, who will help edit my journal into a ten-minute narrative, a cohesive story that I can read in the show. The next day, and in the weeks after, I tell my friends and colleagues that I'll be reading my seventh-grade diary onstage in a couple months, and almost every single person responds with variations on the same question:

Why?! For a long time, I didn't have an answer for them, other than "for research." Most of us build our lives so that we experience as little embarrassment as possible, yet in *Mortified* there is a group of weirdos who intentionally seek out the feeling, who come together to revel in it for three hours every month. What do they know that the rest of us don't?

SECTION 1

Is That What I Look Like?

CHAPTER 2

The Tribal Terror of Self-Awareness

I n 1969 anthropologist Edmund Carpenter and photographer Adelaide de Menil visited New Guinea to study the Biami tribe, who lived on the Papuan Plateau. Carpenter and de Menil, who would later marry, set off on their adventure with a very distinct mission in mind: The time with the Biami would provide "an unparalleled opportunity to step in and out of 10,000 years of media history," as Carpenter later wrote. "I wanted to observe . . . what happens when a person—for the first time—sees himself in a mirror, in a photograph, on a screen, hears his voice, sees his name."

Carpenter, as that passage suggests, was specifically drawn to this group of people on this small island because at that time, he was almost certain that no member of the Biami had ever seen his or her own full reflection. The Biami had only small shards of mirrors, certainly no cameras, and the rivers in their home environment didn't provide clear enough reflections for a proper Narcissus moment. "I doubt if the Biami ever saw themselves at all clearly," Carpenter wrote. It's possible that they could use their own shadows to approximate their size and shape, but Carpenter reasoned that most of their understanding of what they looked like would've come from remarks or actions of others in their tribe. For better or for worse, Carpenter and de Menil's arrival would change that. They brought with them video cameras, Polaroid cameras, tape recorders, and mirrors, allowing the Biami to see what they looked like and to hear what they sounded like.

According to Carpenter's report, when the Biami people saw what they looked like, they expressed what the anthropologist later named his paper: the "tribal terror of self-awareness." That is to say, they freaked. In response to seeing their entire selves reflected back at them in a large mirror, the "tribesmen responded alike to those experiences: they ducked their heads and covered their mouths," he reported. "They were paralyzed: after their first startled response . . . they stood transfixed, staring at their images, only their stomach muscles betraying great tension."

The Biami had a similar reaction to hearing their voices on tape for the first time. "The tape-recorder startled them," Carpenter recalls in his write-up. "When I first turned it on, playing back their own voices, they leaped away. They understood what was being said, but didn't recognize their own voices and shouted back, puzzled and frightened." For the first time, the "me" that each tribal member carried around in his or her own head was juxtaposed with the way they apparently appeared to others. "The notion that man possesses, in addition to his physical self, a symbolic self, is widespread, perhaps universal," Carpenter wrote. "A mirror corroborates this. It does more: It reveals that symbolic self OUTSIDE the physical self. The symbolic self is suddenly explicit, public, vulnerable. Man's initial response to this is probably always traumatic."

The Biami got over their initial apprehension as fear quickly turned into fascination. "In a matter of days . . . they groomed themselves openly before mirrors," Carpenter observed, adding that "in astonishingly short time, these villagers . . . were making movies themselves, taking Polaroid shots of each other, and endlessly playing with tape-recorders." Still, Carpenter was captivated by the fact that they'd at first reacted so strongly, musing:

> When mirrors become a part of daily life, it's easy to forget how frightening self-discovery, self-awareness can be. But in New Guinea . . . mirrors still produce that intense anxiety—that tribal terror—which so often accompanies self-awareness.
>
> When people know themselves only from how others respond to them and then suddenly, for the first time, by means of some new technology, see themselves clearly, in some totally new way, they often are so frightened, so exhilarated, that they cover their mouths and duck their heads.
>
> I think they do so to prevent loss of identity. New Guineans call it loss of soul, but it's the same phenomenon. It's their response to any sudden embarrassment, any sudden self-consciousness.

It's worth noting that some anthropologists are skeptical of Carpenter's report and whether the members of the Biami tribe had truly *never* before seen their own reflections. But even if it's just a parable, it makes for a useful metaphor. In his writings Carpenter's words remind me, somewhat improbably, of a story from a few years ago about a new plastic surgery option called the "FaceTime Facelift." In the early 2010s, this was the kind of "trending topic" that was irresistible to both online editors and TV news producers, something I can say with some authority, as I've worked closely with both. By the spring of 2012, Dr. Robert Sigal, a Washington, D.C.–area plastic surgeon, estimated that of the hundred or so patients he saw annually who requested facelift procedures, about a quarter had come to his office specifically prompted by their hatred of their own appearance on video calls. "What they'll say is 'I don't like the way I look when I'm video chatting,'" he says in a video describing the procedure. "I seem full and heavy under the neck."

To address their concerns, Sigal dreamed up the new procedure, which is similar to a standard neck lift with one important exception: Incisions are made behind the ears, not under the chin, which means the scar is hidden from your video-chat buddies. The trouble with FaceTime, Sigal said, was that it was like "a mirror on steroids." Carpenter was writing about the Biami four decades before the debut of the iPhone, but it seems he was right: The early 2010s did indeed bring about "some new technology" that forced people to "see themselves clearly, in some totally new way."

So many of us want to know ourselves. We track our steps, we keep obsessively detailed bullet journals, we pay $69 to test our DNA. We scoff at *BuzzFeed* personality quizzes and then take them anyway. I'm Missandei, by the way. Which badass *Game of Thrones* lady are you?

We do these things at least in part because we know we can see only so much of ourselves on our own. There's often a stark difference between the way that *you* see you and the way that others see you; the distance between is something the psychologist Philippe Rochat calls "the irreconcilable gap." The term is still fairly new to me, but the feeling is not. Think of the things we call cringeworthy: hearing the sound of your own voice; seeing an unflattering photo of yourself; asking your boss for a promotion. In each of these situations, the version of yourself you think you're presenting to the world is forced to confront the version of you the world is actually seeing. You don't mind your voice until you hear a recording of it. You thought you looked fine until you see an unattractive photo that suggests otherwise. You see yourself as a leader, but your boss still sees you as a junior staffer. It's something that makes you newly conscious of yourself and how you're being seen by others, especially when someone else's perception of you doesn't measure up to the way you see yourself.

Take video calls, for instance, which have been billed as the "next big thing" in tech for decades now, yet have been slower to catch on than many experts predicted. And experts have been predicting this technology would take off for a *long* time: In 1964 Bell Labs introduced the Picturephone, a state-of-the-art video-calling service, at the World's Fair in New York. Six years later, Bell installed thirty-eight of the devices at eight companies in Pittsburgh, a modest enough start. But Bell had big plans for the video-calling sets, envisioning 100,000 in use across the country by 1975 and a million by 1980.

Despite high expectations, the Picturephone was a flop, for

several reasons. For one, the cost. At that 1964 World's Fair, a call cost $27 a minute, or about $200 in today's dollars. Within the company headquarters, engineer Robert Lucky was one of the few to have a Picturephone on his desk, but the only calls he ever got were from his boss, Arno Penzias. "I found it very awkward," Lucky said of this setup, "because I had to stare at him." Four decades later, AT&T corporate historian Sheldon Hochheiser echoed Lucky's perspective, conjecturing that the Picturephone had flopped because "it wasn't entirely clear that people wanted to be seen on a telephone."

Decades later, new video chat apps like FaceTime conjured the same feelings of discomfort. According to a recent Google survey, about one in six Americans say they avoid using video chat apps because it feels "rude." Where are you supposed to look? In the camera so you're looking at the person's "eyes"? Or at the person's eyes as you see them displayed on screen (which will make it appear to them as if you are looking near but not quite at them)? And is no one else bothered by the way the person's face fills your screen, making it appear as if you are standing an uncomfortably intimate ten inches apart?

In addition, people were enormously, and understandably, concerned with how they looked while video chatting. If the FaceTime facelift seems extreme, publications ranging from the *Wall Street Journal* to *SELF* magazine have published explainer guides about video calls that give the reader nonsurgical suggestions on how to look more attractive on video chat. For a while it seemed as if FaceTime's introduction in the fall of 2010 with the iPhone 4 had brought about the "videophonic stress" that David Foster Wallace predicted in *Infinite Jest*, something that would become "even worse if you were at all vain. I.e. if you worried at all about how you looked. As in to other people. Which all kidding aside who doesn't."

———

MANY YEARS AGO NOW, PHILIPPE ROCHAT WAS RIDING THE subway when a group of young women boarded with a packet of just-developed photos, taken at a recent party. "They created mayhem on the train" as they peered over one another's shoulders to examine the pictures, he recalls in his 2009 book *Others in Mind*. When one of the women saw an unflattering photo of herself, she'd snatch it away, trying to hide it from her friends; this, readers of a certain age may recall, was the pre-Facebook version of demanding that your friend untag you. Rochat is a developmental psychologist at Emory University whose work has largely centered around self-consciousness, so that day on the train he observed the group's antics with a scientist's eye.

"The behavior of these women was playful, for sure," he wrote later, "but the force and tension behind it were remarkably powerful." In his writing he seems a little amused by the young women and the way they shrieked and grasped for the photos of themselves they found unattractive. But there was an intensity underscoring their behavior that intrigued him, calling to mind the theory he was currently mulling over: the irreconcilable gap.

It was something he'd been thinking about ever since having a conversation with his mother about her recent cataract-removal surgery. "She suddenly saw clearly the world around her," he told me over the phone in his pleasing Swiss-French accent. (He's originally from Geneva, Switzerland, and trained with the famed developmental psychologist Jean Piaget.) "And she called me in a panic—she was telling me she had passed in front of a mirror and she was completely horrified to see how she was actually looking." She was, she could now see, much older than she imagined herself to be. Rochat is now in his sixties himself, and he knows the feeling. As you get older, he told me, you tend to *feel* much younger than you appear in the mirror.

He drifted into a mini lecture explaining to me the significance of aging and appearance, and I felt a little like I was being pulled into an audio version of the irreconcilable gap. I think he must have seen—well, heard—me as being younger than I really am. I know, from suffering through hundreds of interview transcriptions over my years as a journalist, that over the phone I sound like a teenager. Once I was interviewing a psychologist about people who have a fear of flying. I can't recall the point he was trying to make, but during our conversation, he said something like "I don't know if you're old enough to remember 9/11." At the time, I was twenty-nine. It was 2014. On September 11, 2001, I was sixteen years old. Yes, good god, I am old enough to remember 9/11.

I am now an American lady in her thirties, which means that I do have *some* idea of how it feels to be dismayed at your aging features. For a long time I didn't pay much attention to the faint lines under my eyes, figuring they would just go away after a few good nights' sleep. They haven't. It occurred to me very recently that this may just be what my face looks like now.

But back to my conversation with Rochat about aging. Of his mother he told me, "She was experiencing a gap that is very difficult to reconcile: how you feel from the inside and what you actually project from the outside." Some psychologists who study embarrassment call this the distinction between the lived and the corporeal selves: The former is in your head, whereas the latter is out there in the real world. You can pretend that these two selves are one and the same, until some kind of awkward mishap occurs and yanks you out of that fantasy. You trip over your own two feet, or you walk into an unfairly clean glass door, and suddenly you're aware of how ridiculous you must look, and that the *you* walking around out there does not always do such a good job of living up to the standards of the *you* that exists in your imagination.

It's a deep-seated human fear, Rochat tells me; he believes that it begins to take hold before we turn two. Starting around eighteen months, children start to recognize themselves in the mirror, a classic psychological test that has long been taken to be a sign of self-awareness. Rochat sees it a little differently: He thinks this is when we first begin to feel self-*conscious*. Experimenters test this by surreptitiously placing a sticky note on a small child's forehead. If the baby is younger than eighteen months, she won't seem bothered by it. Babies older than eighteen months, though, seem bewildered by the unexpected sticky note and will try to remove it. To Rochat, it's a sign that babies by this age notice when their internal self-image does not match the image they see in a mirror. The way you see yourself isn't necessarily the way the world sees you, a hard lesson we apparently start learning at a very young age.

This gap between your self-perception and others' perception of you helps explain why socializing with your fellow humans—something that is supposed to feel natural, even *fun*—can sometimes feel so fraught. You want them to see you the way that *you* see you, or at least the way that you are trying to present yourself in the moment, and getting this version of yourself across often involves a fair bit of performing. Ellen DeGeneres used to have a joke that touched on this, about how people will sometimes break into a weird little jog for a few steps after they've tripped. It's like they're saying to anybody watching, *Oh, I was going to start running anyway.*

In that same set, DeGeneres muses briefly about the other thing about tripping and falling that most of us have internalized: Even if you've truly hurt yourself, it doesn't matter. You swallow that pain, and you laugh it off. Physical pain is no doubt felt more acutely, but social pain can sometimes be felt more intensely. It can last longer too. A few years ago I met my early-bird friend Marie for a 6:00 A.M. run on the East River Greenway. I don't think I have whatever biological traits it takes to make a morning person, but sometimes I like to act like one, a pretension that backfired spectacularly that day: About ten steps into our jog, I ran straight into a lamppost.

I *know*. And no, I don't know how it happened either. It hurt like hell, as you might imagine. My right thigh somehow took the brunt of the impact, and when I got home I found an angry purple bruise already taking shape. In the moment, though, I laughed through the searing pain and kept running. "I'm fine," I remember lying to Marie. "No, really, I am. I would tell you."

No, I wouldn't have told her, and I bet you wouldn't have

either. It's a small example of the show we're all putting on for one another. Recall Erving Goffman's idea that social life is a stage. By acting like I was fine that day on the East River path with Marie, I was inviting her over to my side of the gap, where we were just going to go ahead and pretend this moment of astounding clumsiness never happened. With every little performance like this, we build hastily constructed bridges over the irreconcilable gap.

Not only are we trying to present ourselves in a certain way, but we're also simultaneously trying to interpret the impression others are trying to make on us. What was *that* look supposed to mean? And what was *that* tone about? We obsess over these little cues in part because we're trying to figure out what they say about *us* and in part to monitor whether this person is buying the image we're trying to project. This is often difficult work because of that gap between self-perception and other-perception. "Trying to bring these two things together is an infinite quest," Rochat told me. "We are like Don Quixote fighting windmills trying to reconcile that."

Goffman called this the "information game." On the one hand, there are the little things we do on purpose to guide someone over to our side of the gap. Your clothes, for instance, like the hat you carefully tilt just so or the shirt left deliberately half tucked in. You can use things like text messages in this way too: You might override your smartphone's autocorrect to keep your laid-back lowercase aesthetic. But then there are the signals we're accidentally sending about ourselves, nonverbals like our body language, facial expressions, or tone of voice.

To successfully navigate around awkwardness, you have to

buy the scene I'm creating and treat me accordingly, and I have to do the same for you. It's like the cardinal rule of improv: *Yes, and.* Actors in improvisational theater agree to accept the reality their partners present and to respond in kind. If one person starts a scene by pretending to be a school bus driver, only a clueless showboat would jump in and say something like "No, this is a rocket ship. And you're an alien. And we're headed to the moon!" Likewise, if I say I'm fine even though you just watched me run headlong into a lamppost, you'll go along with the story I'm telling if you don't want things to get weird. Awkwardness is the feeling we get when someone's presentation of themselves—either our own or someone else's—is shown to be incompatible with reality in a way that can't be smoothed over with a little white lie. There is a reason that Urban Dictionary's top-ranked definition for "awkward" is "passing a homeless person on your way to a coin star machine." We can relax only "backstage," to carry on with Goffman's theatrical analogy, by which he meant that we can finally stop performing when we're around close friends and family. We can drop the act. In fact, we'd *better* drop the act; no one likes someone who's "on" all the time.

This is the way we've organized our social lives. We're all constructing our identities with one another, lightly tossing ideas of ourselves back and forth like a beach ball at an arena concert. If our idea gets punctured in some way, then what? It's a loss of our identity, as Edmund Carpenter observed all those years ago in New Guinea. It's terrifying in a boundless, existential way to think that we're all pretending. I mean, I know that, and you know that, but, my god, let's not *talk* about it. If you don't see me the way I see me, does it even matter, all this work I'm doing to convince you of who I am? And for that matter—who *am* I?

This discomfort we feel when tiptoeing around the irreconcilable gap gets at our fear of social rejection and the survival instinct that we call an evolutionary holdover. When people talk about this instinct, they tend to characterize it as if it's outlived its usefulness, as if it's just an outdated feeling kicking around in our lizard brains from a time when being cast out of your social group almost certainly would doom you to a lonely death. But isolation is damaging today too, even without the threat of hungry saber-toothed tigers. Contemporary social science has tallied up the potential damage of social isolation and found that loneliness can increase a person's risk of death by 26 percent—comparable to the health risk posed by obesity. We're all trying our hardest to present versions of ourselves that will be accepted by everyone else, and it's no wonder that it can be terrifying when we realize our best efforts aren't being received the way we intended.

When we say things like "I'm so awkward!" I think what we sometimes mean is that we're sensing how tangled and confusing everyday social life can truly be. If you tense up when you're trying to make a good impression, maybe it's not because you're awkward. Maybe it's because you're *right*. This is complicated stuff, much more so than it superficially seems.

It can be miserable to feel hypersensitive to the awkwardness of everyday life, but I'd rather be the sort of person who is aware of it than the sort of person who is not. A contender for most awkward literary creation of all time has to be *Pride and Prejudice*'s Mr. Collins, the "awkward and solemn" suitor of Elizabeth Bennet. Early in the book there's a scene at a Netherfield Park ball where Elizabeth is stuck with Mr. Collins as a partner; he annoys her for two dances in a row by "moving wrong without being aware of it." His obliviousness makes his behavior so much *more* awkward, like his cringeworthy habit of periodically reminding everyone that he's tight with the high-status Lady Catherine de Bourgh. Can't he see how ridiculous he's being?

Contrast Collins with another Austen suitor, this time an ultimately successful one: Edward Ferrars, the gawky romantic lead in *Sense and Sensibility*. "I never wish to offend," he tells the Dashwood sisters, "but I am so foolishly shy, that I often seem negligent, when I am only kept back by my natural awkwardness." Edward is awkward, but he *knows* it. He's also acutely aware of the divide between his intentions and the way others are interpreting those intentions. This is a better place to be, as we'll get into in more detail in chapters 3 and 4. You can't bridge a gap you don't even know exists.

AS I WAS WRITING THIS CHAPTER, THE PUBLIC RELATIONS department at *New York* magazine cheerfully demanded that the editorial staff take new head shots, apparently preferring the idea of uniform photos they could use for publicity purposes over vacation pics swiped from our social media profiles. My longtime go-to, for instance, was a shot of me grinning at the camera while wearing a bright-pink Nike hoodie, hair slightly frizzed after hiking near Snoqualmie Falls in Washington State. It was a fine enough shot for a Twitter profile but didn't exactly scream "serious professional journalist."

The morning my photo was scheduled to be taken, I carefully chose my outfit and spent more time than usual on my hair and makeup. I studied my reflection in the floor-length mirror in my bedroom before I left and was pretty happy with it. Understated but put together. *I clean up nice*, I thought.

And yet I cringed when I saw the resulting photo later that day. My hair was so much flatter than it had seemed in the mirror, and you could hardly tell I was even wearing the makeup I'd spent so long applying that morning (and not in the cool, no-makeup-makeup kind of way). Later my friends and I traded photos, and I complained to them about mine. "I don't see what's so bad about it," most of them said. "You look fine! You look like you." This is the kind of thing that is said to reassure an insecure friend, or else to satisfy a needy compliment fisher, but I've always found it to be a little disheartening. *That's* how you see me?

Seeing a photograph of yourself can be jarring because you really do look different in the mirror according to the aptly named "mirror hypothesis," David White, who studies face perception at the University of New South Wales, told me in an e-mail. People tend to be so accustomed to their own reflections that "seeing themselves left-right reversed appears weird," he told me. It's a workable metaphor for the way our best efforts at self-presentation can fall short in unexpected ways, because sometimes we just *can't* see ourselves the way others do. Isn't it strange to think that you've never seen your face—as in your actual face, unaided by mirrors or pictures or videos? (The "... *man*" at the end of this admittedly stonerish question is implied.)

If you show people two photographs—one of their mirror image, the other in the left-right orientation that appears in photographs (and real life too, of course)—and ask them which they prefer, most people will choose the mirror image. It's the one they're used to. Have you ever seen a close-up of your face—say, I don't know, a professional head shot you had to do for work—and noticed that your face seemed slightly weirdly lopsided? This helps explain why. If you ask other people to judge the photographs, however, they'll likely prefer the non–mirror image. It's maybe the strangest part of being the sort of person who doesn't think they photograph well. Your picture looks bad to you, but others can't see what's wrong with it, which is all the more worrying: By reassuring you, they're essentially saying, *Yes, you really do walk around looking that lopsided.* But at least they seem to like your lopsidedness.

White recently published a study that expands on this photographic take on the irreconcilable gap: He asked people to send him a dozen photos taken from their Facebook profiles, and then he took those photos and cropped them in tight around the face, so that they all looked somewhat alike. Then White and his colleagues asked the owners of the photos to choose which one would be best suited for Facebook, LinkedIn, and a dating site. They also rated how attractive they thought they looked in each photo and how much confidence their faces were projecting.

And then White gave the photos to strangers to evaluate. Their answers were inconsistent with the participants' own ratings, suggesting that we aren't very good at guessing how we're coming across in the photos we choose for our online profiles. This doesn't matter so much for the picture you choose for Facebook or Twitter. On Instagram, for instance, my profile pic has for years been me and my cat making the same sneering face. It is one of my favorite photos of myself, and no one's negative opinion could convince me to change it. But it *does* potentially matter in other contexts, like the pictures we specifically choose to impress job recruiters on LinkedIn or potential dates on apps like Tinder or Bumble. We don't know how we're coming off to others, and we may not even know that we don't know.

On a brighter note, research in psychology suggests that we do tend to be pretty good at picking up on our general reputation, or the way a group as a whole "sees" us—that is, how they're perceiving our personality. Think about your team at work, for example. Not your individual colleagues; picture the group as a whole, the people with whom you work every day. How smart do you think they think you are? Do they think you're funny? Considerate? Friendly? Do they find you defensive? Would they call you a good leader?

The good news is that whatever you're thinking, you're probably right. One recent review of twenty-six studies on meta-accuracy—psychologists' term for correctly intuiting what other people are thinking—suggested that most people are pretty good at knowing a group's overall opinion of them. In one relevant experiment, researchers asked people to work in teams and then asked everyone what they thought about their fellow team members, rating each person on traits like intelligence, sense of humor, consideration, defensiveness, friendliness, and leadership ability. Each study volunteer was also asked to guess how everyone else would rate them on those qualities. In the end, people were pretty good at predicting what their team members thought of them on average, guessing accurately more often than mere chance would predict.

We make these guesses based on our own self-perception, which does tend to be pretty well aligned with how the world as a whole is perceiving us, explained David A. Kenny, a psychologist at the University of Connecticut who studies meta-accuracy. "People who think they generally make a bad impression—they do kind of make a bad impression," Kenny told me. "And people who think they make a good impression do, in fact, make a good impression." I sometimes think about this now when I'm in meetings. If I leave feeling like my presentation went pretty well, then I can safely assume that it probably did. If I leave feeling like it all fell apart, well, at least it always feels good to be right.

And yet there are some parts of our personalities others see that we just can't. A 2013 study explored these blind spots, first asking people to rank themselves on thirty-seven diverse traits and tendencies, including noticeable ones like laziness and punctuality. But the list also included some tendencies that are less observable to an outsider, like how imaginative a person was, or how often they worried. The participants' friends and family members were sent the questionnaire too, and they took a turn ranking the study volunteers' personalities; finally, the participants guessed how their friends and family would rate them.

Interestingly, for many of the traits that could be observed from the outside, the study volunteers were, on average, able to accurately predict how their friends and family would rate them.

They knew how lazy others thought they were, and they knew their friends knew how likely they were to show up late. They might not love what they looked like through someone else's eyes, but they were, at least, aware of it.

But this was less true for the subtler traits, like imagination or a tendency to worry. Your friends and family may not think of you as being very imaginative, for instance, and how could they? They can't see the colorful worlds you're dreaming inside your head, especially if you never tell anyone about them. Or they may think of you as a source of steadiness and calm when in reality you worry yourself to sleep every night. The list goes on, but here are two more notable observations from this study: The participants also incorrectly assumed that others would be able to see how much they liked (or disliked) doing favors and how much they feared rejection.

It all reminds me of an odd exchange I had with a friend a while ago, when she instant messaged me with the link to a quick blog post I'd written on some new research about loneliness. I knew this was you before I clicked, she wrote. Your stories are always the saddest.

Haha, I typed back, but I was thinking, *I'm sorry, what?* Here I thought I was a hilarious blogger who brightened people's days with my wit and wisdom, and meanwhile she thought I was kind of a bummer.

It's impossible to see the whole of ourselves at once, so we depend on the perspective of others to fill in the gaps. This touches on an old idea in social science: that we construct our sense of self in part by incorporating other people's reactions to us. And yet the difference between the way you see yourself and the way that others see you is sometimes so stark that you appear unrecognizable through the eyes of someone else, like an entirely different person. This is difficult enough for adults to wrap their heads around, and it tends to *really* confuse little kids. Jean Piaget once wrote about the way his daughter Jacqueline would refer to her own image, either in a mirror or a photograph. When she was twenty-three months old, the little girl came inside after a walk with her father and her aunt Odette and said that she would like to see the trio in a mirror, but Piaget thought the way that she phrased the request was telling: She said she wanted to see "Daddy, Odette, and Jacqueline" in the glass, as if Jacqueline were a girl apart from herself.

More recently the developmental psychologist Daniel J. Povinelli observed a similar disconnect or dissociation in two- and three-year-olds' relationship to their photographed, videotaped, or mirror images. When three-year-old Jennifer watched a video of herself in which she had a Post-it stuck to her head, she said aloud, "It's Jennifer," and later added, "But why is she wearing my shirt?" It's a strange thing to take a hard look at the version of yourself that everyone else sees. It's you, but it also isn't you. But it is. But it isn't.

It would be insane to suggest that other people's perceptions of you are automatically right, or at least right*er* than your own perception of yourself. That's simply not true, or at least it isn't *always* true. You don't have to take someone else's version of you seriously. But it can be worth shifting your own perspective so you can see what they see in you. Even if it hurts. A good friend will sometimes play the part of your own personal mirror when they tell you that your fly is undone or that you have toilet paper on your shoe. You *expect* a good friend to tell you these things, in fact, and even though you feel stupid in the moment, you're glad they told you.

These metaphorical mirrors surround us, and often in unexpected places. Grades at school can act as a mirror, as can annual performance reviews at work, which serve as evidence that you never, ever stop getting graded on your work (and your worth). Gifts can function this way too. At a former job I struggled with feeling like I was being seen by my colleagues as young and immature, an impression that felt confirmed to me by my boss's Christmas gift one year: a YA novel. It was a *great* YA novel—*The Book Thief* by Markus Zusak—and I read it happily. I also read *into* it, less happily.

Or consider salary negotiations, which are like one of those magnifying mirrors some people use to apply makeup, the kind that shows you every last pore. You're taking a great risk by stating plainly, using the unmistakable certainty of hard numbers, what you believe you're worth; you're risking the rejection of your boss or the hiring manager with whom you're negotiating, who may inform you that, in the eyes of the company, you are worth much less.

An academic study it isn't, but in 2015 the salary-comparison site PayScale conducted an interesting reader survey about this subject. Of about 31,000 respondents, fewer than half said they had *ever* asked for a raise. Of those who'd never asked for a raise, about a third admitted it was because the idea of the conversation made them too uncomfortable; another 19 percent were afraid of being perceived as too demanding. Women and millennials were among the groups less likely to have ever asked for a raise.

Or you could think of a different form of negotiation: the define-the-relationship talk, in which you have to be brave enough to tell the person you're dating, *This is what I think I'm worth to you.* Data from qualitative research, in which sociologists conduct in-depth interviews with people and analyze their answers, suggest that some couples avoid having these talks altogether. When asked by interviewers how they decided to approach major milestones like moving in together, many couldn't recall deciding exactly. It "just happened," they said. Her lease was up, his rent went up, and all of a sudden, there they were at Ikea.

A 2013 study probed this dynamic further, finding that those who drifted into commitment markers like cohabitation and marriage were less happy in their relationships than those who had careful, deliberate conversations about what they and their partners expected from each other. Having the awkward conversation you're dreading is often worthwhile, a subject chapter 4 will deal with in greater detail.

Whereas negotiations and relationship-defining moments are nothing new, the other-people-as-mirrors analogy helps explain why awkwardness has surged into the zeitgeist. We now have so many new ways to see what we look like to others.

––––––

ON A RECENT SUNNY SUNDAY, MY FIANCÉ, ANDREW, AND I were having a drink at a restaurant on one of the busy piers at Brooklyn Bridge Park when we saw a guy get down on one knee and propose to the woman he was with. Her right hand flew to her mouth in surprise, but she offered the left so he could place the ring on her waiting finger when she said yes. It was a lovely moment to watch, and a beautiful setting for it too, with the sweeping skyline of Manhattan across the water.

All of which made the next scene that played out so amusing to observe from a distance. When the boyfriend was proposing, another man with a camera was desperately trying to fight his way through the crowd. By the time he made it to the couple, it was too late; the moment was over. Andrew and I watched the boyfriend and the photographer talk things over, and soon the couple was reenacting the whole thing—him down on one knee, her reacting with surprise—so that the camera could capture it and, presumably, so that they could share the moment with their friends and family members on social media.

We work hard to control the version of ourselves we're presenting to the world, but typically we hide the work we're doing. Goffman extended his stage-play metaphor by calling this the "backstage" action, the things we do in private to construct a version of ourselves fit for public consumption. It's the guy on a date at an upscale restaurant who quickly Googles "how to pronounce viognier" while his date is in the bathroom; it's the college freshman who pretends for the first few weeks of the semester to be neat and tidy so that her new roommate won't know she's a secret slob; it's me when I change my Spotify settings to "public" when I'm listening to something acceptably hip but back to "private" when I get the urge to revisit one of the *Glee* soundtracks. No one needs to see that.

We want the self we're projecting to appear authentic, which means it must also seem effortless. If you've ever cringed at catching someone take a painstakingly posed photo clearly intended for Instagram, Goffman's theory of the backstage helps explain why. Before the proposal on the pier that day, I'd watched a young woman take selfie after selfie, cocking her head this way and that, sometimes posing with a peace sign and sometimes not, sometimes with a smile and sometimes with a silly expression. I don't mean to pick on this person, though, because I do this too. On election day in 2016, in particular, I must have taken dozens of selfies before I finally settled on one to post on Instagram. "Why does it look like you voted in a park?" one of my more observant friends asked me later that day. I was embarrassed. It looked like I voted in a park because the lighting by the church where I actually voted was incredibly unflattering, so I stopped in a park for a better-lit selfie later that morning. Her comment made me cringe, because it was a reminder of all the ridiculous work it takes to be the effortless, authentic person I want to appear to be online. Evidence of all this effort is like an actor's wig falling off in the middle of a scene, an unmistakable reminder to the audience that they're watching a staged performance.

Our relationships are a "potentially infinite cycle" of concealing and revealing our authentic selves to each other, Goffman writes, something that also, by the way, helps explain the awkwardness of trying to mix your friend groups together. The comedian Jim Gaffigan has a bit about this in his 2006 special *Beyond the Pale*. "You ever mix two different groups of friends? That can be stressful," he says. "You always feel like you have to prep 'em. You're like,

'Hey, yeah, um, uh. Uh, these people over here, uh, they don't think I drink." Pause for the kind of belly laughs that can come only from self-recognition. "And don't be thrown by my British accent," Gaffigan adds.

We each construct and play different social roles depending on the group we're with; when these groups are brought together, it's uncomfortable because it's hard for you to know how to behave—*and* because you're confronted with the fact that you were playing a role in the first place. You're seeing yourself through the eyes of competing audiences who each are expecting something different out of your performance. If awkwardness is caused in part by "unfulfilled expectations," as Goffman once wrote, then that's why this situation is so awkward: You've created different roles for yourself to play in discrete social situations, and you can't play them all at once. Somebody's expectations of you are going to be disappointed.

These groups used to collide only at social gatherings like birthday parties or weddings, but thanks to social media, people from different parts of your life can now easily interact every day. No wonder the aughts were so particularly attuned to the feeling of awkwardness; it was in our faces every time we signed into Facebook. Once I posted an article I had written, and my favorite college professor, a former colleague, *and* my mother all commented on it—not only that, they started talking to one another *about me*. Just fifteen years ago or so, this could never have happened.

Sometime around 2009 there was a lot of talk in the newsroom where I worked about keeping separate professional and personal social media accounts, to avoid this kind of uncomfortable clash of selves. Some people still keep these separate, but most people I know have combined them into a single social media self that they're presenting to the world. It's not a perfect solution. My grandmother recently signed up for her first Facebook and Instagram accounts, and she comments adorable things like "Sure do love you, sweetie" on almost everything I post. Yesterday my brother added a new friend on Facebook, to which our grandma commented, "How nice." The challenge now is to build a role for ourselves that we can stand to play in front of a variety of audiences.

I wish it were possible to never again feel embarrassed when you get a glimpse of yourself through someone else's eyes, but the cringey feeling will always return, some way or another. When you've bridged one gap, another one opens. The good news, however, is that you can get used to the feeling it evokes.

Personally, I still hate looking at myself on video chat apps, but this likely represents the concerns of an old millennial, as video calls are rapidly becoming more popular among younger people. In 2016 the NPD Group reported that 52 percent of survey respondents ages eighteen to thirty-four say they now use their smartphone to make video calls, a ten-point increase from the previous year. Just anecdotally, I now see many more people than I did even a year ago walking around New York while making video calls; the other day I ran a 10K in Central Park and at one point passed a man who was FaceTiming during the race. It reminds me of the way mirrors and cameras frightened the Biami at first, but after only a few days, they couldn't get enough. People get used to things in time. Even their own awkward faces.

Or their own awkward voices. An earlier version of this chapter started with pages and pages of angst over hating the sound of my own voice. It was one of the very first things I wrote for the book, and it was true when I wrote it. It's less true now. I do sometimes still cringe when I listen back to recorded interviews, particularly when I ask a stupid question (and there is definitely such a thing as a stupid question). But my voice doesn't bother me so much anymore. It sounds different from the way it does when I hear myself speak, but that isn't such a bad thing. I've even learned to like it a little bit. It still doesn't sound like *me* necessarily, but it doesn't sound awful anymore either.

Besides, cringing isn't the problem. I was so surprised that I could get used to the sound of my own voice that I wondered whether I could go one step further: Maybe I could change the way I feel when I feel awkward.

CHAPTER 3

Making Faces at Emotionally Intelligent Machines

I t seems that I prefer Muppets to humans. I might've been able to guess this about myself, but in this moment I don't have to guess. The evidence is right here in front of my face. The evidence is, in fact, *about* my face.

I'm at the Boston headquarters of Affectiva, a tech company known for developing software that can read emotions in the expressions that flicker across our faces. "I think that, ten years down the line, we won't remember what it was like when we couldn't just frown at our device, and our device would say, 'Oh, you didn't like that, did you?'" Rana el Kaliouby, the company's cofounder, told the *New Yorker* in 2015. This idea of emotion-reading technology fascinates me as a collector of cringeworthy moments, because so much awkwardness arises from *mis*reading other people; there is a fine but crucial line, for instance, between a smile and a smirk. Maybe these emotionally intelligent machines could teach me a thing or two about reading the minds of my own kind.

During my visit I'm told that much of Affectiva's work is with the marketing departments of huge brands like PepsiCo and Kellogg's, which rely on Affectiva to, essentially, tell them whether their ads stink. Test audiences watch a commercial while Affectiva's sensors analyze their expressions; afterward, the tech company can tell advertisers at exactly which parts people smiled or frowned or furrowed their brows. Advertisers can then use that feedback to amp up the sad parts or tweak the jokes, depending on the emotion they want the ad to elicit.

Affectiva claims that its technology can better predict sales than the old-fashioned way of ad testing, in which marketers would simply ask people how they felt about the commercial. According to an internal study Affectiva conducted with Mars, its software was able to predict short-term sales with 75 percent accuracy. Self-reports, on the other hand—that is, relying on people's own recollections of their feelings while watching the ad—predicted sales with 70 percent accuracy. A 5 percent difference isn't huge, true. But it's a little unsettling to think that a machine might know your true feelings better than *you* do.

Like my feelings on the Muppets, for example. During my summer afternoon at Affectiva, my hosts are Jason Krupat, the director of strategic partnerships, and Mahmoud Abdelrahman, who's a product manager. Together the three of us watch an ad Affectiva worked on with Toyota that stars actor and former football player Terry Crews, plus a handful of Muppets. Before he hits "play," Krupat instructs me to stand directly in front of the screen so that the sensors can pick up my expressions as I watch.

In the ad, Crews is a buttoned-up businessman driving a Toyota Highlander, with which he picks up a hitchhiking Animal and his Muppet ruffian bandmates. Honestly, it's a confusing commercial. One moment they're at a bingo hall; the next, the Muppets are performing in a rock concert; the next, they're all at Mardi Gras, I think? I try to smile appreciatively, but I'm not really following the disjointed plotline, though this *could* be because I'm distracted by Krupat and Abdelrahman, whose eyes keep darting over to watch me watch the ad. I also can't stop thinking about this machine in front of me, and the computer-induced irreconcilable gap that has just opened between it and me. What is it seeing—and what is it going to tell Krupat and Abdelrahman about me?

Afterward Krupat pulls up a screen covered in charts and squiggly lines. "So this is going to show you what your emotions were," he explains. We're looking at a graph showing the ups and downs of my "valence," a psychological term meaning positive or negative emotional response. At the moment when the camera switched from the Muppet band onstage to the mostly human audience, there's a huge drop in the line graph. "You really didn't like that," Abdelrahman says teasingly. I guess I didn't, I agree. Maybe I'd rather watch puppets than people.

Most of my emotions stayed in a *meh* kind of middle range as I watched the video. But along with emotions, Affectiva measures a viewer's concentration by tracking how closely people knit their eyebrows together. I'm embarrassed when we pull up this graph, which reveals how little I was apparently concentrating on the ad as it played. I feel betrayed by my own face.

Affectiva's technology is remarkable, but it faces competition. In 2016 Apple bought Emotient, a different artificial intelligence company developing similar emotion-reading tech. Researchers at MIT recently developed a wearable "social coach," a wristwatch-sized device that tracks the emotional tenor of a conversation to tell you whether your chat is happy, sad, or neutral. And as I'm writing this in 2017, Disney has just filed a patent for technology that would use your emotions to control theme park rides. If you're too scared, the ride might give you a break by slowing down for you, but if you're bored, it could wake you up by throwing you some unexpected twists and turns. It reminds me of a video game Krupat and Abdelrahman described during my visit, one that tracks your fear as you play. The more fear your face shows, the more health your avatar loses in the game; in other words, the object is to try not to scare yourself to death.

The idea behind the research upon which all of this new tech is based is that our faces sometimes really *do* betray us by broadcasting our emotions, even the ones we try to hide, and even the ones we are not entirely aware that we are feeling. If we humans can recognize these emotions in others, then we are said to be displaying emotional intelligence. It seems reasonable, then, to assume that more emotional intelligence will result in fewer awkward moments. If you can read people, you'll know how to respond.

And if you can't, well. Here's a quick story about that.

Kate Darling is a researcher at the MIT Media Lab, where she studies human-robot interactions. But this isn't a story about her work. This is a story about sandwiches. A few years ago, Darling was in a café in Boston's South Station, on her way to meet up with the guy she'd just started dating. She placed her lunch order, and the cashier asked, "What's your name?"

"Oh, uh," she stammered. "I have a boyfriend."

A beat.

"For the sandwich," the cashier clarified.

"It was *clearly* for the sandwich," she says when I talk to her over the phone. That day at the train station, she'd been single for the better part of two years, "and I'd gotten really used to being hit on, and hitting on people," she tells me. "So I was just in that mode." By the time we talked, it had been more than four years since the sandwich-shop incident, and yet she says that every time she has to take a train at the station, the memory comes rushing back.

I don't mean to insult Darling's emotional intelligence, because she's funny and charming over the phone. It's just a funny example of how easy it is to misread other people. A friendly customer service smile can look a lot like a flirty smile, especially if you're used to seeing a lot of the latter.

One of the main problems I have with other people is that they have minds of their own. Chapter 2 was all about the gap between the way you see yourself and the way that others see you, and how sometimes this results in people reading you totally wrong. But of course it stands to reason that you're misunderstanding others too, and probably just as often as they're misunderstanding you.

There is an appealing sense of certainty in the promise of parsing emotions algorithmically. I'm drawn to the idea that perhaps I could learn to read other people in the way Affectiva is apparently able to read me. This is the can-do spirit with which I approached the question of "reading" other people, anyway; I thought that if scientists could teach robots to get better at this, then maybe I could use the same principles to improve my own emotional intelligence. And yet the truth ended up being fuzzier and more complicated than I ever assumed it would be. In the end, the conclusion I came to wasn't that I needed to improve my own emotional intelligence. Instead, I started to think that it's time to improve our understanding of emotional intelligence itself.

It feels as if each emotion exists in each of us as a distinct *thing*, a pattern of measurable physiological responses in the brain and body, and that these feelings are expressed on our faces in consistent, recognizable patterns. But what if that isn't true? For the past two decades, researchers in neuroscience and psychology have been systematically poking holes in this conventional wisdom about human emotions. This research suggests that specific emotions *don't* show up in consistent ways on our faces or within our bodies or brains; as the neuroscientist Lisa Feldman Barrett is fond of saying, feelings don't have fingerprints.

The bad news here is that "reading people" is not as simple as memorizing a discrete set of facial expressions. But scientists are uncovering new, less intuitive ways to understand emotions, both in others and in ourselves. To me the most exciting part of this line of research is that it suggests that feelings are not innate; they are something your brain *creates*. With time, you can change the way your brain creates a feeling, which means you can change the way you feel it.

Learning about this research has changed the way I think about emotional intelligence and even the way I think about my own feelings—perhaps especially the cringey one I am so particularly prone to experiencing. But it's also increased my caution in interpreting other people's emotions. It's true that most of us are naturally pretty good at guessing the emotional states of others, and it's also true that there are ways to improve our guesses.

But that's the important part: We can learn to make good guesses about other people's emotions—but they are always, always guesses.

———

AT AFFECTIVA I AM MAKING SILLY FACES AT A TABLET. I'M playing with the app (which you can find for yourself on iOS and Android), grinning maniacally and trying to get it to rate my face at 100 percent joy, but I can't get it to go higher than 98. The app can track six facial expressions at a time, although one has eluded me almost entirely. "I can't get it to recognize contempt—oh! There it goes," I say to Krupat and Abdelrahman, who are patiently indulging me in a conference room.

Right now Affectiva's technology can spot twenty different facial movements: wrinkled noses, pressed lips, furrowed brows, and the like. These combine to express seven so-called basic emotions, which you will recognize as the cast of the 2015 Disney/Pixar film *Inside Out:* There's joy, sadness, fear, disgust, and anger, plus a couple of hangers-on that didn't make the movie, surprise and contempt. (It's a funny coincidence that I had a hard time making the expression for contempt, because it wasn't always counted among the basic emotions.)

Since the 1960s, researchers have studied how well people recognize these emotions. In one common experiment, psychologists show people a picture of a face expressing, say, sadness, and ask them to choose the correct emotion from a list. People all over the world can match the face to the right word, consistently choosing a pouting face for sadness or a scowling face for anger. And if people around the world can recognize these emotions, scientists reasoned, then it follows that these emotions must be universally felt by all of us.

It's undeniable that, despite the occasional awkward moment, we *are* pretty good at reading one another. There's a hundred-year-old theory about this called the social intelligence hypothesis, which holds that our ability to understand one another helps explain why our brains are three times larger than the brains of our closest relative, chimpanzees. Humans came to dominate the planet "not because of our opposable thumbs or our handiness with tools," the University of Chicago psychologist Nicholas Epley has argued, but "because of our ability to understand the minds of others."

And yet we're not as good at reading one another's minds as we assume we are. Chapter 2 focused on the metaperception aspect of mind reading—again, that's what you think someone else is thinking about you. But let's take the focus off ourselves for a moment and put the spotlight on someone else.

In particular, think of your partner, if you have one. This is supposed to be the person you know best, right? Swoony rom-coms like *When Harry Met Sally* often feature speeches toward their climactic endings that are supposed to demonstrate how much Harry loves Sally by showing how well Harry *knows* Sally, right down to her quirks and idiosyncrasies. "I love that you get cold when it's seventy-one degrees out," Billy Crystal says to Meg Ryan in a scene that always makes me cry. "I love that it takes you an hour and a half to order a sandwich. I love that you get a little crinkle above your nose when you're looking at me like I'm nuts." This is the entire basis of *The Newlywed Game:* You and your partner know each other through and through.

Or do you? In his 2014 book *Mindwise,* Epley recounts an experiment designed to function a little like that classic game show. Imagine that your partner is told to fill out several questionnaires about his or her personality; meanwhile, you are asked to do the same, only you are told to answer in the way you think your significant other would. The researchers were interested in part in how well people could intuit their partners' sense of self-worth, and many of the questions asked the participants to rank from one to five how strongly they agreed with statements like "I feel great about who I am."

I'd like to believe Andrew and I would do pretty well at this game. We've been together for more than seven years, during which we've traveled internationally together multiple times and survived one cross-country move in a small car, accompanied by an angry cat. Feeling smug, I scoffed a little at this study's results: People predicted their partners' answers with an accuracy rate of just 44 percent. Amateurs.

And then I kept reading. Like me, the people in the study *assumed* they would be great at this task, predicting that they would be much more accurate than they really were. On average, they told the researchers that they expected their answers to match their partners' about 82 percent of the time, about double the actual average rate of accuracy. "These couples hit a double," Epley writes, "but they thought they'd hit a home run." Also of note:

The longer a couple had been together, the more overconfident they became about how many questions they'd get right, although their accuracy rate did not noticeably increase. The more years you spend together, the more you *think* you know about your partner.

I was thinking about this research while messing around with the Affectiva app, making exaggerated pouty faces at the tablet's camera. The screen read: 96 percent sadness. *No one understands me like you do, Affectiva*, I thought, making a joke for my own amusement as I pressed my lips together. (79 percent anger!) *Not even Andrew.*

———

NOT TOO LONG AFTER I FIRST READ ABOUT EMOTIONALLY intelligent software, some late-night anxiety Googling led me to a link promising "communication hacks for the socially awkward." *Click.* The last one caught my eye: It was about microexpressions, taken from the same scientific literature that Affectiva and the like draw from. "Being able to read them on other faces is like seeing the world in HD—it often feels like cracking a secret code!" the post says. This was what I'd been initially hoping for when I started studying cringeworthy moments: the sweet certitude of science and lists I could memorize that would keep me safe from awkwardness forever.

The term "microexpression" is most often associated with the work of psychologist Paul Ekman, who has argued that our feelings "leak" onto our faces in the form of these microexpressions: In just a fraction of a second, we reveal what we are truly feeling. According to this line of research, there are microexpressions for each of the seven basic emotions—again, that's joy, sadness, fear, anger, disgust, surprise, and contempt. You likely would recognize these: a crinkled-up nose for disgust, a scowl for anger, a smirk for contempt (though the last one looks annoyingly similar to a half smile). Most people recognize these in studies with relative ease, which, again, is why they're considered "basic" or "universal" emotions.

Malcolm Gladwell helped popularize the idea in a 2002 article for the *New Yorker* and discusses it further in his best seller *Blink*. "You must have had the experience where somebody comments on your expression and you didn't know you were making it," Ekman says to Gladwell in the *New Yorker* piece. He isn't asking me, but I will answer anyway: Yes, I have indeed had this experience. A while ago my boss called me into his office for a meeting, and I walked in having arranged my face in what felt to me like a listening expression—so I was surprised when he greeted me by saying, "This isn't bad news. You don't have to look so nervous." Hmph.

But there is a big overlooked flaw in this research on expressions and emotion: It takes an outsider's perspective on someone else's internal state, ignoring the irreconcilable gap in between. Put another way, this research focuses on "emotion *perception*, not emotion production," Lisa Feldman Barrett, a neuroscientist who has spent her career studying how emotions work in the brain, tells me. We might perceive raised eyebrows, for example, as a sign of fear or nervousness, as my boss did. But does that necessarily mean that the person (um, me, in this case) is *feeling* fear?

Scientists have over the years tried to bridge this gap between the observer of the feeling and the feeler of the feeling, notably by using facial electromyography, or EMG. They make their study subjects wear electrodes all over their faces as they watch films or look at photos designed to elicit certain emotions. If people really do always make the same face when feeling fear, for example, then the EMG should pick that up in an objective way. But these studies have failed to find consistent patterns in facial muscle movements.

Or consider a cuter attempt to find out whether these seven facial expressions are truly innate: baby studies. If these expressions are inborn, then you might expect infants to display them even more frequently than adults; as Barrett has pointed out, babies don't yet know how to mask their feelings when socially appropriate. One study looked at this question, alternately angering babies by pinning back their little arms or scaring them with a toy gorilla; later, coders analyzed their facial muscle movements and found no distinction between the faces they made when angry and the faces they made when fearful.

Studies on uniform signs of emotion in the body and brain have come up with similarly inconclusive results. Cringing may make my face flush and my palms sweat, but anger can do that just as easily. Barrett points to four meta-analyses (these are studies about studies) that review hundreds of experiments involving tens of thousands of people, none of which found consistent patterns matching physiological responses to discrete emotions. As for the brain, Barrett's own work has found that no single region of the brain, nor network of brain regions, "contained the fingerprint for any emotion." Sometimes fear activates the amygdala, for example, and sometimes it doesn't. Emotions may not be as predictable as we've long assumed.

So you can't judge someone's emotions simply going by what their face or body happens to be doing; if you have access to a brain scanner, that's very cool, but that may not get you very far in terms of emotion reading either. Then how do we ever get this *right*?

We make good guesses at what others are feeling by taking in the wider context of a situation. I mean, this is obvious, but it's worth stating because you do it without even noticing you're doing it. "It's not just that you see someone's face—you also hear their voice, and you see their body posture, and you have their words," Barrett said. A picture of a person who is wrinkling their nose while holding a diaper, for instance, will likely register as disgust. But if you take that same scrunched-up nose expression and put it on, say, a haughty Regina George type in a high school cafeteria, it will look a lot more like contempt. Studies have done things like this, Barrett explained, and have found that your eyes scan the two faces differently depending on the wider context.

"Even though it's exactly the same face!" Barrett exclaims as we talk. I'm now a little wary of putting a judgment on her voice without seeing the full context of her face and body posture, but the feeling I would wager she is expressing here is exasperation. "If you put the *same* face on two different bodies, the way perceivers look at the face—the way their brains *move their eyes* to sample the face—are so completely different." Our brains use our eyes and ears and memories to take in the whole scene, and consider scenes like it from before, to judge what another person might be feeling. It's an elegant, complex process, and much of the time it does help us make appropriate guesses at someone else's emotional state.

It's just that faces *alone* can't speak for themselves, as Barrett likes to say. It's true that people absolutely do smile in happiness or scowl in anger or pout in sadness, but the point is that these feelings can exist without the expressions, and the expressions can occur without the feelings. I'm sure you've experienced this for yourself. Sometimes we scream in fear, and sometimes we scream with pride; we cry when we're happy and we smile when we're sad. If you are a woman, you have likely had the experience of walking down the street with a neutral expression, only to be told to smile by some male stranger who wonders, "What's wrong, baby? It can't be that bad!" Or perhaps you've been accused of "resting bitch face" when you're just spacing out. Faces are often unreliable narrators.

And yet here I sit in a conference room in downtown Boston, cheerfully making faces at an app that claims to be detecting my emotions as I do so. "What about happy tears?" I ask Krupat and Abdelrahman. "Or my mom had this thing—when she would get really mad at us, she would sometimes *smile*. So . . . what about when your face does weird stuff like that?"

Krupat agrees that incorporating the wider context is key. "Somebody who is playing a game might smile because they're really frustrated—that's probably why your mom would smile, because she's frustrated, right? Not because she's happy," he says.

For now, when Affectiva delivers data on customers' expressions back to its clients, it pairs it with as much context as possible; in the video game example Krupat gave, the company will note the moment in the game when the expression occurred—perhaps it was particularly intense. Or take the Muppet commercial. We could see that I stopped smiling when the camera panned away from Animal on the drums and to the human audience, but it was also, as I said earlier, a really freaking weird commercial that I was having trouble following. Maybe I was more confused than unhappy.

Abdelrahman chimes in to add that the company is starting to do research tracking what faces do in real time—in conversations, for example. This technology is considerably more sophisticated than sticking electrodes all over a person's face; maybe it really will uncover something new about how feelings show up on our faces.

Hearing this, I slouch a little at the conference table, feeling beaten by the machines. Committing the seven microexpressions to memory is something I could actually *do*, and yet, while this would help me ace an "emotional intelligence" quiz online, it wouldn't be much help to me in everyday life, where faces are wont to do the unpredictable. Shortly after this, I leave Affectiva and head to a nearby bar, where I resist the urge to self-consciously analyze the look on the bartender's face to try to tell what he's thinking about my rumpled appearance. (I woke up at 4:00 A.M. to make my bus from New York to Boston.) The robots can keep their facial-expression analysis, I decide, and good luck to them with it.

Anyway, there are more interesting ways to improve our emotional intelligence.

WE UNDERSTAND EMOTIONS AS THINGS THAT HAPPEN TO us. But new research in neuroscience suggests a different story: Emotions are things your brain creates.

In Barrett's view, for example, there are four universal ways for a human body to feel. You can feel pleasant or unpleasant, and you can feel high arousal or low arousal. These are physical sensations, and we use the concept of emotions to make sense of them. If I feel my cheeks burn at a party after I've called someone the wrong name, I recognize that as embarrassment. If my cheeks flush after that party, when I'm riding my bike home and a car cuts me off, I'd call the feeling anger. Emotions are your brain's way of making sense of your physical feelings.

The concept of emotions is not innate. It's something we learn. "At the earliest stage, we are taught these concepts by our parents," Barrett said in a 2017 interview with the online science magazine *The Verge*. "You don't have to teach children to have feelings. Babies can feel distress, they can feel pleasure and they do, they can certainly be aroused or calm. But emotion concepts—like sadness when something bad happens—are taught to children, not always explicitly. And that doesn't stop in childhood either. Your brain has the capacity to combine past experience in novel ways to create new representations, experience something new that you've never seen or heard or felt before."

If you don't have the *concept* for an emotion, you won't feel it as strongly as someone who does have that concept. In the winter of 2016, for example, the Danish word *hygge* was everywhere. Before then, Americans may have enjoyed the calm, cozy feeling of being indoors with good food and good friends when it's freezing outside. But according to the theory of constructed emotions, before you knew that word, "your brain [had] to work really hard to construct those concepts and make those emotions," Barrett said in her *Verge* interview. "You would take a long time to describe it. But if you know the word, if you heard the word often, then it becomes much more automatic, just like driving a car. It gets triggered more easily and you can feel it more easily."

Understood this way, there are endless ways to feel something new. Why would you ever be just plain sad when you could be devastated, crushed, dejected, wretched, gloomy, or comfortless? Why be mad when you could be indignant, vexed, irate, annoyed, disgruntled, or hot under the collar? Each word has a slightly different meaning, and if you know enough emotion concepts, you can choose exactly the right one, which will help you better know how to behave in response to the feeling. If I am at work and know that I'm feeling indignant, then I can take steps toward addressing what I deem unfair treatment. If I'm fed up, then maybe it's time to quietly update the ol' LinkedIn profile.

This is known as emotional granularity, and there is some emerging evidence to suggest that getting better at recognizing your own feelings will improve your ability to accurately see them in others. In a small 2016 study, fifty couples in Belgium received ten notifications a day on their smartphones for one week, each one asking them to rate their own feelings in that moment and to rate how they thought their partners were feeling. The results showed a link between emotional granularity and empathetic accuracy: The more emotions you recognize in yourself, the more prepared you are to recognize them in others. "Even though your brain is always guessing," Barrett writes, "when it has more options to guess with, the odds are better it will guess appropriately." What an exciting new way to think about emotional intelligence. Or is it exhilarating? Intoxicating? Maybe it's galvanizing.

But back to you. Let's accept that framing a feeling differently makes you feel it differently. You can feel cozier if you know the word *hygge*. You can feel a longing as intense as homesickness for a place you've never even been if you know the Finnish word *kaukokaipuu*. Having a single word helps, but an extremely specific phrase will do the job. *The joy of discovering one last fry at the bottom of the bag. The mix of sadness and relief when a houseguest leaves. The perverse pleasure in letting a deadline pass you by.* The better you can pin down a feeling, the more strongly you can feel it.

You can also change an emotional concept you already know. One of the most useful studies I've ever read was published in 2013 by Harvard Business School professor Alison Wood Brooks. In it she showed the benefits of something she called "anxiety reappraisal," a handy kind of emotional alchemy through which you can turn your nerves into something useful simply by whispering three little words to yourself: "I am excited." When you're preparing to do something with a high risk of awkwardness—like going on a first date or getting up the nerve to do a comedy open-mic night, if that's your thing—your palms (and probably pits) sweat and your heart pounds, sensations we understand as nervousness.

But your brain only told your body to do those things because it knows you're gearing up to do something you're going to need a lot of energy for; you'd feel those same physical sensations if you were, say, *excited*. In Brooks's study, people who accepted their jitters but reframed them as excitement performed better on a series of scary tasks (karaoke, public speaking, math) than people who tried forcing themselves to calm down. I've read hundreds of psychology papers over my career as a journalist, but only a handful have stuck with me after filing the piece. This is one.

In the spirit of this book, here is an embarrassing secret: Since reading that study, before I have to do something mildly terrifying, like giving a presentation or attending an important meeting, I go somewhere quiet, put in my earbuds, and listen to "I'm So Excited" by the Pointer Sisters. It is fine if you mock me, but also, try it. I don't even mind if you adopt this habit too, and then continue to mock me; the important thing is that you try it. I'm so excited for you!

The theory of constructed emotion is exciting, though I'm still wary of how this might apply to people with mood disorders like anxiety or depression. Barring mental illness, however, it's a new way of thinking about your feelings. You don't just have to react. You get to direct too. "You realize that if your brain is using your past to construct your present, you can invest energy in the present to cultivate new experiences that then become the seeds for your future," Barrett has said. "You can cultivate or curate experiences in the now and then they become, if you practice them, they become automated enough that your brain will automatically construct them in the future."

You can't just memorize the signs of seven distinct facial expressions so that you know exactly how the person in front of you feels, so that you never misinterpret what they want from you. But you *can* change how you experience the feeling of awkwardness. Cringeworthy moments are those that show you the gap between who you think you are and how other people are perceiving you. But just as there are different shades of sad and mad, there are gradations in the way we cringe. Some of these concepts already exist in other languages: There is *malu*, a word used by the Dusun Baguk of Indonesia, defined as "the sudden experience of feeling constricted, inferior and awkward around people of higher status." I think about this one whenever I find myself alone in an elevator with my boss. Or there is *Fremdscham*, a German word we'll explore in more detail in chapter 7, which means "shame felt for actions done by someone else." This tends to come to mind if I spend more than five minutes reading my Twitter feed.

When I started this curious project of studying to death an emotion that drives me crazy, I understood the feeling of cringing in only one way. It meant shame. It meant run and hide, duck and cover. Rochat's concept of the irreconcilable gap helped add some nuance to this peculiar form of self-recognition. There are times, for instance, when it can feel like *a surprise confrontation with an unflattering mirror.* Mirrors get it wrong sometimes, though. People can send back reflections of you that function like the mirrors you'd find in an Old Navy fitting room: unflattering and harsh, maybe on purpose.

But if what they're seeing about you is unflattering and *true*, then it's the version of cringing I've grown to appreciate, something you could call *the embarrassed relief of being told you have broccoli in your teeth.* You feel stupid in the moment, but wouldn't you rather know?

I would *now*, but I didn't always feel that way. Even about broccoli. I honestly used to ignore it when I saw bits of food between my friends' teeth or on their faces, thinking I was protecting their feelings, and I would get a little resentful if someone informed me of the same. This is ridiculous, I realize in retrospect, and having an aversive reaction to awkwardness is similarly ridiculous, in that it is ineffectual in the long run. Looking at yourself through someone else's eyes can make you feel silly and unsophisticated in the moment. But you *have* to look, if you ever want to become something like the idealized picture of yourself you hold in your own mind.

CHAPTER 4

Your Growing Edge

I t used to be one of his proudest moments as a comedian. In the mid-2000s, W. Kamau Bell was a featured comic on *Premium Blend*, a stand-up showcase series on Comedy Central, and he was great. It was his big break, or at least it was *a* break, one in a series of achievements that eventually led him to the success he has now as host of the Emmy-winning CNN show *United Shades of America*. But these days he can't think about it without cringing.

Not because the jokes were bad. The set is notable even today, more than a decade on, because it happens to include what appears to be the very first Obama joke made by a prominent comedian. True, it's hard to judge whether it's a *good* Obama joke, in part because the punchline—*Boy, isn't this guy's name weird?*—is so tired now. "People say he's gonna be president someday!" Bell says of Obama, then still a senator from Illinois. "My question is— president of what? Because there may be a black president one day, but there will *never* be a black president named *Barack Obama.*

Ladies and gentlemen, that's *too* black. That dude's name may as well be Blackie Blackerson, you see what I'm saying?"

Still: the first Obama joke! That's pretty cool. A few years later, he was still so proud of the clip that he sent it to his good friend Martha Rynberg, whom he'd met when she started taking the solo performance workshop he taught. Rynberg had quickly become one of Bell's favorite students and then one of his favorite people. They're the kind of friends who are more like family: She's godmother to his kids, and he's godfather to hers. At the time, they were working together on Bell's stage show, *W. Kamau Bell Curve: Ending Racism in About an Hour.* "He would come over every Tuesday. You know that book *Tuesdays with Morrie*?" she asks me. "We started calling it Tuesdays with Martha." But she'd still never seen his stand-up, so Bell e-mailed it to her, hoping to impress his dear friend.

But Rynberg never e-mailed back. Later Bell was in her kitchen, the two of them working together on *Bell Curve* as they did every week, and he brought it up again. He was kind of fishing for a compliment, as he remembers it in his memoir, *The Awkward Thoughts of W. Kamau Bell.* "That Barack Obama joke is still good, right?" he recalls asking her.

"Yeah," she said, "but that Condi joke . . ."

That Condi joke. Remembering it now gives him an instant stomachache. The premise of Bell's Obama bit was the underwhelming state of black leadership in U.S. politics in the mid-2000s and how the then-senator could maybe one day shape things up by playing a larger role. But the beginning of the joke is all about Condoleezza Rice. "It used to be that black politicians were our leaders," Bell says in the clip. "Who's the most prominent black politician right now? Condoleezza Rice? Yee-ikes." A brief pause before the big punchline: "Never before has so much evil come together with so much ugly."

The audience explodes in laughter, a hooting, surprised kind of laughter. "That's all I'm trying to say," he adds as the laughter is still rolling in. He pauses again, grinning at the cracking up crowd. He's killing it, and he knows it.

It's the way he'd always seen his *Premium Blend* appearance, as something to be proud of. His first big TV appearance *and* what's considered to be the world's first Obama joke? Get out of here. But his friend sees it in a different light.

Something to know about Rynberg: She is white, and she and her partner were adoptive parents to a little girl named Olive, who is black. "Condoleezza Rice looks like my daughter," she said to Bell in his memory of the conversation. "Is Olive ugly?"

He didn't want to hear this. "What are you talking about?" he remembers saying to her. "She doesn't look like your daughter." But Rynberg didn't relent. "My daughter is a dark-skinned, African American young girl with very, sort of, black features," Bell recalls her saying. "And so when you call Condoleezza Rice ugly, you're calling my daughter ugly."

She kept going. "You don't like Bush's politics, but I bet you wouldn't call him ugly," she told him. "And here's the thing: *She's not ugly*. When you call her ugly, you are just subscribing to a white European version of beauty. And you can't do that. My daughter looks way more like Condoleezza Rice than she does whoever that white woman is on the cover of *Rolling Stone* over there."

Even *still* she kept going. "*And* as a black man who is partnered with a white woman, how could you call a black woman ugly?" he remembers his friend saying. "Like, what is that doing for you? Why would you want to be included with black men who are looked at as actively choosing white women over black women?"

The way Bell talks about all of this, you get the feeling that Rynberg's words are seared permanently into his memory. Maybe they are. In a chapter called "My Awkward Sexism," he tells a couple stories of uncomfortable moments when Rynberg confronted him about sexism in his act. "It was painful," Bell said of those moments when I reached him by phone just before the publication of his book. "It was embarrassing. I was not somebody who thought to describe myself as sexist or misogynist. I thought those were definitions outside of myself."

He's long since retired the Condi routine, and he ends that chapter of his book with a lengthy apology to the former secretary of state. But the mere thought of it is still an excruciating experience for Bell, even now, a decade later. During a question-and-answer session of his live radio show *Kamau Right Now!* in the fall of 2016, an audience member asked Bell to do his Condoleezza Rice bit. "Oh *nooo*, that's not gonna happen," he said. "No, thank you. . . . I've had a good run going the last few years, I don't want to ruin it by bringing back that horrible joke. Thank you for bringing *that* up." He quickly ends the conversation. "Thank you," he says, "give that person a round of applause for embarrassing me about a joke I wrote years ago that is horribly horrible horrible!"

Kamau Right Now! consists of a rotating panel, and one of the panel members asks, understandably, for Bell to explain what that was all about. You can *hear* the cringe in his voice as he says, "I used to have a horrible joke about Condoleezza Rice, it was really bad, and I don't wanna think about it because it makes me feel sad! And I have daughters now!"

His conversation with Rynberg forever changed the way he saw that joke and, at least for those few uncomfortable moments, the way he saw himself. Back in the kitchen with Rynberg, he remembers, "It got super awkward. I wanted to run away from the conversation.

"But I also wanted to maintain my friendship with Martha," he continued. "So in that moment, instead of running away, I sort of sat in the awkwardness and leaned into it, and then eventually could very clearly hear that she was right. . . . She was one hundred percent right. And it changed the course of my career."

He's not exaggerating. Bell now describes awkwardness as a central function of his work. "I've spent a lot of my life talking about the power of awkward conversations, a lot of my professional life," he told me. "When I really think about the work that I'm doing, that's what it is—it's encouraging people to have different conversations." It's an example of the discussion from chapter 1 about "awkward" being asked to shoulder more weight than it used to: On his CNN show, he's had conversations with members of the KKK and the prominent white supremacist Richard Spencer, to name just two extreme examples.

When I heard Bell talk about his work, and in particular how that uncomfortable conversation with his friend changed his life so many years ago, a phrase I recently came across came to mind: "your growing edge." When you say something kind of shitty without *knowing* that what you said was kind of shitty, and someone calls you on it, it forces you to peer into the irreconcilable gap, true, but that's not the phrase I mean. When this is done with empathy and compassion—as Rynberg did back then, and as Bell does in his work now—it's an opportunity to begin to *bridge* that gap. You can see yourself from their point of view and take a hard look at what needs to improve. "By the end of [that conversation], I was changed," Bell told me. "And I was also determined to make sure I learned from that and did better. But you don't get there without awkwardness."

As we saw in the previous chapters, one way to understand awkward moments is that you're confronting who you're not. And yet another way to understand them is that they may also be showing you what you *could* be. But first you have to find your growing edge.

———

IN HINDSIGHT, THE ARRANGEMENT OF THE CHAIRS IN THE seminar room was a clear sign of what was to come. It's 6:35 on a Friday night, and I am five minutes late for a workshop called "Undoing Racism," put on by a group called the People's Institute for Survival and Beyond (PISAB). It's been described to me by past participants as a weekend full of, among other things, flustered, faltering white people awkwardly attempting to talk honestly about race in America.

I'm looking forward to what I imagine will be a series of smart lectures. I'm also exhausted from the workweek so, frankly, I'm looking forward to a bit of solitude: I imagine the next few days will be filled with lots of thinking and careful note taking, all done quietly on my own in the very last row, preferably somewhere near the door. An awkward introvert's paradise. I enter seminar room B to find that the class hasn't started yet, but—oh no—where I expected to find rows of chairs and tables so that I could hide in the back behind my laptop, instead I see that the chairs have been formed into the very worst shape that you can arrange chairs in: a giant circle.

Inside the conference room, about forty people are seated around the ring of chairs. The workshops aren't intended specifically for white people, but this weekend most of us—I'd say around 70, 75 percent—are white. Some are chatting, some are silently staring off into space, but many are sitting perilously close to the edges of their chairs with their arms and legs tightly crossed. I make my peace with the circle and take a seat. Soon the session begins.

"We're here to talk about racism," one of the workshop leaders, an amiable young white man—I'd place him in his early thirties—named Justin says to the room. Justin has a folksy habit of droppin' his *g*'s when he speaks, and his good-natured earnestness gives off a certain church-youth-group-leader vibe, as if any minute he may pull out an acoustic guitar and lead us in worship songs. He warns us that the next two and a half days will often be uncomfortable. To underline this point, he asks the room, "Show of hands—how many of you have had conversations with friends and family about racism?" About half of the participants raise their hands. "And how did that go?" We laugh nervously in reply.

A second leader—a funny, sharp woman named Annie, who is

Latina and whose demeanor brings the phrase "doesn't suffer fools gladly" to mind—joins in, mimicking the folded-over posture of those in the room who are already obviously uncomfortable. This, she says, gesturing at her own hunched-up body, is nothing new. She and the other trainers see this all the time. "They're so tight— they're, like, falling off their chairs," she says, pretending to fall off her own. We laugh again, and the sound chases some of the tension out of the room.

If a circle of chairs is introduced at the start of an evening workshop, the sentence "Let's all go around the circle and share" must be used by the evening's end. We close the night with all fortyish of us, one by one, answering three questions: who we are, what we do, and why we're here this weekend. I learn that about half of the attendees are from a social-work graduate program in the city; these were the chatty people from the beginning of the night—they all knew each other already, which hardly seems fair. The rest of us came alone, and we work in a variety of fields: advertising, education, academia.

We all came for our own reasons, but as each of us speaks, a theme emerges: Over and over, people confess that they want to start having difficult conversations about race and racism in themselves and in this country, but they feel too nervous to know where to start. I scribble down some of the things they say:

"It's a little touchy."

"It's just weird to deal with."

"Not knowing how to name uncomfortable experiences—it makes you feel like you're crumbling under it."

"I feel tongue-tied, or frozen."

"I feel like I *have* to feel uncomfortable—like it's the least I can do."

"I feel so anxious. . . . It makes me want to avoid talking about it."

"I'm here to try and make myself constructively uncomfortable."

When it's my turn, I mumble something about being a writer who's working on a book that is in part about how to have awkward, uncomfortable conversations. I've never been good at the elevator pitch. By the time we're done, about half the group has said that they're here this weekend because talking about race makes them deeply uncomfortable, and they'd like to know how to get past this. As it happens, PISAB has a term for this, the awkwardness that arises when well-meaning people stumble around when trying to talk about racism: They call it "your growing edge." It's something to watch for, they say, because it signals an opportunity. "That's the moment to sit with it," Justin says. " 'Why do I feel this way?' Check in with yourself. There's the most amount of possibility to grow when you're in that discomfort."

I love this phrase: "your growing edge." I love its sincerity, I love its unpretentiousness, I love its gentle corniness. But I also love it for its sheer utility. PISAB recognizes that the feeling of awkwardness may never disappear entirely, so you may as well change the way you conceptualize it. In my mind, this connects with the idea of reframing emotions that we covered in chapter 3: Change the way you conceptualize a feeling, and you can change the way you feel it.

PISAB has been around for more than three decades and was founded in 1980 by a pair of community organizers in New Orleans and Yellow Springs, Iowa. In the years since, half a million people have taken one of the organization's workshops. It is nothing new, in other words, but as I've been researching this book, I've been interested to note how many organizations like it exist *and* how many of them have essentially said that their mission is to promote awkward conversations about uncomfortable but consequential subjects like politics, religion, and race. All of the things the ghost of Emily Post would rather we avoid.

There's Living Room Conversations and Village Square, both of which help people facilitate talks among friends or acquaintances about touchy subjects like money, mental health, and the environment. There's also Hi from the Other Side and the American Dialogue Project, both of which connect people of different political persuasions for a short phone chat, accompanied by a trained facilitator. I did one of these recently and had a nice, if not life-changing, conversation with a farmer in Nebraska who talked a lot about his pride in his Finnish heritage.

I'm also a little surprised at how often representatives from these groups use the word "awkward," which, as I've noted a few times already, can at first blush seem woefully inadequate. Maybe that's by design, though: a name we've settled on for something unnamable. Early in 2017, for instance, journalist Ana Marie Cox launched a new podcast, *With Friends Like These*, which she often describes as being devoted to awkward conversations. And in the fraught week after the 2016 election, the hashtag #MakeItAwkward circulated on Twitter, with people urging one another to call people out when they said something sexist or racist. As of this writing, that online encouragement was set to move offline in early 2018, with the Canadian city of Edmonton hosting a conference called the MIA Summit (that's MIA as in Make It Awkward), which promises to help its attendees learn how to "disrupt the status quo and create lasting social change."

That's a lot of people counting on the power of awkward conversations to change minds. Are they right?

THERE ARE TWO MAJOR RULES AT EVERY PISAB WORKSHOP, Sandy Bernabei tells me. Bernabei is a New York City social worker and the founder of the Antiracist Alliance, a group that partners with PISAB to put on these events, and I spoke with her before attending the workshop to get a preview of what it might be like. The first rule you could call the butt-in-chair rule: Everyone must agree to stay the whole time. Sometimes, she says, deep discussions of race—particularly in a roomful of strangers, who often have different cultural backgrounds—can become so profoundly uncomfortable for attendees that they slip out the door during a coffee break and never come back. A seat at the workshop will set you back a hefty $350, but that can start to seem like a small financial sacrifice if it'll buy you a one-way ticket away from the awkwardness.

The second rule goes beyond just showing up. It's this: When you reach your growing edge, keep going. "We're comfortable talking about what we know about, right?" Bernabei said. "But the minute you hit something you don't know about, you shut down. You don't want to be exposed." It's the irreconcilable gap again. Maybe, according to your own self-concept, you are an informed, enlightened, *woke*-type person. Bernabei is white, and so am I, so she's talking to me specifically about the perspective of many white participants in PISAB workshops. Part of the point is to help us see a more accurate view of ourselves, and to help us understand how much we still have to learn here.

There's an apartment building I run by often, an oddly shaped one in that an eye-level block of concrete juts out, encroaching onto the sidewalk. I've never hit my head when turning onto the block, but sometimes I think it's just a matter of time. I realize at some point during the weekend workshop that I'm picturing the edge of that building when I hear the phrase "growing edge," and several times over the course of the weekend I smack my face right up against this metaphorical concrete.

On the second day, we break into groups to discuss media portrayal of class in America. My group, without realizing we're doing it, ends up mostly discussing race instead. So when I am called on to stand up in front of the room and give an overview of our group discussion, I do what our group did—and then, with all those eyes staring at me, my mistake dawns on me. "I . . . just realized I'm conflating these things," I say when it hits me. I apologize and add for good measure, "I, um, hate talking in front of people." There's a smattering of kind laughter, but my error hasn't gone unnoticed. Later a group leader named Diane says in a review of the discussion, "We're so used to conflating race and class, and some of you did." I shrink a little in my seat and can feel my cheeks burn. "To the rest of you, good job staying away from that."

After Diane says this, I think, *Sandy was right*. It *did* feel like being exposed, like a spotlight shining on my uglier impulses—

even ones that, before this weekend, I would've argued that I didn't *have*. It's not that I'm trying to argue the feeling of awkwardness is the *only* thing that keeps well-meaning white people like myself from acknowledging their own patterns of racist thoughts or actions. But I do think it's at least *part* of the problem. Forget "gap"— there is something more like an irreconcilable psychic *chasm* between how I see myself and my words and actions and how people of color may perceive me and my words and actions. When those two yous collide in a Skype video chat, revealing that you are having a weirder hair day than you thought, it's disappointing. When these yous collide in the context of discussing something like racism, it's sickening.

"But wouldn't you *want* someone to help you see it?" Robin DiAngelo, who studies race and racism at Westfield State University, asks me. In a 2011 paper, DiAngelo coined the term "white fragility," which she described as "a state in which even a minimum amount of racial stress becomes intolerable, triggering a range of defensive moves." She uses the same broccoli-in-your-teeth metaphor that I used at the end of chapter 3, to describe the way you can learn to be thankful for having someone point these things out to you. "Most of us have the experience, if we're even minimally open-minded, of realizing that something we used to say or do is kind of cringeworthy, now that we understand it— jokes we used to tell, or assumptions we used to make," she says. "And we're so grateful that we know not to say or do those things anymore—and yet we're so defensive when somebody tries to help us see." But wouldn't you rather know when there's a little racism stuck in your teeth?

Confronting your hidden biases—and misconceptions and misunderstandings—is difficult, exhausting, embarrassing work, and I should point out that I'm not claiming to be an expert here. White people like me, and like Bernabei, often simply do not know what we are talking about. "This is an area that white people can never be experts on," she tells me. "People of color are the experts, *and* they have the lived experience." That ambiguity makes us uncomfortable, she says, and in response, "we tend to divert the conversation, back to something where we have some expertise."

On that very first evening, Annie and Justin prepared the group for confronting that discomfort. "We *hope* that at some point [this weekend] you feel uncomfortable," Annie said, to which Justin added, "It would be strange to be in the room for two days and talk about racism and everyone walks out comfortable." After all, chickening out is not an option for everyone, a point Bernabei made in our earlier conversation.

"Shutting down is a privilege," she said. "So we invite everyone to experience that growing edge and to *not* shut down and to just push through."

"Okay," I said, trying to envision this in action. "But . . . *how* do you push through?"

"You take a deep breath," she answered. "You try not to react right away. You hang in there. And you get better at it." Still, I assume that *some* discomfort must always be there. Is the answer, then, learning to live with that discomfort?

"Listen to me. Do I sound uncomfortable, talking about all of this?" she asked me.

"You don't, actually," I said.

"I've become totally okay saying 'I don't know," she said. "We really have to become brave and to admit this is one area we can never be experts in. You can learn to be comfortable."

Other people who are much more knowledgeable than me on this subject have pointed out that feeling a little uncomfortable is literally, laughably, the very *least* white people like me can do. But after Bernabei and I got off the phone, I started rereading some of the notes I'd assembled during the time I'd spent researching the feeling of awkwardness. One of the definitions I'd settled on, which I noted in the opening chapter, is that it's self-consciousness tinged with uncertainty about how to proceed, which gets at why we nervous white people so often reach for the word "awkward" in this context: *What* are we supposed to say or do next? Figuring that out isn't easy. But it's not impossible.

———

FOR SOME TIME AFTER ATTENDING THE WORKSHOP, I flounder around searching for a clear answer to the question I posed earlier in this chapter. It certainly *feels* like challenging yourself to have more awkward conversations could help change minds—both others' and your own—but human intuition has an unfortunate way of being wrong when you'd least expect. The science journalist part of my brain craved data and the reassurance of confident charts and line graphs.

And then I remembered one recent, and remarkable, paper published in *Science* in 2016, called "Durably Reducing Transphobia," which describes one of the most optimistic studies I've ever come across. In it, researchers partnered with canvassers in order to discover whether brief conversations *are* enough to change attitudes about sensitive, controversial subjects in a real-life setting. At the heart of this study is the successful application of two important psychological concepts: active processing and perspective taking. Understanding both of these ideas has helped me figure out where to start in my own mind when I want to speak up but don't know how.

In Miami in December of 2014, local law officials had just passed an ordinance that would protect transgender people in Miami-Dade County from discrimination in housing, employment, and access to public places (this included things like hotels, restaurants, libraries, and stores, but not public restrooms, by the way). Local LGBT groups feared that the law would spark a backlash against the trans community, and so they set out—unannounced— to knock on area voters' doors and gauge their opinions by having some brief conversations. The canvassers asked voters what they thought of the new antidiscrimination law; they also asked if the voters could think of a time when they had felt discriminated against. Finally, after the canvassers asked the person at the door to recall a time they'd felt misunderstood or judged, they asked again: What did the voters think about the new ordinance? Most of these conversations lasted only around ten minutes.

But that was enough, it seems, because the results of the field experiment are impressive. The researchers used something called a "feeling thermometer" to gauge people's attitudes toward trans people before and after these short conversations and found the voters' positive opinions increased ten points on average. To put that insane jump in perspective, let me ask you this: Do you remember how much American attitudes toward gay and lesbian people changed from the late 1990s to the early 2010s? In 1998 we were just one year out from the controversy over the "I'm gay" episode of *Ellen*. In 2012 Obama became the first president to publicly support same-sex marriage. Opinions in the United States toward gay people changed rapidly in those fourteen years, but these conversations in Miami were able to produce even *bigger* increases in positive attitudes toward trans people. In ten minutes.

What's more, these changes in attitude outlasted the moment at the door. Three months later, the researchers checked back in with the voters and found that they still had more positive opinions toward trans people than they had in the beginning.

It's just one study. It's a very cool, very hopeful study, but it's just one study. It's not clear yet whether it really proves the power of awkward conversations to change minds, although David Broockman, a professor at Stanford University who coauthored this paper, tells me that he's interested in further investigating that question. It's also not clear whether this approach could be applied more widely, to contentious subjects beyond transphobia. But at least for now, the lessons from this research have given me a place to start.

I mentioned that the canvassers drew on two well-established ideas in social psychology. One of them is perspective taking: Toward the end of the chats, the volunteers asked the voters if they could think of a time they'd been treated unfairly, and from there the canvasser gently helped the voter see how that personal experience of theirs connected to the need for antidiscrimination laws. You will no doubt recognize this as empathy, or the ability to imagine and then feel what someone else is feeling. As we saw in chapter 3, it's not always so easy to accurately guess someone else's emotions. So whenever you can, ask.

And this too is a key component of successful so-called awkward conversations. In the *Science* study, the researchers theorize that what may have contributed to the canvassers' success was the second psychological concept at work here: active processing. It's a term that means abandoning your gut instinct in favor of carefully thinking something through. In these conversations, canvassers asked the voters a couple different times to explain—perhaps for the first time out loud—their beliefs about transgender people.

In their paper, Broockman and his coauthor theorize that this may have helped voters tap into what the behavioral economist Daniel Kahneman has famously called System 2 thinking. That's your cooler, rational side, as compared with the heated, impulsive System 1. There seems to be something special in combining these two concepts, something that takes people from shallow arguments based on gut instincts toward real understanding and empathy, maybe even compassion.

And yet awkward conversations can be so stressful. It's so easy to feel in over your head. I know myself, and I know that if *I* get into a conversation about something huge and uncomfortable with someone who sees the issue differently than I do, my mind will go blank, and more often than not I'll say nothing. I'm not sure how much muttering jargony words to myself (*Active processing!!*) would help me when I'm feeling nervous.

It's tough, because in a way, this is far too complex to be explained in some kind of prescriptive rule book. But some social psychologists, like Alana Conner at Stanford, are at least trying to give people a place to start. Conner is the executive director of SPARQ, a Stanford think tank that seeks to apply social science to the real world. (Its mission is in its name: Social Psychological Answers to Real-World Questions.) When I reach her by phone, she tells me she's been putting together a "tool kit" that she hopes will help people who are interested in having more awkward conversations about big issues but don't know where to begin.

"The first step is actually *not* to try and persuade anybody," she tells me. Instead, she says, approach the conversation as if you were an anthropologist: Try to understand, to the best of your ability, how the other person sees the world and how that compares with your own point of view. "Think of it as an occasion to really learn how people different from you think and feel," she says, "rather than an opportunity to change their minds." It's a cooler, calmer way to talk about difficult subjects, and it's one way to help both of you keep an open mind. This is often also a pathway toward active processing.

If you still need more advice, Conner has some practical tips on how to think like an anthropologist: Ask questions, particularly ones that start with the word "why." This serves the dual purposes of helping you to better see the world from the other person's point of view *and* giving you something to say when words are failing you.

She also urges people to seek common ground—there's perspective taking again—and to respond with "I" statements: *When you say X, I feel Y.* This way, it becomes less about throwing facts at each other or, as Conner put it, it's less about "me trying to beat you into submission with my fact stick." Instead, she said, it changes "the discourse to 'We are two people who care enough about each other to try to see why we disagree.'"

"HI, GAB?"

I'm on the phone with Gabrielle Bosché, a high school classmate (though she's younger than I am) who has grown up to author several books about millennials in the workplace, and who regularly speaks at big conferences about the same. More recently, though, she has become at least a minor figure in the conservative and far-right media landscape, with appearances on the SiriusXM Patriot Channel and bylines on Breitbart.com.

I was always fond of her; I have a soft spot for overachieving women. If I'm honest about it, maybe that's why I find her so interesting—she reminds me of me, at least a little bit, so it's been strange to watch us drift further and further apart ideologically.

It's one thing to want to have more so-called awkward conversations, or to believe in the power of them as W. Kamau Bell does. It's another to initiate them. So many of us were raised not to make waves or rock boats, yet this is increasingly seeming like an inert approach to life. But where do you even begin, especially if you're naturally shy?

When I interviewed Bell, he pointed out that you don't have to overthink this, especially these days. "Donald Trump is basically, every day, inviting people to have uncomfortable conversations," Bell said. "And if you only have those on Facebook threads or on Twitter, then you're doing it wrong. You have to actually have those conversations with people in your real life . . . who don't agree with you."

And so here we are. Bosché is generous enough to agree to a phone call, and when we chat, it's just a couple weeks after the August 2017 violence at the white nationalist rally in Charlottesville, Virginia. Two nice white ladies talking about the rise of white nationalism in the United States. This should be a sufficiently uncomfortable place to start.

Before I call her, I scribble down in my notebook the rules as described to me by Stanford's Alana Conner and others: Seek common ground. Ask "why" questions; make "I" statements. And be an anthropologist—try to understand instead of convince. On the opposite page from my list of instructions is a list of possible subjects to bring up, the last of which is "on both sides . . . ?" And then Bosché quickly steers the conversation there without my having to.

"I believe President Trump came out and said, 'I condemn violence on both sides,' . . . because he saw that there was instigation—and not only violent rhetoric but violent action—on both sides," she says. She can't see it, but I raise my eyebrows in disbelief when she says this.

"Frankly," she continues, "I think he really showed a lot of leadership."

Listen, I am not expecting any awards for courage here. Everything in me at this moment is telling me to *be polite* and paper over the fact that I find this equivocation offensive. Lately, though, politeness seems overrated. "I guess for me," I start slowly, going for a version of an "I" statement, "that was a surprising thing for him to say when, like, there was one person dead, and it was pretty clear—"

"— who did it," she interjects.

"Well, yeah," I say. "And that's why the 'on both sides' thing made people so mad. But that's not—I take it that's not how you read that?"

"When I was listening to his press conference, I wasn't considering, 'Oh you know, clearly he should say that the white nationalist who killed someone—we especially [don't] condone him,'" she says. "Should he have said that? Probably. But I think that this is an example of how we never saw this kind of speaking down to the office of the presidency with George W. Bush, certainly not with Barack Obama."

And on and on she goes, changing the subject without my quite realizing that's what she's done. Listening back to my recording of this, I'm furious with myself for my timidity. I kept trying to ask those "why" questions to get her to explain her views, but I'm not sure, in retrospect, that she was interested in having a conversation at that active-processing level; either that or perhaps I didn't phrase my questions clearly enough. (At one point I blurted out, "Do you—do you *like* Trump?" So, yeah. It might be the latter.)

After we hang up, I feel ill. We got nowhere. Why even bother?

Much of the media coverage of that *Science* paper mentioned earlier in this chapter focused heavily on the fact that this *one* ten-minute conversation was enough to change people's minds, in the short and the long term. But despite his own conviction about the importance of awkward conversations, Bell knows it's not that simple.

"I've heard this from people: 'Kamau, I listened to you about the awkward conversations, and I tried to talk to my grandfather once, and it was so bad, it didn't work, so I don't agree with you anymore!'" he tells me when we chat over the phone. "Like, who are you to think *once* is going to help?" Also, as I just demonstrated, if you only bother to have the conversation once, chances are you will be terrible at it.

Bell tells me he's been thinking about this lately, the power and the limits of uncomfortable dialogue. Just a few nights earlier, he'd recorded an episode of *Kamau Right Now!* in which his friend Nato Green, a comedian and community organizer, challenged him on his belief in the power of awkwardness. "He believes you have to have boots on the ground," Bell says. "He believes that sometimes you have to just run at the doors of power . . . and awkward conversations aren't necessarily going to get you the change you want fast enough."

Bell agrees. Kind of. But to him, movements like the March on Washington or the Women's March can fit into his definition of what it means to be unafraid of awkwardness. It's someone having the courage to say, *Hey, uh, this thing you're doing? This isn't really working for me.*

"I mean, Occupy Wall Street was just a way to have an awkward conversation," he tells me. "And guess what? Now every politician knows how to say 'wealth inequality.' Nobody knew how to say that before! So as much as people think these things were failures, everything doesn't happen the way you expect it to. Everything moves at different speeds. Now people on the right and the left regularly say 'wealth inequality.' Whether they actually want to do anything about it . . . At least the beginning is having the term in your brain."

And by the way, it's really nice to be able to choose to avoid many of these conversations, or to have one exactly once and then give up, Bell points out. Not everyone has that option. "I think that people of color, gay people, gay people who are people of color, disabled people—we're all used to having these conversations a lot, you know?" he says to me. "Those of us who are sort of allowed to float through the world and just worry about things like rent and our jobs—we *have* to get used to having more awkward conversations."

It's scary and disorienting to feel like your self-concept is being challenged. I like to imagine the irreconcilable gap as if it were a physical place, some shadowy abyss that opens up in the ground between you and another person. You know how we say things about awkward moments like "I wanted the ground to open up and swallow me whole"? Maybe that's what we mean. Or, to use a different metaphor introduced in chapter 2: If we sometimes use other people to see our own reflections, then initiating an awkward conversation can feel like entering a hall of mirrors. You're getting a glimpse of how they see you, and meanwhile you're watching them realize how you see them, which probably shifts the way they had previously seen you—it's head spinning. It's intimidating. But it's worthwhile. At the very least, in my conversation with Bosché, I realized that my mind shuts off at the mere mention of Trump's name, which is also not exactly useful. I could stand to improve at that, if only so I can better fight through the brain fog that came over me as we spoke.

Also: If we can't read each other's minds or emotions as well as we think we can, as discussed in chapter 3, then we're going to have to learn how to talk about difficult subjects. I keep mentioning how the word "awkward" can feel too slight to be applied to heavier subjects, but I've started to wonder whether that's to our benefit. Using the word can make the discomfort feel more manageable, perhaps especially for those of us who are not naturally bold. It's just a little awkward. That's all. "For me," Bell says, "leaning into the awkwardness and facing the fact that it's going to be awkward makes it clear that that doesn't mean *bad*. It just means 'Okay, I'm going to feel uncomfortable and embarrassed,' and not naming those things as negative. That's just part of an awkward conversation."

SECTION 2

Is Everyone Staring at Me?

CHAPTER 5

The Awkwardness Vortex

Sorry, just quickly . . ." the businessman says to the business-woman. They're in a beige, bland conference room, and he's in the middle of conducting an interview; she, meanwhile, has just arrived from headquarters and is there to observe and take notes. The man is of average height; the woman is a little person. This becomes important.

"How should I refer to you?" he asks her. "Do I . . ." He trails off.

"Ah—Fran," she supplies.

"AFRAN?" the interviewer repeats. "Is that an acronym, or . . . ?"

"No," says Fran. "That's my name." I hit "pause." Fran and the unnamed interviewer are actors in a short film that I have watched in horror on YouTube at least a dozen times. In just under four minutes, it makes me cringe almost as much as I do when watching the worst Larry David moments from *Curb Your Enthusiasm*, to the point where I keep having to stop the clip to collect myself. After a few seconds, the cringe dissipates. I hit "play."

"Oh, okay," the man is saying. "Well. Welcome! Fantastic. Take a seat!"

"Thank you," Fran responds, smiling warmly and extending her right hand.

"Oh! Sorry, yes," the nameless man says, and he then hooks both of his hands underneath Fran's armpits, hoists her off the ground, and plops her down in the chair behind her. From her new, seated position, Fran freezes for several long moments, with wide eyes and incredulous eyebrows.

"A handshake would've been fine," she finally says.

"No!" he replies, waving her off. "It's no problem, really."

It's not real life, but it's based on a series of real-life stories from disabled people who've had to weather the awkwardness created by the nondisabled. It's part of the "End the Awkward" campaign, launched in 2014 by Scope, a British disability charity. It was inspired, public relations manager Danielle Wootton tells me, by the group's own research on attitudes toward disability in the UK. "One of the most interesting insights was the fact that a lot of the attitudes nondisabled people were expressing was . . . awkwardness around disability," rather than outright discrimination, she says. Scope also works to combat structural problems the disability community in the UK faces, such as accessibility, employment, and housing. But this seemed like a subject worth taking on too, an opportunity to address a largely unspoken problem in a light, comedic tone.

According to Scope's own research, about two thirds of Britons surveyed said that they felt awkward or uncomfortable around disabled people. Young people ages eighteen to thirty-four were twice as likely as their older peers to feel this way, and one fifth of this age group said that they'd purposely avoided interacting with a disabled person because it made them so uncomfortable. Often, Wooten says, "nondisabled people end up panicking, or being awkward, because they're scared of being offensive." Many nondisabled people "don't want to acknowledge that this is an issue," she continues. "It's not very nice to hear that you're making disabled people feel socially isolated with your social awkwardness."

I must admit that I've wandered into this kind of awkwardness myself, and recently, when talking to a woman on whom I was developing a giant friend crush. Not long ago, I was on the phone with a writer named Emily Ladau describing the Scope ad I mentioned at the start of this chapter. Ladau is an activist and public speaker whose work on disability rights has been featured in places like the *Washington Post*, *BuzzFeed*, and the *New York Times*, though I confess I am most impressed by her 2002 appearance on *Sesame Street*, when she was just ten. She also keeps an entertaining blog, *Words I Wheel By*, which centers on what her life is like as a woman who uses a wheelchair, on which she wrote a post recommending the "End the Awkward" campaign. Ladau is witty and charming, and I had so much fun interviewing her that I basically ended the conversation with something extremely chill and laid back, such as, "Can we please hang out?!"

But as I tried to tell her about the ad, I faltered. I know the term "little person," of course, but detectable panic crept into my voice when I tried to describe the guy. I recorded the conversation, and listening back to it makes me cringe so hard at myself that while I was transcribing it, I had to turn the volume all the way down until the moment passed. "It's, like, uh, a little person," I say in the recording. "And, uh . . ." Uncomfortable pause as I dive deep within my own brain in a desperate search for the right words to use for the interviewer in comparison to Fran. "Normal"? No, I knew it obviously couldn't be that. "Tall"? Eventually I land on "the, uh, not-little person." I was so nervous about saying the wrong thing.

This sort of thing happens to me, and perhaps also to you, in countless other contexts. It happens when I overthink what to say at a party and blurt out something weird; it also used to happen a lot in meetings earlier in my career. I would sometimes get so self-conscious when presenting that it was like part of me had split off from my physical body and was seated with the rest of the editors, most of whom were at least two decades older than me. Phantom Me was now watching Actual Me badly explain the details of my team's next-day lineup, in a kind of self-inflicted irreconcilable gap. *What is this kid trying to say?* this split-off version of myself wondered with the rest of them. *What is going on with her eyebrows? Is that the third time this week she's worn that cardigan?*

It sometimes feels like I could get a grip in these situations if only I could better control my words and my behavior, yet this instinct isn't often much help in real life. When I find myself in awkward situations, my nerves usually cause extreme self-consciousness, which makes me that much more nervous, which makes me that much more self-conscious, and round and round. If the way *you* see you is on one side of the irreconcilable gap, and the way everyone else sees you is on the other, then in between is where I often feel myself getting stuck, especially when that nervous/self-consciousness loop picks up. It's a place I've started calling the awkwardness vortex.

RESEARCH CONFIRMS THE EXISTENCE OF THE VICIOUS CIR-cle of self-focus and awkwardness in everyday life. I could tell you about all the academic articles I've read about it, with titles like "Effects of Focus of Attention on Anxiety Levels and Social Performance of Individuals with Social Phobia" and "Anxious and Egocentric: How Specific Emotions Influence Perspective Taking," or I could tell you about one TV scene that captures the idea of the vortex perfectly, and in fewer than fifteen seconds. In a season-three episode of *30 Rock*, Liz Lemon tells her boss, Jack Donaghy, that she has developed a little routine for psyching herself up before attending parties where she doesn't know anyone. "Stop sweating, you idiot," she pleads with herself in front of a mirror. She's dripping with sweat as she says this and is frantically mopping it away. "What is *wrong* with you, you stupid bitch?!" Weird that this doesn't seem to help her much.

Liz Lemon's sad preparty ritual got me thinking again about the "End the Awkward" campaign and of myself in those early-career meetings. Truthfully, my interest in studying awkwardness began as an attempt to permanently banish the feeling from my life—*with science!* By now I've lost count of how many old articles I've read in obscure psychology journals that dissect the social interactions most likely to be fraught with awkwardness, things like the ways people insert themselves into already-ongoing conversations or the tactics people tend to use to exit them. Many of these also include confusing diagrams or mathematical formulas, making them too complicated to be much help in countering the everyday embarrassment of being human. I began all of this by looking for answers, for instructions, for the sweet certainty of scientific conclusions that would protect me from the excruciating discomfort of social missteps.

In the 1970s, for example, a handful of social psychologists took on a question that will surely be of interest to anyone who has ever attended a networking event, cocktail party, or really any gathering of humans ever: What is the best way to end a conversation? After eavesdropping on dozens of exchanges between both friends and strangers, these intrepid academics came up with a few extremely specific formulas that denote precisely the best ways to do this. A team of behavioral scientists from Purdue University, for instance, observed that in the final forty-five seconds of a conversation, people tend to start using "reinforcement" phrases (like "yeah" or "uh-huh") before using some kind of transitional word or phrase (usually something like "well," or perhaps an inelegant "uh"); from there, some type of appreciative phrase was used in closing.

A similar study in 1978 also came up with a formula for gracefully exiting a conversation. After listening in on telephone calls between twenty pairs of friends and twenty pairs of strangers, Stuart Albert of the University of Pennsylvania and Suzanne Kessler of SUNY-Purchase dreamed up this formula:

Content Summary Statement → Justification → Positive Statement → Continuity → Well-wishing

In real life it might sound something like this:

Person A: "Well, we talked about all the things we wanted to cover [content summary statement], so let's call it a day. I have another appointment anyway [justification]."

Person B: "Yes, I really enjoyed getting together [positive statement]."

Person A: "Let's try to do it again next week [continuity]."

Person B: "Okay. Take care [well-wishing]."

In recent years, books and videos and articles promising to teach you how to avoid awkwardness have kept popping up, and they often contain outrageously specific instructions on navigating everyday life, usually citing studies like these as examples. Nothing like the addition of equations to make a social encounter less awkward. I first came across those above formulas, actually, on a *Fast Company* site called *Co. Design* under the headline "The Science of Politely Ending a Conversation." A few weeks ago I came across a video promising to reveal how you can tell whether someone is going in for a hug or a handshake. The big secret: If they want a handshake, they'll come toward you with one hand outstretched. If they want a hug, they'll come toward you with *both* arms outstretched.

To be fair, I've run plenty of similar articles as a health and science editor over the years. One I did a while ago asked people whether they could guess the exact moment that silence in conversation turns awkward—it's four seconds, according to a 2011 study published in the *Journal of Experimental Social Psychology.* But what good could knowing that possibly do you in real life? Was I arguing that if a lull in conversation occurs, you should make damn sure the silence doesn't last for four seconds—and, what, are people supposed to be *counting* the seconds as they tick by? That does not seem like a *great* strategy to make social interactions less awkward. Although, come to think of it, this could suffice as a fun fact to puncture an awkward silence, so maybe it is useful after all.

Another popular post we've done on *New York* online was headlined "How to Deal with the Eye-Contact Awkwardness of Walking down a Long Hallway or Street toward Someone You Barely Know." The piece quotes Ronald Riggio, a psychologist at Claremont McKenna College who studies nonverbal communication and had this advice to offer: "Make eye contact at 30 ft., break eye contact, brief eye contact and eyebrow flash at 10 feet and then look straight ahead."

I've read so many articles like this; I've *written* so many articles like this. But I have to imagine that paying such close attention to yourself and your behavior would backfire. It reminds me of another aspect of the neuroscientist Lisa Feldman Barrett's critiques on microexpressions, one I didn't much touch on in chapter 3. The idea of microexpressions is alluring to self-conscious people like me: Memorize these seven expressions, and then rest assured that you're coming across the way you intend. Make sure not to knit your brows together unless you want to show that you're angry, don't wrinkle your nose unless you want to broadcast disgust, and so on. Barrett's issue with microexpressions is that she's not convinced they really do map so closely onto emotions, but even if they did, wouldn't concentrating so hard on what your face is doing distract you from the conversation you're trying to have? *And now I shall raise only the left side of my mouth, thus creating a smirk.* It seems to me that you'd be in danger of creating a social version of paralysis by analysis.

It's a version of what psychologists call explicit monitoring theory, the idea that if you are especially skilled at some action— golf is a go-to example—too much self-focus will cause you to screw up. Rich Masters, who studies human performance at the University of Hong Kong, devised a questionnaire to determine which athletes were more likely to choke under pressure; those who were tended to agree with statements like these:

- "I am self-conscious about the way I look when I'm moving."
- "I sometimes have the feeling that I am watching myself move."
- "If I see my reflection in a shop window, I will examine my movements."
- "I am concerned about what other people think about me when I am moving."

I feel so known.

Sian Beilock—formerly a psychologist at the University of Chicago, now the president of Barnard College—is one of the most prominent experts in explicit monitoring theory, and she was game to speculate a little about a potential social application. She agrees that this is a plausible explanation of awkward moments, though she cautions that this is just a hunch and has not been tested. Her research on human performance has suggested that paying close attention to every little thing you're doing is a great way for novices to learn. If you've never played golf before, then you have to start by focusing on exactly the right way to hold the club or exactly the right way to position your feet. But studies by Beilock and many others have found that once you develop expertise, too much self-focus can cause you to fumble. In extreme cases it can even give experts a case of the yips, the shorthand description for the way that, for instance, a baseball player—like Chuck Knoblauch of the New York Yankees—can suddenly become unable to successfully throw the ball to first.

It's not a bad metaphor for social life. Maybe it is possible, as those videos and online articles and self-help books suggest, to think deeply about the intricacies of everyday interactions. Erving Goffman observes as much in *The Presentation of Self in Everyday Life*, writing that in order for someone to give "a talk that will sound genuinely informal, spontaneous, and relaxed, the speaker may have to design his script with painstaking care, testing one phrase after another, in order to follow the content, language, rhythm, and pace of everyday talk. Similarly, a *Vogue* model, by her clothing, stance, and facial expression, is able expressively to portray a cultivated understanding of the book posed in her hand; but those who trouble to express themselves so appropriately will have very little time left over for reading." You can overthink your behavior *before* an awkward situation, but if you overthink while you're in the middle of it, that's a good way to give yourself the social yips. Sometimes I get so focused on making it look like I'm listening in a meeting that I forget to actually listen. Maybe you can relate to that, the times where you spent so much of a conversation worried about how you were coming off that you can barely remember anything that was said.

Beilock writes that this is because worrying about your performance is so psychologically taxing that your mind doesn't have enough capacity to be fully engaged in the task at hand. "Worrying (and trying to suppress your worries) uses up working memory that could otherwise be used to maintain several pieces of information in mind at once," she writes, meaning that you're so focused on making a good first impression on a first date or a job interview that you aren't able to devote adequate attention to making conversation. "Indeed, in many situations where people are faced with difficult thinking and reasoning tasks," she continues, "worrying can harm performance by diverting brain-power."

It's kind of like when you think about breathing, and then for a few minutes you have to *remind* yourself to breathe, until it becomes an unconscious process again. Or, to make a second *30 Rock* reference in one chapter: There's a scene in a season-one episode called "Jack-Tor," in which we see how Jack Donaghy falls apart while he's filming an instructional video. "It's weird," he says. "What do I do with my arms? I've never thought about that before." He takes a turn across the office, robotically moving each arm in synchrony with its corresponding leg. "Is it this?" he asks. "Or, if I may, this?" He tries again, this time bringing his arms up a little higher with each step. "Maybe I should just hold something." The scene cuts to Jack smiling while holding a coffee mug in each hand. "Okay, yeah. This feels more natural. Is this right?"

Being human is exhausting and embarrassing.

—————

AT TIMES THE "END THE AWKWARD" SPOTS REMIND ME OF scenes from the British *The Office*. It's something about the way the clips use silence, like audible white space that serves to highlight the cringeworthy lines. And, just like *The Office*, the campaign has an American knockoff.

"Just Say Hi" is an ad campaign introduced in 2015 by the Cerebral Palsy Foundation that features actors like William H. Macy and *CBS This Morning* cohost Gayle King in ads "about the unnecessary hesitation some people feel around disabilities." In his, Macy speaks directly to the camera in front of a soothing fireplace. "The Cerebral Palsy Foundation has asked me for a good way to start a conversation with a person who has disabilities. Um," he says, pausing for a moment. "Hi!" The intent is so similar to "End the Awkward," and it's a worthy one: Nondisabled people, don't let your fear of saying the wrong thing to someone with a disability prevent you from saying anything at all. Also, don't overthink this! Just say hi.

And yet Emily Ladau, the writer and disability rights activist, insightfully critiqued the message on her blog. She gets that the point is supposed to be that the nondisabled simply shouldn't behave any differently around the disabled, but for her, these PSAs miss the mark. As she points out in a blog post, "No one's ever created a 'Just Say Hi to Every Single Person You See' campaign."

The funny thing, she tells me, is that the ads technically worked. "My disabled friends told me that after those ads went live, a couple of them had people that came up to them and were like, 'I'm just saying hello!' or 'I saw a campaign that I should just say hello!'" she said. "They were like, 'Why are you talking to me? This is uncomfortable.'" It felt forced, unnatural. All most of us want while walking around in public is a little civil inattention, sociologists' term for the way city dwellers acknowledge one another's existence with quick eye contact and then politely go back to ignoring one another.

I wasn't there, of course, but it's probably safe to assume that these people didn't mean to make Ladau's disabled friends uncomfortable. Maybe they just couldn't see past their own point of view. Beyond the notion of the social yips, one interesting recent theory proposed by psychologist Adam Galinsky and his colleagues holds that nervousness can trap people inside their own perspective, making it less likely that they'll be able to see the world from someone else's point of view. "When you get anxious, it narrows your attention," Galinsky told me when I interviewed him about his research for a brief *New York* blog post. "You feel like you've got to go back inside yourself and figure things out—*Do they really like me? Am I really a good person?*"

There's a nice example of this in the "End the Awkward" ad, the one I mentioned at the start of the chapter, with Fran observing the job interview. The interviewer, speaking to the candidate, says, "So, should you be invited to join the company, I think it's important to try and take baby steps—" He cuts himself off. "Sorry, Fran. No offense." Fran briefly pauses in her note taking but otherwise lets the moment pass.

"Because the job itself can stretch you—" He stops and says to Fran, "Again. Sorry." "You don't have to apologize for saying everyday words!" she says, flashing him and the job candidate a big, and only slightly irritated, smile. "Please, just try and relax," she tells him.

This advice reminds me of the blog post that first led me to Ladau, about "Just Say Hi." "I'm not a celebrity," she writes, "but I know a thing or two about disability, so here's my PSA: just act normally around me." (In hindsight, she tells me, she wishes she had used the word "naturally" over "normally.") And yet recall Jack Donaghy and his two coffee mugs or Liz Lemon, sweaty and terrified in front of the mirror. Willing yourself to act naturally— *Stop sweating, you stupid bitch!*—is a good way to land yourself in the awkwardness vortex, which is something I believe I need to clarify with Ladau.

"If you were just meeting a new person for the first time, and maybe there was something particularly noticeable about their appearance—would you immediately blurt that out or say, 'What happened to you? What's wrong with you?'" she says. "Or, alternatively, would you just go up to a person who is not visibly disabled and talk in a sort of singsongy voice and go"—and here she uses the kind of tone you might use when addressing a toddler— "*Hiiii*, nice to meet you! I'm Emily!'"

"Wait," I say. "Does that happen to you?"

"Oh, yeah," she says. People see her wheelchair and assume she must have a cognitive disability too. "For me, 'Just act naturally' is 'Just act like you would with anyone who doesn't have a disability'! If you're a jerk to everyone, then, I guess, be a jerk to everyone. Otherwise, just be chill."

In the next several chapters, we'll get into some ways to prevent getting lost in the awkwardness vortex. But there is something fairly simple you can do when you feel like your nerves are narrowing your attention in on yourself. "I think it goes back to the advice in athletics," Sian Beilock, the psychologist and Barnard College president, told me. If you take a group of soccer players who are all about equally skilled, and tell them to dribble their way through an obstacle course of traffic cones, they'll all do about equally well. But if you tell half to focus on the mechanics (*Keep loose and bend your knees*) and the other half to focus on the outcome (*Try to keep the ball close to the cones*), the latter half will do better.

The same principle applies to awkward moments. "In situations where you're well practiced," Beilock said, "focus on the outcome," not the mechanics. And come on: Barring anxiety disorders or similarly serious issues, she pointed out that *most* of us are already pretty well practiced at talking to other people; the mechanics are the same, whether you're talking to your closest friends and family or your boss at your company holiday party or someone who is visibly different from you. Whatever the case, she said, "keeping in mind the goals you want to achieve can sort of lift you out of the details" so you can focus on the person in front of you.

It's up to you to decide what the goal is. Maybe, Beilock suggests, you decide you want to "learn one thing about this person," and you want to learn that thing as deeply as you can. Even if you try and it feels awkward, you can at least rest assured that you will likely not cause as much weirdness as some of the things Ladau has experienced. "I remember I went down to DC for a job interview," she tells me. "And I was at the hotel, eating breakfast right before the interview—trying to pump myself up, minding my own business." As she was eating, a little girl came over with her mother, and the girl started to chat with Ladau. "And then, all of a sudden," she says, "she asks her mother if she can pray for me."

"Oh, no," I say, feeling queasy with secondhand embarrassment.

"Yeah," she says. "And it's in front of the whole sitting area, where everyone is eating breakfast." Everyone could see, and everyone could hear, as the girl—encouraged by her mother—started saying a prayer. It would have been one thing if Ladau had asked for this, or if they'd asked her permission. But she didn't, and they didn't, and now Ladau was in a strange spotlight she hadn't asked to be in. "And I just kind of sat there and took it," she says. "And then afterwards, I felt so ashamed, and like I really should've stopped her. But I was so uncomfortable in the moment that I just sort of lost all ability to communicate."

There is a generous way to interpret this: that the girl and her mother no doubt believed that they were doing a good thing in praying for Ladau. To be clear, Ladau wasn't upset at the kid, but she thinks the mother should've known better; shouldn't a grown woman be able to imagine Ladau's perspective and recognize that putting her in the spotlight like that might humiliate her?

Again, it helps to keep in mind Beilock's advice, to keep out of the self-consciousness vortex by keeping your goal in mind. One "End the Awkward" clip features a woman at work who is about to greet a man who is missing his right hand. In the ad, the woman simply offers her left hand to shake instead of her right; perhaps you could say she decided that her desired outcome was to make the interaction go as smoothly as possible.

Ladau, by the way, does this for me when she hears me struggling toward the beginning of our conversation, when I fumble around and somehow decide the best of all possible options is the cringeworthy "not-little person."

"If it helps," she says, "I think the term you're looking for is just 'average height.'" It did help. Which, by the way, you're allowed to ask for. If you can't remember a person's name, you can ask! If you need the word for someone's disability or impairment and can't find it in your own brain, you can ask! We are mutually obligated to help one another end the awkward, because the only way out of the vortex is through the help of other people. Who, as we'll see in the next chapter, are often not as bothered by your awkwardness as you think.

CHAPTER 6

Dance Like No One's Watching,
Because No One Is!
Except When They Are

Before he gets into it, Stephan Aarstol wants me to know one thing: It's not that he's afraid of public speaking. After it happened, he tells me, everyone assumed it was stage fright. "I was, like, my class president in high school," he says, "and I've spoken in front of thousands of people on several occasions." He isn't bothered by the spotlight.

Out of the blue one day in 2011, Aarstol got a call from a producer for *Shark Tank*, the hugely popular ABC show in which entrepreneurs pitch their companies to wealthy business types, who may then choose to invest. Or not. Such is the drama of reality television. Didn't it seem for a while there, earlier on in this decade, that all of us would eventually get our shot at reality TV fame? There were just so many of these shows, and only so many of us Americans in that prized eighteen-to-forty-nine demographic. It's not like I ever would've auditioned for one of these things, because in contrast to Aarstol's Southern California chill,

I *loathe* the spotlight, even lower-wattage versions of it. Once I saw a friend's band play at an Irish pub in Midtown, and between songs he called out to me from behind his drum set, asking if I had any requests. "Um," I said, stalling, staring down into my IPA. My mind was suddenly blank, and I imagined every person in the bar was watching me, growing increasingly weirded out the longer it took for me to name a single song, *any* song. "How about . . . uh . . . the Beatles?" I eventually called back feebly. No specific tune. Just "the Beatles."

And yet if someone asked me nicely to appear on reality TV, even I might've considered it. This, Aarstol tells me, is pretty much exactly what happened in his case. "They said they'd like to get a stand-up paddleboard company on the show," he tells me, "and we were a stand-up paddleboard company." His company, Tower Paddle Boards, is a direct-to-consumer online surf shop, and it was already doing pretty well, turning enough of a profit that Aarstol had recently hired his very first employee. He wasn't looking for reality TV exposure, but reality TV came looking for him. It seemed foolish to say no.

A few weeks later he was on set. For hours. He was bored, frankly, sitting around all day at the Sony Pictures Studio lot with nothing to do but mentally rehearse his pitch, which he'd already gone over again and again in his hotel room the night before. People tell you not to memorize your presentations, but Aarstol was wary of winging it, especially when he'd be appearing in front of a prime-time television audience of six million viewers. Anyway, there was nothing else to do. For the most part, the producers left him on his own.

Seven hours later he was summoned to the set's giant doors, which in just three minutes would swing dramatically open so that he could walk onstage to deliver his presentation and confront the sharks. After whiling away most of the day by himself doing nothing, Aarstol was amused, and mildly annoyed, at the sudden burst of last-minute activity that transpired behind the doors. One of the producers noticed a logo on Aarstol's flip-flops and sent a gofer running off to find a piece of fabric and a pair of scissors to fashion a quick bit of camouflage. Now there were two minutes to go.

"And then a guy hands me this—it looks like a garage door opener," Aarstol says. It was the remote for his slide-show presentation, and the producer quickly ran down the instructions: *Press this button to go forward, this one to go backward, got it?* "And then," Aarstol says, "the doors open."

He walked forward, toward the sharks and the *X* on the floor where he was supposed to stand, worrying the remote in his hand and repeating to himself the hasty directions: *This button goes forward. This button goes back. Okay. I get it.*

He did not get it. "And so I go yada, yada, yada—boom, I hit the button for the next slide," he says. "And instead it shoots through *all* my slides." For several long moments, Aarstol was silent in front of the sharks, with the cameras running. When I've delivered PowerPoint presentations, the slides are the only way I have any hope of remembering my place in a talk, and Aarstol apparently functions the same way. Onstage he fumbled fruitlessly with the clicker as ten seconds of dead air ticked by.

"My, uh—" There's a bleeped expletive here, after which Aarstol looks down at the floor, like maybe he hopes the text of his speech will be there. "My company is, uh . . ." He trails off again, then tries a different strategy, repeating lines he's already said. "Stand-up paddleboarding is the fastest-growing water sport in the world—"

"We know that," Mark Cuban, the billionaire owner of the Dallas Mavericks and one of the regular sharks, interrupts.

"Don't worry," the Canadian business owner Kevin O'Leary chimes in, "it's only the biggest moment of your life."

On the show, all of this lasts for about a minute. In real life, Aarstol stammered and sputtered for at least three, maybe four minutes, a rare example of a reality show being edited to appear *less* embarrassing than actual reality. But it's too late for Aarstol. He doesn't know it yet, but six years later this moment will be a popular video on YouTube: "Man Freezes Up During Pitch on ABC's *Shark Tank*" has been viewed 250,000 times and counting.

Then again, maybe he does already sense that this is in his future. "I'm thinking in my head, as it's all coming crashing down on me, 'I just made an ass of myself on TV. And this is a reality show—they can do whatever they want with this footage,'" he remembers. "'You need to pull it together.'"

LONG BEFORE I TALK TO AARSTOL, I KNOW HOW HIS STORY ends. I start Googling him with an intensity I usually reserve for tracking down information about people from my past who were vaguely mean to me once. I know, for example, that he got a great deal from Cuban, who offered him $150,000 for a 30 percent share of Tower Paddle Boards plus right of first refusal for any business venture Aarstol made going forward. Since that episode aired, the company has pulled in more than $25 million in revenue, and Cuban now calls it one of the best investments he's ever made on the show. I find a recent interview on *The Howard Stern Show*, in which Cuban mentions Aarstol, but only for his success, not the screw-up. "He's killing it," Cuban told Stern. "He's been growing so fast, I've been giving him some additional money."

Look, I'd love it if the point of this story were that withstanding awkward moments will make you rich and successful 100 percent of the time, but if that were true, then where is my check? Instead, Aarstol's story demonstrates a high-stakes, televised version of something called the spotlight effect.

Have you ever read something that altered the way you thought about your life and the way you lived it? I hope so, and I hope it was a passage from a novel, or an ancient philosophical text, or maybe a story from a religious book like the Bible. I've found profound insights in all of those places too, but a few years ago I came across one in a somewhat dorkier place: An article in a 2000 issue of the *Journal of Personality and Social Psychology*. It's a soothing read for the overly self-conscious. Writing about this research in 2015 for the *Atlantic*, the Yale psychologist Paul Bloom suggested the same, and that the ideas it puts forth could change your life. He's not wrong.

The experiment at the heart of this paper is a simple one, and it's also pretty funny. The researchers—led by Thomas Gilovich of Cornell University—set up an unfortunate few of their volunteers for awkwardness, starting by purposely telling them the wrong start time for the study, to ensure that they arrived five minutes

later than everyone else. Upon his or her late arrival, the researchers insisted that the volunteer change into a goofy, oversized T-shirt
with a giant picture of Barry Manilow's face printed on it. (An
aside: Manilow pops up a lot in psychological studies of embarrassment. If these experimenters aren't making people wear a shirt with
his face emblazoned on it, they're making people sing his songs—
"At the Copa! Copacabana!"—in front of a stony-faced audience.)
After putting on the shirt, the accidental latecomer was sent into a
classroom where the rest of the study participants were already
gathered—but before this poor person could even sit down, the
experimenter interrupted. On second thought, the researcher said,
the rest of the group was too far ahead. It would probably be best,
in fact, if the be-Manilowed individual left the room and instead
continued with a private, one-on-one version of the study.

You have to imagine this person was incredibly confused at
this point. But they turned around, left the room, and in the hallway were greeted by a different experimenter. This one started
asking a bunch of questions, purportedly to test the subject's
short-term memory, but there was really only one answer the researchers were interested in. How many people in the room did
this study volunteer think noticed his goofy T-shirt, to the extent
that the others would be able to name the famous person whose
face had been screen-printed upon it?

About half would probably remember, most subjects guessed.
In reality, only about a quarter recalled the Manilow shirt. The
subjects' guesses, in other words, were excessively high. True,
some people did remember the embarrassing T-shirt, but not
nearly as many as the subjects predicted. Gilovich and his col-

leagues call this cognitive bias the spotlight effect: our tendency to overestimate how closely others are noticing what we do or how we look. It's a welcome thought for people who struggle with self-consciousness. The entire point, after all, of the Manilow shirt was that it was an odd, eye-catching thing to be wearing—my cool teenage cousin might call the shirt cringey, if she had any idea who Manilow was. But if hardly anyone noticed something that was *purposely* embarrassing, then why should we assume people notice, or care, when we do something that is accidentally embarrassing? Give yourself a break about the coffee stain on your shirt or the weird comment you made on a first date or, say, the slideshow gone haywire. Fewer people are keeping track of your foibles than you imagine.

Also interesting to note about the Manilow shirt study: The results held true even if the shirt wasn't purposely ridiculous. In another version of the same experiment, the researchers gave the latecomers a Bob Marley T-shirt, which had been rated prior to the experiment by a panel of college-kid judges as an acceptable celebrity face to wear on one's shirt. And here too people greatly overestimated the extent to which other people were noticing what they were wearing. Anyone who has ever excitedly gone to work with a new haircut, expecting compliments that never materialize, can confirm that this result also sounds about right. It all calls to mind that well-worn quote: "You wouldn't worry so much about what others think of you if you realized how seldom they do."

Sometimes, though, Gilovich tells me, retellings of this research seem to flatten its findings into a kind of superficial social nihilism: *Nothing matters! Do whatever you want! Nobody is paying attention, anyway!* Or maybe *Dance like no one's watching, because no one is!* And yet something has always bothered me a little bit about this understanding of the spotlight effect. How do I square that interpretation with the fact that I feel like I pay *extremely* close attention to the people around me? Just the other day I was walking behind a teenage couple. The boy took the girl by the arm— actually, he took her by the elbow. His hand resting there caused her forearm to bend at an uncomfortable-looking negative forty-five-degree angle in front of her. They walked this way for half a block. But then, with considerable grace for someone so young, the girl gently straightened her arm, and the boy got the message: He let go of her elbow and took her hand instead. They turned left on the next block, and I continued straight toward home.

They never saw me, the weirdo watching them from behind and reminiscing about her own first awkward teenage love. (We were on his couch watching *Meet the Parents* on DVD when he went to put his arm around me for the very first time. He elbowed my head instead.)

Some newer research, published in early 2017, adds nuance to the spotlight-effect phenomenon. Not to be outdone by Gilovich and his colleagues, these researchers—led by Erica J. Boothby, who conducted the study as a graduate student in psychology at Yale University—coin their own kicky term for the slice of social interaction they're interested in: the "invisibility cloak illusion." It's their name for the paradoxical notion that most people engage in a fair bit of people watching when out in public, while at the same time assuming that no one is watching them. "This is an illusion that prevents you from realizing that, whether you are on a plane, in a restaurant, or at a rodeo, when you stop watching people . . . when you turn your attention to whatever else you are doing—the people around you are likely to raise their eyes from whatever they were doing and watch you," Boothby and her colleagues write.

I frequently observe people closely, and yet I never imagine that others might be watching *me* in my day-to-day life. If I'm observing people on my commute to work, shouldn't it follow that others are doing the same to me? And why is it that I sometimes assume I'm drifting through life unobserved, and other times I feel like all eyes are on me? How, in other words, am I supposed to reconcile the spotlight effect with the invisibility cloak illusion?

So many questions, all of which Boothby and her colleagues attempted to answer in a series of experiments, the results of which were published in the *Journal of Personality and Social Psychology*. In one study they asked their volunteers—two at a time—to report to the social psych lab, only to be told that the experimenter was running late. The study participants were told that they could pass the time while they were waiting however they chose: They could read a newspaper, fiddle with their phone, or just stare into space—whatever they wanted to do. After five minutes went by, an apologetic experimenter showed up and ushered each person into a separate room so the experiment could begin.

In reality, though, the waiting room *was* the experiment. In their private room, each person was given a questionnaire, where they had to answer questions about how much they remembered about their waiting room buddy. They also were asked to rate how closely they had observed the other person—and how closely they believed the other person had been observing them. "Although people surreptitiously noticed all kinds of details about each other—clothing, personality, mood—we found that people were convinced that the other person wasn't watching them much, if at all," Boothby wrote in an op-ed column about her research for the *New York Times*.

Sometimes you feel like you're the center of attention, whereas other times you're minding your own business and assuming that you're drifting along unnoticed by others. The problem is that you assume other people are fixated on the things that *you* are fixated on. Often they are not.

Both the spotlight effect and the invisibility cloak illusion can be explained by something psychology researchers call "anchoring and adjustment." To bridge the irreconcilable gap between your mind and someone else's, it makes sense to begin with what's going on in your own head. That's the "anchoring" part. From there you make adjustments: You try to shift your point of view to see what the world looks like through someone else's eyes. The problem, both research and my own past experiences have shown again and again, is that you often don't adjust *enough*.

This sort of thing has been demonstrated in the laboratory; in his doctoral dissertation Kenneth Savitsky—now a psychologist at Williams College—made his research subjects prepare and deliver a speech, always a mildly intimidating endeavor. Many of the study participants were nervous, and they assumed those in the audience would register their nerves. They didn't—or at least not to the degree that the speech givers assumed that they would.

In another, related experiment (and this is a particularly odd one), researchers asked students to come into the lab, one at a time, and had them take a seat at a table where fifteen identical cups sat. Each cup contained a mysterious red liquid: Ten cups were filled with cherry Kool-Aid, whereas the other five were filled with a questionable combination of "water, red food coloring, and the vinegar brine solution in which pickled grape leaves are packed." *Mmm.* The students were asked to try a sip from each cup and were assured that though each cup would taste different, all were harmless. All of this was filmed, and after the taste test, the students were told that a different set of students would be watching and guessing which cups contained the briny solution and which cups contained regular old Kool-Aid, judging only by the looks on the drinkers' faces. They were asked to guess how many out of ten observers would guess correctly, and on average they thought about five people watching would get it right.

The results showed that the study participants consistently overestimated how many people would correctly interpret the looks on their faces, and the researchers hypothesize that this is because they couldn't separate what *they* knew about themselves from what *others* could actually observe about them. "Participants knew when they were tasting pleasant or unpleasant drinks and it may have been difficult for them to get beyond that knowledge when estimating what the observers were likely to know," the study authors note.

Psychologists call this phenomenon the illusion of transparency: Because *we* feel an emotion so strongly, we expect that other people can read it on our faces. Most of the time, that's simply not true. You could call this the curse of self-knowledge.

Think about it. What is the subject that you are *most* familiar with, the one thing that is nearest, if not always dearest, to your heart and mind? *You.* You have been studying you your whole life. You are the world's leading expert on you. You know so much about yourself that you can't help expecting others to see you the way *you* see you, which is yet another reason why the irreconcilable gap can come as such a shock. If you're embarrassed about wearing a huge T-shirt with Barry Manilow's face plastered on it, it's hard for you to step out of that feeling and into the minds of others in the room. If you're nervous while giving a presentation, you imagine others can read those nerves all over your face. You imagine that others register your awkwardness and that because this moment is standing out to you, it will stand out to them too.

Think about what expertise allows in other disciplines. "If you're an expert physicist, for instance, you can notice all kinds of small minute details that nobody else can notice. If you're an expert mathematician, you can look at a formula and notice all of its intricacies in a way that a novice can't," University of Chicago psychologist Nicholas Epley told *Nautilus* in 2015. "The same thing is true with yourself. You're an expert about yourself—you saw yourself yesterday; you know what you look like when you go out to a party versus when you just get up in the morning out of bed; you know so much about yourself. . . . You can judge yourself like an expert does."

I wish, for the sake of Stephan Aarstol, the guy who froze on *Shark Tank*, that the lesson here were that no one noticed his screwup. A quarter million views on YouTube prove that wrong. People certainly notice you, especially when you are doing something in an *actual* spotlight. When Jennifer Lawrence tripped and fell up the stairs when going to accept her Oscar for best actress at the 2013 Academy Awards, people definitely noticed. Thinking back to those awkward meetings early in my career that I mentioned in chapter 5, I know now that my inner turmoil wasn't always noticeable from the outside. Then again, there are times I *know* it was. Once, my entire upper body flushed—not just my face but my neck and arms too. My best work friend, Carissa, was sitting beside me that day, and after I finished speaking, she reached over and pressed her forefinger down on my forearm, like you'd do to demonstrate how bad a sunburn was. Both of us watched the skin beneath lighten for a minute before quickly returning to pink.

But here is more good news for the overly self-conscious: Even when people do see your screwups, they aren't judging you as harshly as you think.

A follow-up series of experiments detailed in a later paper—also lead authored by Gilovich—applied this to another area of everyday awkwardness: the bad hair day. Over the course of a semester, an experimenter popped into a psychology seminar at Cornell on five randomly chosen days, handing out surveys to the students that asked them to rate the appearance of their fellow classmates relative to the way they looked on a typical school day. Additionally, they were to rate their own appearance on that day relative to a typical day—but they were to try to do this from the perspective of their classmates. Here again, Gilovich and his co-authors found evidence of the spotlight effect: The students saw their own flaws and expected their classmates' ratings of them to vary accordingly. But their assessments of their classmates stayed consistent through all five sessions. "The blemishes and cowlicks that are so noticeable and vexatious to oneself are often lost on all but the most attentive observers," Gilovich and his colleagues write. Most people are too busy paying attention to their own blemishes and cowlicks.

The spotlight effect study was inspired by Gilovich's work on regrets, I learn in a conversation with him. You know that quote people like to post on Instagram and Pinterest? "Twenty years from now you will be more disappointed by the things that you didn't do than by the ones you did do." It's often mistakenly attributed to Mark Twain, but its actual origin is the 1991 memoir by H. Jackson Brown Jr., *P.S. I Love You: When Mom Wrote, She Always Saved the Best for Last*; it's a word of encouragement from Brown's mother. But the actual content of the quote turns out to be true. According to research conducted by Gilovich and others, people really do tend to regret inaction more than action. Often a decision against taking action is made out of fear of the social consequences: If you speak onstage, if you say "I love you" first, what will people say? What will people think? "If that's the concern that one has—you know, how will it look to others—what one needs to factor into the equation is—you know what?—many fewer people than you think are likely to notice in the first place," Gilovich tells me. Do the awkward thing that's pulling at you, if only so that you won't later regret *not* doing it.

––––

I FIRST FOUND THE CLIP OF AARSTOL'S *SHARK TANK* AP-pearance on an online forum on which I have been spending entirely too much time lately, the subreddit /r/cringe. Its theme is awkward, cringeworthy moments, and I'm hooked on it. I started regularly visiting the page in the early spring, when it still had a banner up that read MERRY CRINGEMAS! I gathered that it was left this way on purpose, to add that extra cringey touch. In the very first comment on the thread about Aarstol, I discovered the Mark Cuban interview with Howard Stern, where the billionaire investor praises Aarstol. Further down someone says, "Looks like a good idea, guy has a legit brain-freeze (happens to the best of us)." Not every comment is as earnest as these, but most are, and none of them are outright cruel or mocking.

The night his episode aired, in March of 2012, Aarstol tells me, he heard from many old friends who saw him on TV. But many of them saw more than that; they saw themselves in him as he stammered awkwardly on national network television.

"I had a bunch of people after it aired call me the night of and say, 'Oh, I watched you on TV, and I just wanted to say you did excellent—I've dealt with stuttering my whole life' or 'I hate public speaking too,'" Aarstol said. These weren't accurate reads of the situation; the funny thing about putting yourself in someone else's shoes is that it's still *you* in there, using your own emotions and experiences to contextualize what you see from the other person's vantage point. Still, he said, their words were reassuring somehow. "All of these people really had a lot of sympathy toward me," he said. So many of us waste so much time worrying what other people will think of us, but the truth is that they are mostly *not* thinking of us.

And even when they are, they might be thinking about how they see themselves in us.

CHAPTER 7

Your Flaws Are My Pain

Jim is thirty-two, and in his Tinder profile picture, he grins in the middle of a grocery store produce section, holding up a pineapple. He looks pleased with himself, and with his pineapple. It is . . . not a *great* look, truthfully, but what do I know—maybe it's fine when seen the way a Tinder profile is supposed to be seen, on the smallish screen of a smartphone.

But, oh, poor Jim. I'm taking in an oversized version of his Tinder profile, displayed on a five-foot projector screen for the viewing pleasure of a buzzed, cackling audience at a theater in Brooklyn. I'm in the back, by the bar, where it's standing room only. Around me people are drinking, laughing, talking, and only half listening to the blond woman onstage, whose phone is connected to the projector, displaying Jim and his pineapple.

"What I wanna know is, who took that picture?" she asks. Her name is Lane Moore, and she's a stand-up comedian, writer, musician, and actor in New York City. She has some impressive credits to her name, including a memorable cameo in the fifth season of *Girls*, but this thing I'm at tonight might be what she's currently best known for, at least in the city. It's called *Tinder Live*, a monthly comedy show with a simple but brilliant concept: She uses the dating app live onstage. The audience decides, reaching a consensus through drunken shouts, which men Moore dismisses by swiping left and which ones she pursues by swiping right.

She keeps up a running narration as she does this, helped along by a panel of fellow comedians. Tonight one of the panelists is Danny Tamberelli, a former child actor whom older millennials like me will remember fondly as Little Pete from the 1990s Nickelodeon show *The Adventures of Pete and Pete*. In response to Moore's question, he imagines what the unseen photographer might've said to Jim.

"You're gonna get *so laid* from this picture, bro," Tamberelli says. He's adopted a voice that sounds like a macho, gym-going guy, the kind who could lecture ad nauseum about the merits of the ketogenic diet.

"Yeah, man," Moore continues, taking on the same vocal affectation. In her dude-bro voice, she starts listing the photo's merits. "It shows *depth*," she says. "It shows . . . *fruit*." The list ends there, and the crowd cracks up.

Earlier this week I read a *New York Times* story on Moore and *Tinder Live* that called the comic "ingenious" and praised her show as a paragon of cringe comedy. As I said in chapter 1, a big part of the reason I was drawn to researching awkwardness in the first place was because no one else was, or at least they weren't studying it in the way I understood it. But I kept finding confirmation that I wasn't the only one drawn to various aspects of this feeling: I found it in *Mortified*, I found it in W. Kamau Bell, and now I think I've found it again, at this *Times*-approved show in Brooklyn.

I down what's left of my wine, throw the cup away, and stare at Jim. I don't know the guy, but I imagine he thought the photo would be a quirky-cute way to catch a lady's eye as she thumbed through the hundreds of other identical dudes on the dating app. *A pineapple, huh? How unique!*

I recently helped an elder friend redo his résumé, and he trusted everything I said. One of my suggestions was to put a picture of himself at the top. It's not a professional portrait, but it's recent, and it's nice, taken in Hawaii. He looks bright-eyed and happy, with his face framed by a lovely hibiscus tree. I thought it might catch the eye of a busy recruiter or HR representative and help him stand apart from other applicants.

And now Jim is making me question that decision, in particular the hot-pink hibiscus part. Was that bad advice? Is my friend now, because of me, in danger of appearing on some kind of corporate spin-off of Moore's show, like *LinkedIn LIVE!*? I start to think the chatty people around me who paid to see a show they are mostly ignoring are onto something, because it physically pains me to look at Jim's photo for too long. I've never even been on Tinder, and still I'm cringing on his behalf, or maybe my friend's, or maybe my own. My cheeks are burning and my gut is clenching almost as much as they might if it were me up there, smiling stupidly, flaunting a tropical fruit.

I decide to return to the bar for another glass of wine, mostly to distract myself for a moment, because I'm starting to feel a little queasy. This particular cringey feeling has plagued me as long as I can remember; I tend to feel extreme embarrassment on behalf of other people, even people who don't know they're embarrassing themselves, even people I've never met. The night NBC aired *The Sound of Music Live!* in 2013, my Twitter feed was filled with people watching and tweeting snarkily along. I tried to join in the fun, but sometime within the first few bars of "My Favorite Things," I turned it off. I couldn't take it. A similar feeling overtook me in early 2016, when a video circulated online of Jeb(!) Bush begging a silent crowd at a town hall in New Hampshire, "Please clap."

Moore's voice breaks through my reverie as she asks the crowd to weigh in on Jim. It's true that the people immediately around me seem more interested in one another than in the show, but those who managed to get a seat closer to the stage are clearly engrossed in its innovative, interactive form. Throughout the night, a pattern has emerged: People tend to reject the boring profiles, preferring instead the particularly ridiculous or embarrassing ones—the better, presumably, to toy with later, if Moore gets a match.

"Right or left, guys?" Moore says to them about Jim.

"RIGHT!" they yell back.

I take a small sip from my glass of mediocre pinot noir and try for the zillionth time to imagine what could possibly be the purpose of this emotion swirling around in my body and brain, and whether I'm even feeling the same thing as the gleeful crowd up front. If this feeling is making me want to curl up and die, then why does everyone else here seem to be energized by it?

As it turns out, two neuroscientists across the Atlantic once wondered almost the exact same thing.

⸻

YEARS AGO SÖREN KRACH AND FRIEDER PAULUS—BOTH OF the Social Neuroscience Lab at the University of Lübeck in Germany—were watching someone give a presentation. This person, they tell me, was bragging about himself and his work in a way that made it clear to both Krach and Paulus that he had *no* idea how irritatingly self-important he sounded. (There's that annoying irreconcilable gap from chapter 2 again.) They squirmed in their seats as he spoke. "I've always been very sensitive to embarrassing things," Krach tells me, but this time he wasn't embarrassing himself. So what, they both wondered, was with this feeling?

Early on in my awkwardness research, I e-mailed Krach, because he is the lead author of one of my favorite psychology papers, one he cowrote with Paulus and a few others. I love this paper so much I stole its title for the title of this chapter: "Your Flaws Are My Pain." As far as I could tell, he and Paulus were two of the only scientists in the world who were as obsessed as I was with the question of what makes people cringe.

I reached out to Krach to ask for a copy of his newest paper on cringing, the kind of routine e-mail a science journalist sends dozens of times in any given week. He and Paulus had been on my radar for a while, but I was feeling shy about requesting an interview; I get a little starstruck around my favorite researchers sometimes. And so I was surprised, and flattered, to learn when Krach wrote back that I'd been on their radar too.

Hi Melissa,

Very funny—my colleague (Frieder Paulus) and me just recently tried to get into contact with you. We read your articles in the past and were always very excited!

In Krach and Paulus, I soon realized as we started a months-long e-mail correspondence, I had found two more kindred spirits in cringing.

Eventually we decide that I should visit their lab in Lübeck, a picturesque town that's a two-hour train ride away from Berlin. Andrew and I skip American Thanksgiving and instead fly to Germany that Thursday; a few days later we meet Krach and Paulus at a Berlin bar, where we exchange stories about our lives and our work and our mutual obsession. It's thrilling to be around people who *get it*; at times this has been a lonely process. "I guess there isn't exactly an awkwardness conference to attend," people would sometimes say when I complained about this, usually adding something like "Well, there's always Comic-Con!" as if they were the first to think of the joke. (Awkward people attend sci-fi conventions. Get it?) But at the bar that night over Thanksgiving weekend, it *does* feel like I'm at my own private version of Comic-Con, like Krach and Paulus and I are all dressed up as the same obscure comic book character, like we clearly belong together.

Andrew, meanwhile, has a great time chatting along with everyone but is not quite as excited as we are to discuss the more arcane aspects of cringe-ology. "I'm just glad you guys found each other," he says later.

During our first round, Krach describes to me what to him is the ultimate in *Fremdscham*, a German word that is an almost direct translation of *cringe*, at least the way I've come to define it: *Fremdscham* means shame felt on behalf of another, or embarrassment by proxy. Krach waves his hands around as he describes what is, to him, a nightmare of a person—someone who would pull up to this casual bar driving something impractical and flashy. "Like a Ferrari," he says. *Oops, can't find a parking spot! Better do a couple extra loops around the block*, Krach imagines the imaginary driver thinking. *This way everyone gets a chance to see and admire me!* "It's a misperception of the audience," Krach says. You're playing the wrong part for the crowd, to dip a toe back into the dramaturgical theory of social life from chapter 1.

This imaginary Ferrari driver can't see that no one in the bar is impressed by his fancy car. Instead the bar patrons are taking the Ferrari as evidence of his ridiculousness. Again, this is all hypothetical, a made-up scenario to illustrate a point. But even so, it twists Krach's stomach into knots just describing it—the same feeling he got while watching the presenter give that completely un-self-aware speech years ago. Like me, Krach and Paulus wanted to know: What could possibly explain this feeling?

Unlike me, however, Krach and Paulus had access to an fMRI machine. The cringey feeling they experienced while watching that awkward presentation became the inspiration for that paper I love, which was published in 2011 in *PLOS ONE*.

In it they describe one experiment in which they asked people to read little scenarios or look at sketches that showed people embarrassing themselves. In one, a person walks around unaware his fly is open. Another described a person just, you know, nonchalantly wearing a T-shirt with the words "I am sexy" printed on it. Rereading the paper long after I return home from my trip to visit Krach and Paulus, I notice another scenario with Krach's fingerprints all over it: a person who gives a speech that swerves into "extensive self-praise." Most research is me-search, goes a little joke in the world of academic psychology.

Their subjects studied these vignettes or images while inside an fMRI machine, which scanned their brain activity so Krach and Paulus and their colleagues could peek inside. The results showed increased activity in the anterior cingulate cortex and the left anterior insula, two structures that, according to other research in neuroscience, may be involved in pain processing. But these brain regions aren't just associated with a person's own pain; they also become active when you're feeling someone *else's* pain. Experiencing social pain, then, whether first- or secondhand, may be interpreted by your brain as at least a little like physical pain. If this is true, then there's a good reason we say things like "That was excruciating" when we watch someone else embarrass themselves.

Just for fun, when I visit their lab in Lübeck, they have me do a version of that initial cringing experiment. I lie in the fMRI, and I read the short descriptions of some classic cringeworthy moments that are flashed on the screen, though in truth none of them affect me too much, no doubt because I *wrote* all these descriptions. I did try to include my own personal greatest cringe hits: Seeing someone walking out of a restroom not realizing that their skirt is tucked into their tights. Running into your boss on the subway and not knowing whether to say hi or to ignore each other. That time at brunch when my friend accidentally called her boyfriend "Dad." At this point, though, I've been studying awkwardness for so long that I think I've developed a kind of immunity to it. Everything I read seems funny instead of cringey.

Afterward I stay in the fMRI while Paulus and a lab assistant alternate making horrible noises—a fork scratching a plate, literal fingernails on a chalkboard, a fork scratching the chalkboard—with the comparatively soothing sounds of a plush toy brushing against the chalkboard or a dishrag gently wiping the plate. It's a way of simulating something unpleasant that isn't physically painful. The experience is fun, but mostly what I gather from my personalized experiment is that being in an fMRI is in itself an incredibly awkward experience. As I lie inside, it occurs to me that these nice scientists are looking inside my head, a part of me that even I've never seen. What if, I don't know, my sexual-arousal brain blob "lights up" while I'm in there?

In that initial experiment, in addition to having their brains scanned, all the study participants also took a survey called the E-scale, a set of twenty-five questions designed to measure a person's empathy. Their instructions were to rate how much they agreed with statements like "I feel sad if I see a lonely person in a group of people" or "sometimes I try to understand my friends better by seeing things from their point of view." Those who scored highest in empathy also tended to have the most activity in these particular brain regions when seeing those embarrassing images or stories.

From their research, Krach and Paulus have come to understand cringing as an empathetic reaction, a way of experiencing someone else's awkward moment as if it were your own. I felt un-bearably smug the first time I read this. Clearly, the depth of my emotional reaction to things like *Tinder Live* mirrored the depth of my good character. It's *science*, you see. That's the way we've long defined empathy, anyway, as a kind of synonym for compassion. Yet empathy and care for others are *not* synonyms, not necessarily. Empathy isn't inherently good, Krach and Paulus tell me later on in my visit with some exasperation, and it isn't inherently bad either. It *can* be a route to compassion, but understanding how someone else feels can also lead to something darker, something more like contempt. Empathy itself, my new neuroscientist friends tell me, is simply something healthy brains do automatically, in order to help us better socialize with others. On its own, it's just a cognitive process.

What matters is what you do with it.

IN BROOKLYN SEVERAL MONTHS LATER, THE *TINDER LIVE* crew has moved on to a twenty-seven-year-old named Kyman, whose photo makes the crowd burst into laughter and jeers the moment it appears on the projection screen, without Moore or any of the other panelists having to say a thing. Kyman stands about waist deep in what looks to be a lake, and he's leaning to one side as if he might be in the middle of a game of volleyball. He is also shirtless and in swim trunks, a combination that accentuates his . . . If he were a woman, I'd call them curves. I don't know what the euphemism is for a man. Moore is less concerned with polite language.

"That's a *butt*!" she exclaims. "That's a *buuuuuuuuutt*!"

"Get in that butt! Get in that butt!" chants the third panelist, another New York comedian named Janine Brito.

"I mean, okay," Moore says after a few moments of this. "Obviously right, right?"

"Yes!" the crowd agrees, and what do you know: We have a match. Moore starts typing out a message to Kyman. So you should know I'm very classy or whatever but THAT BUTT THO, she writes.

This is how the night has gone: Pull up a profile, spend a few minutes mocking the guy behind his back, swipe right or left, and then, if it's a match, mock him to his face (or at least to the Tinder avatar version of his face). From my long chats with Krach and Paulus, I recognize that this is bugging me because I'm feeling empathy for these guys, but I think you could also argue that everyone else in the room is too. Understanding how confused Kyman might feel when receiving a message like THAT BUTT THO is the whole joke—and understanding how he might feel is, of course, empathy.

Some psychologists account for this difference by splitting the concept of empathy into two: One of these is cognitive empathy, which means recognizing and understanding someone else's feelings but keeping those feelings at a distance. You can imagine what someone is likely going through, in other words, but you don't let it in; you don't feel it yourself. The other kind of empathy is affective empathy, or compassionate empathy, and this one is the way we usually use the word: It's understanding someone else's experience *and* internalizing what they are likely feeling. You feel what they feel.

One isn't necessarily better than the other. For nurses and other health-care practitioners in particular, cognitive empathy can be essential in protecting against "compassion fatigue," burnout that comes from constantly internalizing patients' emotions. Some recent evidence suggests that if health-care workers instead engage in cognitive empathy, keeping a little distance between themselves and their patients while still understanding their emotional needs, this can lead to lower burnout rates and higher well-being.

But there are times when cognitive empathy can turn darker. A recent study tested the difference between these two branches of empathy in the context of Internet trolling and found that Internet trolls tended to score higher in cognitive empathy than compassionate empathy. That might, in fact, be how they knew how to be so mean—they can guess at what the other person might be feeling, so they can plan their attack accordingly.

It's true that you can't walk around 24-7 with a wide-open heart, your feelings pushed and pulled by those of everyone else around you. You have to know which type of empathy to use and when. It's worth remembering the theory of constructed emotions from chapter 3: Emotion isn't something that happens to you. It is something your brain creates, which means you have some agency over your feelings. My instinct is that the crowd around me at *Tinder Live* is cringing while tapping into their cognitive empathy, perhaps in a way that's curdled into something more dismissive, like contempt.

Lately, though, I've been experimenting with choosing compassionate empathy whenever I can: I know how you feel because

I *am* you, or at least I can see some version of myself in you. It's easier, of course, to do this with people I feel some kind of connection to, something Krach and Paulus confirmed in a follow-up study to that initial 2011 paper: Your empathetic reaction to someone else's embarrassment is stronger the closer you are to that person. It's why husbands and wives are so likely to be embarrassed by each other, or why your family's weirdness, particularly in public, never fails to make you cringe. They're a part of you; you've incorporated them into your self-concept. And then these people go, out there in the world doing god knows what, making you look embarrassing by association.

I thought about this finding of theirs—this particular paper is titled "When Your Friends Make You Cringe"—when I read a piece published in the spring of 2017 by *The Cut:* "When You Love Your Friend But Hate Her Social-Media Presence," by Hayley Phelan. In it the writer is weirded out by a new friend's online persona. She would post "multiple times a day, increasingly in nausea-inducing poses with her boyfriend that looked about as staged as a rom-com poster: laughing and eating soft-serve on a stoop, holding hands while walking over a bridge, stealing a kiss post-run. Soon, they had their very own hashtag. It involved the word 'lover.'"

But you can have embarrassment by association for something bigger than a corny hashtag favored by an Instagram addict. Your entire country can make you cringe. Australians have long lived with the scourge of the "cultural cringe," a term coined by Aussie writer and critic A. A. Phillips in a 1950 essay. He used the phrase to describe the embarrassment many Australians felt at the time when comparing their artistic efforts with those of bigger countries like Britain; in the second half of the twentieth century, it began to be used more often to describe the deflating way Aussie pop-culture exports never quite lived up to the cooler TV shows and films and pop stars coming out of the United States. "And so all too often, whenever we see Australian movies, TV, music, art, awards shows, slang, food, and fashion, we cringe," Australian writer Jenna Guillaume wrote in a recent essay for *BuzzFeed*. "Or rather, when we choose not to see them, because we reject them on face value as bogan (unfashionable, uncouth, unsophisticated) and avoid them altogether. It flattens our culture, this deep-seated cringe."

As I'm writing this in the upside-down world of 2017, Americans are experiencing our own cultural cringe, though it's over politics, not pop culture. In February, just a few weeks after Trump's inauguration, the *New Yorker* published an essay titled "The Embarrassment of President Trump"; a few weeks earlier, *Vanity Fair* had called his plan to keep his businesses a "national embarrassment." In May *Paste* magazine published a listicle headlined "The 8 Most Embarrassing Moments from Trump's *One Day* at NATO"; the *Nation* used that same trip to argue that "Our Embarrassment in Chief's International Trip Is No Laughing Matter." It isn't just headline writers who feel this way; a poll from the McClatchy Company and Marist College released in early 2017 found that nearly 60 percent of those polled said they were "embarrassed" by the president, compared with 33 percent who said they were proud.

I can't predict what the country will be like by the time this book is in your hands. Hello from the past. It's pretty weird here. How is it when you are? A brief dispatch from 2017: The talk right now is all about how divided this country is. If we are going to get emotionally granular about it, as we discussed in chapter 3, then the emotion I might choose to describe the national mood is something bordering on contempt, just like the vibe I was getting from the crowd at *Tinder Live*. Contempt is a powerfully negative emotion, one that the psychologist John Gottman has found to be among the biggest predictors of divorce. The behaviors associated with this feeling are eye rolls and the silent treatment, both of which can be understood as ways to shut out the targeted person, all the way out. Some psychologists who study emotion have theorized that these are embodied ways of refusing to acknowledge the offender's existence. By the time a relationship gets to a contemptuous state, reconciliation is likely to be extremely difficult, if not impossible.

This is why I'm oddly cheered by these headlines and that poll that suggest the prevailing national mood is one of embarrassment. Embarrassment implies compassionate empathy, or feeling what someone else is feeling. The relationship hasn't completely dissolved yet. Sometime around the fourth month of the Trump era, Krach sends me the latest paper he and Paulus and a few other colleagues have published, on how engaging in mindfulness may decrease the pain associated with *Fremdscham*. In a Twitter direct message, he advises, Next time you cringe because of Trump—just meditate before :-).

As the sociologist Neil Gross observed in the *New York Times*, it's unlikely that these cringing Americans are reacting this way because they're embarrassed *for* Trump. It's much more likely that they're embarrassed for the nation as a whole—which, in the tacit, paradoxical way that cringe theory works, implies a feeling of connection to this country. The deeper the cringe, the more you care; that's one way to look at it.

"Embarrassment of the sort that's bubbling up today is tied to national pride and patriotism, which the right often accuses the left of lacking and which cosmopolitan liberals sometimes fail to notice in themselves," Gross wrote. Pride and embarrassment are what the research typically classifies as self-conscious emotions, which would suggest that you wouldn't feel them unless you had some kind of personal investment in the thing that is making you cringe. "Time will tell whether embarrassment over Mr. Trump proves a galvanizing force for political change," he continued. "Either way, in these rancorous times, embarrassment is a healthier, more civic-minded emotional basis for dissent than hatred."

I wondered, at certain points while watching *Tinder Live*, if my problem with the show might be more simply expressed this way: *I am no fun.* Moore and her panelists are sharp, skilled comedians, and I'm not opposed to poking fun at people. I did grow up with a little brother, after all, so I know that teasing the people you love is a great way to bond.

Even so, at the Tinder show I keep trying to get into the joke, but I just can't. I feel so upset for the guys they're mocking. Everyone's secret fear when putting a social media persona together is some version of "Is everyone going to laugh at me?" For Jim and Kyman and all the guys in between, the answer tonight is "Yeah, actually, everyone is *definitely* laughing at you." All of us are afraid, to varying degrees, of social rejection or ostracism, and when we sense that fear in others, we can choose to respond with contempt or compassion. Both are ways of processing that automatic empathy response, the developmental psychologist Philippe Rochat has theorized. You feel the ostracism right along with the ostracized, and you can either bring that person in or push them out. In this way contempt can function as a defense mechanism. "Contempt turns social rejection the other way around," Rochat argues. Instead of feeling rejected yourself, "now it is the self that rejects others." *Tinder Live* felt like contemptuous cringing, an expression of the rejection all of us fear in love and relationships, only turned outward. *We are safe, and we are superior—it's these guys who are the loser weirdos, amirite?*

The unspoken statement being made by the comedians onstage read to me like a message to the Tinder guys: *You are totally ridiculous, and thank god I'm not you.* A more compassionate (and probably more truthful) point to make is the opposite: *You are totally ridiculous. And so am I.* The appeal of processing vicarious social rejection through contempt is understandable, because it turns the feeling outward, which keeps you at a safe distance from feeling rejected yourself. A compassionate response, on the other hand, invites the rejection inward by recognizing yourself in the rejected. At first I wasn't sure why you'd want to respond to someone else's embarrassment in this way, with a compassionate cringe, but then I realized that the explanation is simple: It helps you feel less alone. To cringe compassionately is to realize that we are more alike in our weirdness than we are different. And this, by the way, is a lesson I ended up learning in an unlikely place: Reddit.

THE YOUNG MAN ON THE PHONE DECLINES TO GIVE ME HIS real name. It's too risky, he says. Better—safer—to go by the name he uses on Reddit: drumcowski. There are some out there, he tells me, who "actively hate" what he does. It adds a dramatic element to our conversation that I was not exactly expecting.

I called him—fine, I'll play along: I called *drumcowski*—to talk about the origin story of /r/cringe, the subreddit he brought to life in the summer of 2012. A few years ago, /r/cringe was among the most popular subreddits on Reddit, and it's still an active community today, with more than 600,000 subscribers. It was inspired by a local TV news report on "teen werewolves," high schoolers who like to wear fake furry tails, prosthetic fangs, and colored contact lenses; drumcowski came across the video when he was dog sitting and bored at a friend's apartment in Manhattan.

"It hit me with a wave of embarrassment," he remembers. "I had to pause it every five seconds just to try to gather myself and get the courage to kind of keep going through the video. In a way, it was kinda fun to watch it, but awful at the same time, you know?" I *do* know, I tell him. In drumcowski, I discover as our conversation continues, I have found another cringe enthusiast. "It was kind of putting myself through this punishment, but—I don't know," he said. "There was something interesting about it."

From the way he describes it, it sounds like drumcowski is more likely to respond to vicarious embarrassment with a compassionate cringe rather than a contemptuous one. He internalizes the person's pain—it's "awful," he says, like a "punishment"—and yet he is clearly getting something out of it, to the point where he decided to set up a site so that he could collect more videos that would trigger this feeling on purpose.

I stumbled onto /r/cringe early on in my awkwardness research, and while I've never actively participated, I am a constant lurker. I visit the site almost every day, in part because I find it so amusing to eavesdrop on fights within this odd little online community.

"This isn't cringe," one user wrote on a post titled "Taylor Swift Fans Have a Message for Her as She Walks In." The "message" turns out to be a song that the enthusiastic fans sing to Swift when they see her, which, this Redditor concedes, is "a little hokey," but isn't *cringe*. Including the video on /r/cringe is tantamount to "making fun of them just cause they wanted to sing to their favorite artist," this commenter argues.

"Why are there always comments saying 'this isn't cringe,'" another Redditor responds, seemingly too exasperated to end the question with a question mark. "You don't choose what's cringe, and neither does logic. Some people will watch it and cringe, some won't."

A third pipes up. "Actually," this one begins, causing me to picture someone pushing their glasses up their nose before typing, "cringe was clearly defined on this subreddit, once upon a time, as a feeling of empathic embarrassment for someone who is being publicly embarrassed. This isn't cringe as no one is embarrassed, and certainly no one is empathically embarrassed in these comments." And on they argue about the nuances of what it means to cringe. That's just a randomly selected example; arguments almost exactly like this one are a regular occurrence on the subreddit.

They're the aftershocks of a long battle waged on the subreddit, which quickly took a turn for the trollish. It was meant to be about the universal awkwardness of everyday life, like someone "telling a bad joke" or "tripping in the middle of graduation," an early user of the subreddit recalled. ("When it hurts just to watch" is /r/cringe's tagline.) "It was about cringing out of empathy," this user wrote, "not laughing out of spite." But by early 2013, as the page grew, the spirit of the thing had changed. Some subscribers defined the emotion it was designed to elicit in a very different way, and the subreddit "became a place to laugh at teenagers posting awkward videos to youtube," that Redditor continued. "That was never what it was supposed to be."

It turned from a place celebrating compassionate cringing to one that dealt in contemptuous cringing. This crowd got its kicks from laughing *at*, not with, these unlucky stars of awkward You-Tube clips, many of whom were just kids. On a video of a teenage girl scream-singing to a One Direction song: "Imagine having to be out in public with her." On a different teen girl's selfie: "You look . . . like Beavis in drag." It does sometimes seem to me like contempt is the easy route, the path of least resistance when encountering something that makes you cringe. If you distance yourself from it, you're protecting yourself, and you can delude yourself into thinking that you're safe from rejection or ostracism (*and* that you're not the kind of person who would ever embarrass yourself like that).

At the time, however, drumcowski was not interested in philosophical meditations on the nuances of cringing; he just wanted the bullying to stop before someone got hurt. In 2014 drumcowski brought on *sixty* moderators to try to combat the bullying on /r/cringe. These days, drumcowski says, "we're known on Reddit for having some of the most strict rules, and we get a lot of criticism for it." The maddest users went rogue, forming their own twisted version of drumcowski's idea, /r/CringeAnarchy, where contempt cringing continues to flourish. "They make posts talking about our subreddit, and [the moderators], and they actively hate us here," he tells me, explaining why he doesn't want to give me his real name.

I was taken aback to learn about the history of the subreddit, because by the time I stumbled on it, it seemed to me to be so welcoming—weird, for certain, but warm too. I think this might be because drumcowski and the rest of the moderators insist that every posting has to invoke compassion cringe, the kind where you internalize the other person's awkward moment and feel it as if you were right there with them. One video that is regularly posted and reposted is one of YouTube's oldest: "Boom Goes the Dynamite." It's three minutes and fifty-four seconds of a college sports news broadcast, featuring a nervous college freshman named Brian Collins, who stumbles over his words as he tries to keep up with the Teleprompter. In the comments, the majority of Redditors post about how clearly they can see themselves in Collins. "I know exactly how he's feeling," writes one commenter, who goes on to describe a similarly tongue-tied moment from his high school debate class. Another writes, "Having social anxiety and having had panic attacks when things don't go as expected . . . holy shit I feel for this guy."

Recently people have started posting fewer videos and more

personal anecdotes, which often make me laugh out loud. One of my favorites is from a children's tennis instructor who was about to teach a private lesson for an eleven-year-old girl. "Christmas was coming up, so I asked if she was excited about Christmas," this person wrote. "She said she was, and then I looked at the mother and said, 'So eleven years old, does she still believe in Santa?' in a really pleasant, upbeat voice. The mother just looked at me with disgust and said 'yes she does.' I didn't break character and said, 'That's great!' After a long silence I said, 'He's real!'"

One does not expect to find a sense of deeply felt common humanity on Reddit, but that's exactly the feeling I get when I visit the site. The literal meaning of "compassion" is "to suffer with," and whether he intended to or not, drumcowski created a place where you can find this feeling on demand. *I've been there before*, the commenters tell one another. *You'll be okay.* The more I read through these comments, the less I feel like awkwardness is my own unique problem. How can it be? I can't be that out of the ordinary if all of these people confess to feeling this way too. "I bet things would be easier for you if you either realized you're not that weird or realized that being weird isn't bad," the love interest in Curtis Sittenfeld's 2005 novel, *Prep*, tells the protagonist, and this is what this odd little online community has inadvertently taught me. I'm not that weird, and anyway, being weird isn't that bad. And this, I think, is the secret appeal of the compassionate cringe: Feeling embarrassment for someone else can help take some of the emotional charge away the next time you feel it for yourself.

CHAPTER 8

Cringe Attacks

The other day I was putting away laundry, my least favorite chore. It's already *folded*, dammit. What more do you want from me? As I worked, my mind was wandering this way and that when, out of nowhere, a memory pulled me back to the summer of 2007, to the carpeted hallways of building 25 on the Microsoft campus in Redmond, Washington. Suddenly I'm twenty-two again.

I'm also nervous. I was always nervous back then. Just days after graduating from college in northern California, I packed everything I owned into my Toyota Corolla and drove north to Washington State, where I'd gotten an internship in the health section at MSNBC.com. In retrospect, I was terrifically underqualified for the role. All day I would nod along in meetings while the rest of the editors discussed things like hormone replacement therapy or hospital-acquired infections or the obesity paradox, and then, back at my desk, I would conduct quiet, frantic Google searches to figure out what on earth they'd been talking about. There were so many things to worry about.

Lately, though, I'd been worrying about my clothes. The newspapers where I'd interned throughout college were very come-as-you-are, but people dressed better here, or at least my boss sure did. Sometimes, I noticed, if I showed up late *but* was wearing something nice, she would tacitly dismiss my tardiness. I started copying my roommate, who at twenty-five seemed infinitely wiser and more worldly than me and who on weekdays favored mid-length American Apparel jersey skirts in dark, office-approved neutrals like navy and black.

But in this memory the skirt betrays me. I leave the restroom, preoccupied by all of the obscure medical terms I need to look up later, and walk back toward the newsroom. That's when I hear a shriek of laughter to my right, coming from down the hall. I look toward the sound and see three people staring back, one of whom is *literally* pointing and laughing at me. I look down and—oh . . . my god.

My new skirt is tucked into the back of my tights.

In my apartment ten years later, I know I'm far away in space and time from this moment, and yet it still makes me wince. I even shake my head back and forth a few times, as if I think I can use physical force to remove from my brain the image of the office hallway, the laughing coworker, the traitorous skirt. "How embarrassing," I whisper, out loud, to no one.

This reaction, the way I will often respond physically to a cringeworthy memory, has always seemed like an odd personal quirk of mine. But drumcowski, the king of online cringe himself, told me he reacts the same way when his mind sees fit to replay his own embarrassing memories. "You're just sitting there and your brain decides to throw it in your face for no reason," he says. "For me, if I'm alone, I just start shouting, '*NO! No no no no no no no.*'"

Really, I shouldn't have been so surprised to hear that others react this way, because the physicality of the cringe is captured in its actual dictionary definition: "to draw in or contract one's muscles involuntarily; to recoil in distaste." Check and check. Online I came across a name for these memories that I quite like: cringe attacks. They're the little humiliations from your past that come back unbidden, sometimes years after they first occurred.

I recently spoke with James Danckert, a psychologist at the University of Waterloo, about this. I'd called him to talk about his research on boredom, but during our chat, we wandered off topic to discuss other emotions we don't pay much attention to, and I told him about my preoccupation with awkwardness. Later that year, he and I were both invited to speak at a small psychology conference at the University of Louisville called the Conference on Neglected Emotions. It's a title I find so endearing, as if it promises a showcase for the feelings that didn't *quite* make the cut for a featured role in *Inside Out*.

As for the neglected emotion of awkwardness, he says, "The reason I hate it—you really relive past embarrassments." This is less true, for example, of the emotion he studies: boredom. I can remember feeling bored in my high school economics class or at my after-school hostessing job, but the *feeling* of boredom doesn't come back with the memory. Not so with embarrassment. "When you think about it again," Danckert points out, "you get embarrassed all over again."

But . . . *why*? These memories are painful, but they're not exactly traumatic. They're often not even objectively all that embarrassing.

Recently, for instance, I had coffee with a former colleague who told me that a couple of weeks earlier, she'd been innocently standing in front of her bathroom mirror when she flashed back to Halloween 2015. "I did ecstasy and made out with two guys on the same improv team," even though she really liked another person at the party, she told me. For her, this was enough to cause a cringe attack so strong that she yelled at her reflection: "Oh my god oh my god oh my god why did you do that?!" I understood the reaction, but truthfully, the memory itself didn't sound *that* bad. And yet I have some like that too, that would be hard to explain why I find so embarrassing. So what's causing these memories to rush back at seemingly random times, like when I'm mindlessly doing household chores, and is there any way to prevent them, or at least remove some of their sting?

And then a thought occurred to me that I couldn't let go: What would a cringe attack be like if you remembered, in astonishing detail, almost *every day* of your life?

I didn't get the answer I was expecting, but what I found instead was so much more interesting, and genuinely useful for anyone who regularly feels under attack by embarrassing memories from their past. The first step: Learn how to be nicer to yourself.

And the second: Learn how to forget yourself.

I HAVE ASKED NIMA VEISEH A SIMPLE QUESTION, ESPE-
cially for someone with his, shall we say, skill set: I want him to tell
me about an awkward or embarrassing memory from his past. He's
had time to think about it too, because I asked the same question
in the e-mail I sent several days ago to schedule the FaceTime chat
we're having now on a summer Friday night. And yet he can't answer me.

Veiseh is one of just sixty or so people in the world who is
thought to have a highly superior autobiographical memory, or
HSAM, a condition discovered in 2006 by scientists at the University of California at Irvine. He remembers nearly every day of his
life in vivid detail. I, in contrast, could not tell you what I published on NYMag.com just last week. Mine is only an average
memory, and yet I often feel haunted by cringeworthy jolts backward in time. The more I thought about it, the more I was dying
to know: What would it be like to remember your embarrassing
moments when you remember virtually *everything* that's ever happened to you?

Before chatting with Veiseh, I had coffee with Joey DeGrandis, who has HSAM *and* who happens to work just down the street
from *New York*. We had a great talk about memories and our relationships to our past selves, but he too struggled with my question
about embarrassing memories. He and Veiseh used different analo-
gies for their memories; Veiseh seems to think of his like a highly
organized file cabinet, while DeGrandis thinks of his past selves as

being perpetually connected to his present by thousands of invisible threads. But neither of them seemed to be able to use their superpower to summon an awkward moment from their past.

Isn't this your whole thing?! I shouted inwardly, while outwardly keeping quiet as they consulted their memory threads and file cabinets. I knew I couldn't assume that everyone with HSAM would necessarily have as much trouble recalling cringeworthy moments as they did, but even so, I was baffled. How could it be possible that I can't stop remembering embarrassing episodes from my past when these two guys—who supposedly remember everything they've ever said or done—struggle to think of even *one*?

To understand this, let's return for a moment to those of us with ordinary memories. Research in neuroscience might categorize the cringe attack as an example of "persistence," which means pretty much what it sounds like—it's a memory that persists over time and is often involuntary and recurring. Persistence is often associated with traumatic experiences, but as the neuroscientist Dean Burnett explains in his book *Your Brain Is an Idiot*, these memories don't always come from some dramatic life event.

"You might be wandering along the road on your way to somewhere," he writes, "casually thinking about nothing in particular, and your brain suddenly says, 'Remember when you asked that girl out at the school party and she laughed in your face in front of everyone and you ran away but collided with a table and landed in the cakes?' Suddenly you're racked with shame and embarrassment, thanks to a twenty-year-old memory, apropos of nothing."

But why do these memories so often seem to come back out of nowhere? Burnett, in his book, describes the brain not as a supercomputer that should be revered but as a dotty, irrational thing that sometimes works in mysterious ways. Imagine, he says, "a computer that kept opening your more personal and embarrassing files, like the ones containing all your erotic Care Bears fan fiction, without being asked, and at random times." To Burnett, that's not a bad metaphor for your brain.

It's a funny image, but Lia Kvavilashvili, a psychology researcher at the University of Hertfordshire, believes that memory, at least, is more orderly than that, even if it is often in ways we can't immediately understand. Kvavilashvili has made a name for herself by studying what she calls "mind pops," those thoughts that seem to come to you out of the clear blue sky. One of her study subjects is herself, and early on in her research on mind pops, she wrote down every single one that happened to her over the course of nine months, during which she experienced some four hundred of these cognitive mysteries. She found some commonalities: 90 percent of the time they happened when she was alone. And 80 percent of the time they happened while she was doing some kind of mindless routine, like chores or personal grooming.

She's replicated those results by looking beyond herself, studying people who kept diaries of their random memories. "Always, people reported being engaged in an undemanding activity, just being in a relaxed state of mind," she tells me, which sounds about right: I was dragged back to 2007 while putting away laundry, and my former coworker flashed to a 2015 Halloween party in the middle of her morning routine.

Kvavilashvili and her colleagues have also tried to induce these mind pops in the lab by parking people in front of computers and asking them to watch something very boring, like a series of identical vertical lines that marched across the screen. Interspersed with the lines were phrases: "crossing the road," "mug of coffee," "broken glass." The study volunteers were to hit a button every time a memory came back to them, and jot down a few notes about what the memory was. In a fifteen-minute session, people tended to report seven memories on average, which suggests to Kvavilashvili that these memories "happen much more frequently than we thought."

At this point in our conversation, she gently breaks it to me that so far no one has yet studied specific emotions attached to mind pops, so she can't tell me exactly why embarrassing memories come back to us in this way. But she floats a few theories.

For one, some memory researchers argue that even the memories that seem completely random are in fact usually triggered by something in the environment. She tells me about a colleague of hers who would obsessively dictate his random memories into a voice recorder while he drove; in reviewing the recordings, he could see how a street name or a particular car make or model brought the memory forth. "So even at times when it seems completely random," she says, "it seems like they are not *really* totally random." Maybe something about the T-shirts I was putting away that day reminded me of the feel of the turncoat jersey skirt.

For another, think about how often your first response to someone who's witnessed an awkward moment of yours is something like "This isn't what it looks like" or "I can explain." If you never actually get to *make* that explanation, the moment likely feels unresolved in your mind, and some researchers believe that interrupted moments stick with us longer than those that feel completed.

Or else there's the fact that, as chapters 2 through 4 suggested, awkward moments often cause you to see yourself, if only briefly, from someone else's point of view. Studies have shown that self-defining memories tend to stay more vivid in our minds across the life span—as you may recall from chapter 1, this is also one explanation for the reminiscence bump, the reason your teenage experiences still carry so much weight even many years after you've graduated from high school. You see yourself in some brand-new way, and those moments tend to stick around.

Even so, there may be a much simpler explanation for the neurological mechanism behind cringe attacks (in people with typical memories, that is): Your emotions dictate what your brain decides to hang on to. The stronger the feeling, the stronger the memory.

"I'VE ONLY TALKED TO YOU FOR A COUPLE MINUTES," JAMES McGaugh, a neurobiologist at UC Irvine who studies memory, said to me on the phone. "And, you know, I'm sorry—you're really stupid."

I knew he was only saying this to illustrate the link between memory and strong emotion, particularly in moments of surprise. He'd given me a heads-up that he was about to say something purely for the sake of creating an example, and that he didn't mean it. Still. It kind of hurt.

"You may well remember that the rest of your life anyway, even though I said it's not true," he acknowledged, and though it's only been a few days since our interview, I suspect he might be right. As he said it, my eyes were resting on the latest *New York* cover, which featured the model Ashley Graham clad in a leopard-print top and matching fur coat. Check back with me in a few years to see whether I've developed an aversion to animal prints.

"It was unexpected," McGaugh explained, and it was highly emotional, both of which cause the brain to say to itself, *Capture that moment, whatever that was.* He takes me through a simplified version of the neurobiological processes at work here. Something excites your brain, which triggers the release of adrenaline, which in turn releases another substance called noradrenaline, a neuro-transmitter that then perks up the amygdala. "That's a region of the brain which gets excited by emotional arousal," he said. The amygdala then communicates "with almost every other region of the brain, and it says, in effect, *Something important happened. Make a strong memory.*"

This happens in moments of embarrassment or humiliation, but it's not limited to these emotions, and it's not, as I initially assumed, limited to negative emotions either. If someone told you that you'd just won the lottery, you'd remember that moment for-ever. I can still vividly remember the moment Andrew told me for the first time that he loved me. All of these things, McGaugh said, are evidence that "we have a built-in system which helps to ensure that the important experiences in our lives are remem-bered better than the boring ones, because that will help us adapt in the future."

Interesting, all very interesting. But here's a practical applica-tion of which you might want to take note: For those of us with typically functioning memories, this link to strong emotions may be the key to combatting a cringe attack. According to one recent finding by neuroscientists at the Beckman Institute at the University of Illinois at Urbana-Champaign, it helps to try to recall other, nonemotional details about a highly emotional memory. Can you remember what you were wearing? Who else was there? What did it sound like? What did it smell like?

In a 2015 study, these researchers found that when people took a few moments to mentally flesh out the details of a memory that caused them pain, it helped to dull the sting. "Sometimes we dwell on how sad, embarrassed, or hurt we felt during an event, and that makes us feel worse and worse," Florin Dolcos, one of the researchers, said in a statement. This is, in fact, what often happens in people with anxiety and depression: Dwelling on painful memories can drive you deeper into mental-health issues. Focusing on the unemotional aspects of the memory, on the other hand, should help tamp down the emotion attached to it. "Once you immerse yourself in other details," Dolcos explained, "your mind will wander to something else entirely, and you won't be focused on the negative emotions as much."

And this brings us back around to Veiseh, DeGrandis, and others with HSAM. McGaugh was part of the team of scientists who first discovered this remarkable memory ability back in 2006, and he explained to me his theory about why the two HSAMers I talked to likely had such a hard time recalling an embarrassing episode from their past. One reason their memories may work the way they do is that *everything* is registered at the same emotional level. It's why the mundanities of their day-to-day lives are so readily recalled; I offhandedly mentioned a date in the mid-2000s to DeGrandis at one point, for instance, and he immediately knew that was the day he saw *A Beautiful Mind*.

But if everything is emotional, then nothing in particular is. "If you have a strong memory that just takes everything up to a high level, then there's no differential," McGaugh said. "So you're not going to say, 'Oh, I remember the embarrassing experiences better than I remember the nonembarrassing ones.'" It isn't that DeGrandis and Veiseh can't remember embarrassing moments; it's just that those moments don't stand out more vividly than any of their other memories, even memories as bland as "that time I saw an overrated Russell Crowe movie."

For some with HSAM, this means they're haunted not just by a few painful moments from their past but by almost all of them. "The thing is with HSAM: You can't hide from anything," Veiseh told me. "Every beautiful moment, every demon, is persistently and constantly present." Some with this unusual ability are more troubled by their pasts than others, just like those of us with regular old memory capabilities. "It comes down to the individual," McGaugh said, "and how they handle their memories."

My own memory will never work the same way as Veiseh's. But as he and I talked, his conceptualization of his own amazing memory made me realize that I could borrow from his perspective on his past. Nearly an hour into our conversation, a suitable cringeworthy moment finally emerges: the time he was really into competitive karaoke, and his partner bailed on the championship, leaving him to sing a duet in the citywide championship with someone who didn't know the words.

I award him bonus awkward points for merely having belonged to a competitive karaoke league, but overall I'm underwhelmed. To be fair, so is he. He admits it wasn't all that embarrassing in the moment, and it's even less so when he recalls it now. I ask Veiseh to speculate on why he had such a hard time coming up with something embarrassing from his past.

"To be disciplined against embarrassment with HSAM, you kind of have to accept yourself," he said. "Which is a fundamental thing about embarrassment in general—the people you find who are least [sensitive to] embarrassment are either total jerks, or else they're very self-accepting. HSAM *forces* you to be self-accepting. There's no time decay of memory. You don't forget." The rest of us could learn a thing or two from this mind-set.

———

"**SOME PEOPLE ROLL WITH LIFE'S PUNCHES, FACING FAIL**-ures, losses, and problems with equanimity," begins an article subtitled "The Implications of Treating Oneself Kindly" published in 2007 in *Personality Processes and Individual Differences*. That line continues by contrasting the roll-with-it types with those who "exacerbate their distress by ruminating excessively about life's calamities, castigating themselves for their shortcomings, and catastrophizing about their problems." It brings to mind the phrase "There are two kinds of people in this world. . . ." Since about 2003, a handful of psychologists—most notably Kristin Neff of the University of Texas at Austin—have been dividing the world in two in this way: those who practice self-compassion and those who do not.

The term "self-compassion" has a somewhat cornball feel to it;

the 2007 article referenced earlier was published in an academic journal, but it at times reads like something out of the Personal Growth section at Barnes & Noble. I don't mean that as an insult exactly, because I've read and enjoyed many of those books. (I also have a hunch that's where you might've found my book.) But the fact is that it's also a confusing term, because it sounds as if it means something like self-esteem. Children of the 1990s like me will remember sitting through classroom exercises in which we were told how *special* we were and how we should always, always love ourselves. This is not that.

Instead, it's something better than that. Neff's research suggests that self-compassion helps you see yourself accurately—or, more specifically, it allows you to see yourself the way that others see you. It reminds me of Nima Veiseh's comment that self-acceptance is so important when you have an overly ambitious memory like his. After I talked to Veiseh and DeGrandis, they started to seem to me like exaggerated examples of a broader truth: None of us can truly escape our past selves, so it would be best if we could learn to be a little more objective about Past Us. This is, I think, at least partially what Veiseh means by self-acceptance: recognizing your former self for who you truly were, instead of trying to forget or fudge the details. Neff's studies suggest a way to achieve this, a path to self-awareness that can function as another way to build a bridge over the irreconcilable gap. Because this is the aspect of the concept that is most interesting to me, and because I can't stomach typing words as hokey as "self-compassion" over and over again for five pages, I'm going to instead use the term "self-clarity."

In one relevant study, Neff rounded up some college students who had just learned that they'd done poorly on their midterm exams and she measured each person's individual level of this particular type of self-awareness using a short questionnaire. It's a simple way of gauging whether people understand their place in the world. Do they just see themselves? Or do they tend to place themselves within the wider context of others' experiences?

Early on in this book, I talked about how awkwardness can feel like an isolating emotion. If it does, this research suggests that it's worth remembering that all people are total social dummies sometimes. People low in self-clarity tended to agree with statements such as "When I think about my inadequacies, it tends to make me feel more separate and cut off from the rest of the world" or "When I fail at something that's important to me, I tend to feel alone in my failure." Someone high in self-clarity, on the other hand, tends to agree with statements such as "When things are going badly for me, I see the difficulties as part of life that everyone goes through" or "When I feel inadequate in some way, I try to remind myself that feelings of inadequacy are shared by most people."

Students who scored higher in self-clarity were also more likely to *accept* their poor grades. In contrast, the others were more likely to engage in "avoidance-oriented coping"—they tried not to think about it. In the context of a cringeworthy moment, as we saw in chapter 4, avoidance is a tempting but ultimately useless strategy. You can't fix something if you never look straight at it.

In a weirder study, researchers asked people to come into the lab and take a seat in front of a camera, which would record them as they made up a fairy tale or some other kind of story that could be told to children. The only rule: It had to start with the sentence

"Once upon a time, there was a little bear. . . ." After they told their made-up stories, the researchers played them a recording—either their own or that of a different participant in the study—and asked them to evaluate the bear story.

Overall, people who did not have much self-clarity hated their own recordings, which would suggest another reason why some people cringe at their appearance on FaceTime more than others. These participants were more likely to call their own made-up stories "very bad" or at least "somewhat bad"; they also tended to describe their personal demeanor in the recordings as awkward or foolish. They were embarrassed, irritable, and nervous while being made to watch themselves tell their stories about the little bear, and they scored their own performances lower on average than others scored them. People high in self-clarity, in contrast, weren't as bothered by watching themselves on video, *and* they tended to rate their own recordings just as other people rated them.

This is important, because it contrasts self-clarity with self-esteem. Studies on self-esteem and performance evaluation usually find, unsurprisingly, that people with a lot of self-esteem *really love* themselves and their performance on a given task, tending to rate their own performance and personalities much more favorably than others do. Self-esteem inflates your ego, which can make the reality of how others see you harder to bear. And yet: "In contrast to the self-enhancing tendencies of people who are high in self-esteem," as the authors of that 2007 journal article wrote, those who are high in self-clarity "appear to judge themselves as others do." You can see and accept yourself, even your flaws.

But this form of self-acceptance doesn't leave you there, gaping at your imperfections. Returning again to the bad-midterm-grade study, the students in that report who had a lot of self-clarity were more likely to exhibit signs of what's known as mastery orientation—that is, their behaviors and attitudes suggested that they wanted to know *why* they screwed up, so that they could get better. *What happened here? Why didn't this go as well as I expected it to?* In turn, their curiosity motivated them to make an effort to improve. Those without a lot of self-clarity, on the other hand, were incurious and more likely to become defensive when probed about what might've gone wrong.

If self-clarity doesn't come naturally to you, there are ways to learn it. In her 2011 book, *Self-Compassion*, Neff suggests that you try behaving toward yourself in the same gentle but no-nonsense way you would behave toward a close friend. I'm lucky enough to have several close friends who keep me grounded, telling me plainly but kindly when I am being ridiculous. That's the kind of friend you should be to yourself, not the kind who means well but is so protective of your feelings that she minimizes your bad behavior by telling you it wasn't that embarrassing. It's important to acknowledge that, actually, maybe it *was* that embarrassing. But pair that with a reminder that you're not the only human on earth to have done something like it. Be the kind of friend to yourself who would tell you that you have spinach in your teeth but would also tell you about the time she herself walked around all day with a giant coffee stain on her shirt.

It's a skill worth learning, as there is even some evidence that people who are high in self-clarity may be better able to withstand a cringe attack. You can try this right now, if you want: Think about some awkward moment from high school or college, something that really made you feel bad about yourself. (I have several to spare, if you need to borrow one.) Think the moment carefully through: What happened right before? Who was there? How did you feel at the time?

While it's true that focusing on the unemotional aspects of one of these memories can help lessen their impact, as I mentioned earlier in this chapter, there's also a case to spend a little time doing the opposite: Let the feelings in! Let them all the way back in. "Give it a full seven seconds, and release it," advised a viral 2017 Jezebel post on dealing with awkward memories. It's a great start, but for me it doesn't seem like an effective long-term strategy. It'll just keep coming back.

Instead, once you let the awkwardness back in, put the memory in its place with these three questions. First, how many times have other people experienced the same thing or something similar? Or, to get more specific about it: How many times have other people, say, exited a public restroom with their skirt stuffed into their tights? A lot! It was embarrassing, sure, but it's also kind of a cliché of embarrassing moments.

The second question: If a friend came to you and told you about this memory, how would you respond to her? In this situation, I think I'd say that if she told it right, it could be a really funny story; beyond that, I'd probably tell her it's endearing.

And the last one: Can you try thinking about the moment from someone else's point of view? Let me try to project myself into the mind of the woman who pointed and laughed when she saw this happen. Maybe she was surprised, and grateful for something to have upended the workday monotony. Or, now that I'm older, I know how out of place interns sometimes seem in an office environment, like they're travelers from some faraway country: They barely speak the language and struggle to understand the culture. Sometimes, to those of us who feel at home in an office environment, watching interns try to get the hang of things really *is* amusing, even if we feel like jerks laughing about it.

This three-questions advice is the gist of that same 2007 paper that found that the above exercises are a much more effective way to process a negative personal memory than some other methods that are more intuitive. Here's what doesn't work: Convincing yourself it was someone else's fault. Distracting yourself by focusing on your positive characteristics. Telling yourself that the memory "does not really indicate anything about the kind of person I am."

It's a version of self-awareness that allows you to acknowledge that you *are* the "kind of person" who makes mistakes while also putting those mistakes in perspective. You definitely tucked your skirt into your tights that one time, and people definitely saw. You're kind of a screwup sometimes. But so is everyone else! As Neff has said of her research, when we arrive at this kind of self-awareness, then "when we fail, it's not 'poor me,' it's 'well, everyone fails.' Everyone struggles. This is what it means to be human." It helps you see yourself. It also helps you see beyond yourself.

EARLIER THIS WEEK, I WAS WASTING TIME ON TWITTER when I came across a tweet that helped me pull together some loosely held thoughts that had been knocking around in my mind. It was from my colleague Olivia Nuzzi, the Washington correspondent for *New York*, and in it she had screencapped a Lena Dunham quote: "I AM a model. I am Rihanna to myself." Nuzzi, who is always entertaining on Twitter, responded to this in one run-on sentence: "I'm so over the self-love movement I think we need a self-hate movement."

I realize she wasn't serious, but it caught my eye, because I'm similarly bored with people promoting excessive self-love. And yet (. . . obviously) advocating for self-hate would be absurd. Instead, lately I'm interested in something I've started to call self-indifference.

To me, self-indifference is the comfort of realizing that you are simply not that big a deal. I'm sure my attraction to this idea is at least in part a reaction to a childhood steeped in the self-esteem movement, which I already mentioned once in this chapter. We were constantly told how exceptional we were, how special we were. The adults in our lives meant well, but what did it do to us? As we've just seen, the psychological science on the subject has shown that when you try to make yourself feel better by shaking off criticism and zeroing in on your positive aspects *only*, it backfires. The best, if counterintuitive, way to truly feel better about yourself is to see yourself as you really are. As Nima Veiseh and his extraordinary memory reminded me, even those of us with normal memories will never really escape our past selves, an idea chapter 11 explores more. So it's best to simply acknowledge the things about yourself and your past that make you cringe and address what you can—but then shrug. Who out there hasn't done something equally ridiculous?

I just tried this, actually, with a cringe attack that occurred during a long walk. Something brought me back to several years ago, when I was blogging three to four science posts a day, many of which embarrass me now. I had to dash them off so quickly so many times a day, and the quality sometimes suffered. I was thinking of one that, in retrospect, was particularly shoddy when my gut clenched up, as it always does in a cringe attack. But then I had this thought: *Literally everyone who writes on the Internet has some subpar stories from their past that they regret. You are not unique.* I don't know which muscles in my stomach had twisted up when the first thought occurred to me, but with the second, they instantly untwisted.

C. S. Lewis once wrote about what I mean by self-indifference, only he called it humility. They're different names for the same thing. A truly humble person, as he says in *Mere Christianity*, "will not be the sort of person who is always telling you that, of course, he is nobody." Instead he "will not be thinking about himself at all."

Humility is a misunderstood concept, the psychologist Jennifer Cole Wright has said. We often understand it as if it meant having a low opinion of yourself and your status, but Wright and other contemporary scholars studying the attitude see it differently. As the anthropologist Alan Morinis once wrote, humility allows you to "occupy a rightful space, neither too much or too little." Humility is knowing your place.

Humble people tend not to focus on themselves, according to the modern scientific literature on the subject (not to mention thousands of years of philosophical writings). Wright explained that a little humility helps you keep your natural talents and honed skills in proper perspective: The fact that I'm able to string coherent sentences together as a professional writer isn't valuable because of what it says about me and how awesome I am, for example. What matters is what I *do* with that ability.

What humble people *do* focus on, then, is other people. They look outward, to those around them, just as often as, if not more often than, they do inward, to themselves. "This is not to say that a humble person fails to care about her own welfare or pursue her own interests—it is simply that she sees these as being deeply intertwined with the welfare and interests of others," write the authors of a 2016 philosophy paper called "Some Varieties of Humility Worth Wanting." Humility allows you to see yourself as part of an interconnected whole. You matter because of the way your actions impact everyone else.

The research suggests that humble people are more likely to remain open-minded when dealing with someone whom they're disagreeing with, a quality that will serve you well when handling awkward conversations like the ones we saw in chapter 4. Recent research on intellectual humility, which could be loosely defined as knowing that there are limits to what you know, has suggested that people with this quality tend to be more open to new ideas, which means they're likely to be better learners, even finding something they can learn from those they disagree with. In a recent paper, Wright and her colleagues explained that "humility is a corrective to our natural tendency to treat our 'selves' as special." It sounds like the antidote to the self-love movement that both Nuzzi and I were searching for.

If you are sensitive to awkwardness, then you're already in a great position to start becoming a little more humble. By now you are aware of the role of empathy in awkward moments, in that these instances briefly shift your perspective as you imagine what you must look like from somebody else's point of view. In an instant, you're freed from your own perspective. So a cringeworthy moment, then, can be used as a reminder that yours is not the only perspective. Likewise, a cringe attack could become a reminder that you *aren't* alone in your awkwardness. It's not a feeling that is unique to you. Everyone shares it, to some degree or another, and reminding yourself of that may be one way to minimize the impact of these memories.

It sounds abstract and lofty to talk about a moral virtue like humility, but learning to be more humble can help you endure everyday awkwardness. When you meet someone for the first time, you are, obviously, trying your hardest to make yourself look good. You're trying to present the best version of yourself, and so you make sure to mention things that will give the person a good first impression of you—maybe the last good book you read, or a shoehorned-in reference to the years you lived in Europe. That's nothing to be ashamed about—we all do it. In one study, for instance, researchers analyzed conversations among bar patrons and found that two thirds of the time, people talked about themselves. We do it because we want to fit in; we want to be liked.

But the research consistently shows that this tactic backfires. Talking about yourself is a good way to leave a bad first impression, a depressing finding when you consider the research that shows people talk about themselves because they think that's the best way to get people to *like* them. A better thing to do when you don't know what to say: Ask a question instead.

More specifically, some recent research by Harvard Business School doctoral student Karen Huang and her colleagues found that the more questions you ask people, the more they tend to like you. In an experiment, the researchers told some participants they were to ask at least nine questions; others were told they could ask no more than four. They chatted with a partner for a while, and then everyone ranked how much they liked the person they'd been paired with. In the end, the people everyone liked best were the ones who asked a lot of questions. Not just any questions would do, however: The researchers found that people liked being asked follow-up questions the best, no doubt because it proved they were being listened to. Most people just want to be heard.

The secret to feeling less awkward in everyday life, then, isn't to closely monitor your own behavior so that you do and say the right thing at every turn. This is highly unnecessary, anyway, because—as you'll recall from chapter 6—most people aren't judging you as harshly as you think they are. Instead of focusing inward, turn your attention outward, onto the people in front of you. While you're at it, maybe help me spread the gospel of self-indifference.

SECTION 3

What Am I Supposed to Do Now?

CHAPTER 9

Awkward Silences at the Office

It was a snowy day in March, the kind that was severe enough to trap most everyone at home, but not so severe that their homes had lost power. The modern knowledge worker will immediately recognize this as a textbook work-from-home day: You don't get the day off, but you also don't have to change out of your pajamas. Small victories.

On this particular day, a woman began her snow day / workday in her bedroom. She shared her home with several roommates, although this group also lived with their landlord, who enforced some unusual house rules. Among them: No laptops allowed downstairs. It was an annoying mandate but not a huge deal, and so, from her room, she dialed into a conference call.

The guy who lived in the room next to hers had gotten a *real* snow day, an actual day off work, as had his girlfriend. The two celebrated their surprise day of freedom by having sex—very loud, very obvious sex, the kind that could be very clearly heard through thin walls. The kind that could also be heard on this woman's conference call, an ordinary meeting suddenly soundtracked by moans and heavy breathing. She scrambled to hit mute as soon as she realized what was happening, but it was too late. Everyone had heard everything.

The next day the icy weather had subsided, so everyone returned to work, where she was met with a metaphorical kind of iciness. The colleagues who had been on that call seemed to be avoiding her all day; several times one of them would be walking toward her down a long hallway when they would notice her, abruptly about-face, and head back in the opposite direction.

"This is," Alison Green tells me, "probably the most awkward situation I've ever had on *Ask a Manager*." And that is saying something.

Since 2007 Green has answered thousands of questions about workplace weirdness on her blog, *Ask a Manager*, a popular online advice column. Green started the site when she was still a manager at a nonprofit in Washington, D.C., when she realized that the biggest question most of us have at our jobs is *What is my boss thinking?* followed closely by *What am I supposed to do now?!* The idea behind *Ask a Manager* was to provide people with some new insight into those questions.

It was a good idea. The site now attracts about 1.1 million unique users per month, and Green also writes for places like *Inc.* and *Fast Company;* in 2016 she became a colleague of mine, kind of, in that she writes a weekly column for *The Cut* called Ask a Boss. Some of the letters she gets are more unusual than others. "I had one person write in who had an employee who was telling her coworkers that she was casting magical curses on them," she said. In another, someone wrote to complain that she was pretty sure her colleague was moonlighting as a sex worker and using the office bathroom to meet clients. "[S]he didn't even sound that put off by it," Green said. "She was just annoyed that she was having to cover [for her]—she was having to do her coworker's work at those times."

The oddball queries are entertaining, but my favorite columns tend to be rooted in the more everyday forms of office awkwardness: What should you do if you realize everyone at work is hanging out without you? Or, uh, what is the best way to politely tell someone that *you* would really rather not hang out with *them* outside work? How can you tell when it's the right time to initiate a salary negotiation? And when you do, what are you supposed to say?

So many questions and so few clear answers. Even Green is sometimes momentarily stumped by some of the letters she receives, like the problem of the sex-noises conference call. "Do you follow up and say something later, like 'Heyyy, that was my roommate'?" she said. "Because *that's* super awkward too." Or should she just advise the letter writer to do nothing and let it blow over?

The best and the worst thing about the uncertainty aspect of awkwardness is that it is so easy to avoid, something that is often less true about the other two aspects. It doesn't take much more than a simple conversation to shift your perspective in the way that the irreconcilable gap does or to cause the nervousness that leads to the self-consciousness vortex. You'll often get plunged into those kinds of cringeworthy situations whether you're trying to or not, but uncertainty is easier to keep at arm's length. If you don't know what to say or do, there is always nothing. Nothing is always an option.

This is true in so many different parts of our lives, but in this chapter I'm going to focus on uncertainty in the workplace, partly because it's where most of us spend most of our time and partly because, on the job, the stakes are so high and so clearly defined. For many of us, work provides a measure of our self-worth; for most of us, it also provides our financial worth, and probably also our health insurance. It can seem smarter to suck it up and say nothing (or else just vent about the problem on Slack) than to address the issue directly.

Off and on as I chat with Green, my memory flashes back to my own uncomfortable work problems. I have a spotty track record of rising to the moment of awkwardness at the office. Once, after being told I was receiving an unexpected promotion, I had the presence of mind to ask for an increase in compensation to match the increase in responsibilities. I didn't really know how to ask, and I'm sure I didn't phrase it in the most eloquent way possible, but I blurted out what I meant, and it worked. (It didn't happen instantly, but I did get a raise a few months later.)

Then again, there was the time when several people in different parts of the company privately contacted me to complain about one of my direct reports. This person, they told me, was disrespectful and rude and had a habit of flouting officewide rules in ways that created more work for others. In our next check-in meeting, I meant to bring this up; I wrote it down and everything. Toward the end of the half hour, I stared down at my notebook, where I'd scrawled something like "address attitude??" in ballpoint ink. But I didn't know how to say it. So I didn't say anything.

If social life is a performance, then these are the unscripted moments. Uncertainty might be the aspect of awkwardness with the highest stakes, perhaps *because* it's so easily avoidable. You didn't *have* to say or do anything. Most people would understand and perhaps even expect you to sense an opportunity but ignore it, because your next move is unclear. But when that's what you choose to do, what do you stand to lose?

IT'S COMMON SENSE THAT NOT KNOWING TENDS TO MAKE people uneasy, and it's also a well-established finding in psychology research. Consider a classic 1960s study, for example, in which people received several rounds of small but still painful shocks of electricity. Little warning bells went off several times throughout the study period, sometimes followed directly by a shock and sometimes not. Overall, people told experimenters that they preferred when the warning was followed by the shock over when it wasn't. Other research has suggested that people report feeling unpredictable pain more strongly than pain they saw coming, a finding that's hard not to read metaphorically. It's easy to see how that relates to some of life's most painful moments, like the way we say things like "At least we knew it was coming" when someone dies after a long illness.

But for me, this also helps explain the social pain of awkwardness, and why one of the most obvious awkward-moment coping strategies often works so well. Sometimes if you just *say*, "This is going to be a little awkward," it turns out not to be so bad after all. It's nice to get a little heads-up.

Or here's another example. Not long ago I made myself go to a networking event. I know these things are annoying, but they are also annoyingly useful; I've met people at book-launch events or journalism meet-ups whom I ended up working with later. At this one I was standing alone, waiting for my friend to show up, when I noticed another solo woman. "Hi," I said to her, "I notice that you too are standing awkwardly alone." That was all it took to break the ice. We started chatting so animatedly that when my friend finally got there, she assumed this random stranger and I had arrived together._

We all react to ambiguity differently. In the 1990s, a pair of psychologists developed something called a "need-for-closure" scale, which measures how much individuals are bothered by uncertainty. Many of the questions are straightforward enough—*Do you like structure? Do you dislike unpredictable situations?*—that I would think most of us could intuit where we stand on our own, without taking the questionnaire. If you crave tidiness, order, and resolution, it's likely that you have a high need for closure; if, on the other hand, you change your opinion easily, are okay with mystery and messiness, and are more open-minded, you likely have a low need for closure. But other, related research has shown that certain situations increase the need for closure even in those of us who mostly don't mind loose ends. Stress makes uncertainty feel more unpleasant, and so can feeling rushed.

The downside of really needing closure is that sometimes uncertainty feels so unpleasant that you'll make any decision just so that you can move forward in certainty, even if it's a rash or wrong one. There are times when it's worthwhile to dwell more in the interesting questions than in the correct answers; sometimes there *are* no correct answers.

This makes for an interesting thought experiment, but I sometimes get caught there, considering at length all the ways I *could* move forward and never making a move because I can't settle on only one. None of them feels exactly right, and none of them feels exactly wrong. An unimportant but irritating example of this is the boss who gave me a nickname I hated. She said the nickname for the first time, and two paths appeared. Either I could have the awkward conversation and say that I'd rather she called me by my actual name, or I could just put up with it. I spent so much time imagining all the ways I could bring this up that I forgot to ever actually bring it up. And *then* the thing happened where it had gone on for too long, and with every day, week, and month that went by, it felt like too much time had passed to bring it up *now*. (For what it's worth, I do think it's sometimes fine to ignore a problem if it's trivial—but if you do, you also have to relinquish your right to complain about it.)

Learning to become comfortable with ambiguity doesn't have to mean leaving awkward situations unaddressed; it often just means picking *a* path forward while acknowledging that it may be an imperfect path. It's simply the best choice you could make in the moment. Or perhaps you'd like to borrow my go-to tactic for dealing with office ambiguity: Googling my very specific problem and "Ask a Manager." After more than ten years of answering reader questions, there's a good chance Alison Green has addressed at least some version of your issue. After reading her for years, I think I can distill her advice down to this: In awkward work situations, be as straightforward as possible. Her letters often include variations on this message: *The way to address this is by talking to her. Talk to them now. Just talk to her! Do it ASAP, though, because it's going to get weirder with each passing day.*

So you don't know what to say. Okay. But you know what's bothering you, right? That's a start.

About the woman at the start of the chapter, whose coworkers were acting strange after overhearing her roommates having sex on that conference call, Green was flummoxed for a while but eventually advised the letter writer to address the situation head-on: *I really apologize for the background noise on our call the other day. I have roommates and thin walls, and they clearly weren't working that day. I was mortified, and I'm sorry it disrupted the call like that. I'll be more careful about work calls when they're at home!* The letter writer wrote back a few days later to report that, first of all, her colleagues had assumed that she'd been home watching porn on her snow day, which, yikes. But Green's advice worked. The tension was gone, and the unspoken problem became an inside joke.

It's why so many people love Green's approach to workplace awkwardness. She sees direct paths that cut through the ambiguity described by every letter writer. The question may be head spinning, but you read her response and you think, *Of course—clearly, that was the answer.* "I've always been pretty eager to tackle the awkward," Green tells me, "but I don't think that's normal behavior on my part." Those of us who respond to uncertainty at work (and elsewhere) by avoiding it are often imagining all the ways we could make things worse by addressing the situation: We could offend someone or cause tension or just risk looking really stupid.

"So often," she said, "awkwardness is being direct about something that people aren't normally direct about."

She can't tell you for certain how it will turn out once you go the straightforward route, but she thinks it's always better to be honest and ask for what you need rather than hoping in vain that someone will see you struggling and offer a solution. Be direct, she encourages her readers, and remember that this is not the same as being rude. Stay professional, of course, and be as kind as you can, but when it comes down to it, you just have to say the thing. You have to speak up, because, as we saw in chapter 3, people are harder to read than we tend to assume. The problems at work that feel so obvious to you are often invisible from the outside.

And yet it makes sense to leave some room for ambiguity in a discussion of how to handle ambiguity. In most instances of office awkwardness, it helps to minimize uncertainty by being as straightforward as possible. *This is what I need, and this is how I think we can make this happen.* It's not personal, as the cliché goes. It's business. But that's not always true, is it? Sometimes it's both.

———

DID YOU THINK I COULD MAKE IT THROUGH A CHAPTER about the awkwardness of the office without mentioning *The Office*? The UK version gives me such strong secondhand embarrassment (shades of chapter 7) that I can hardly stand to watch it, and one of the scenes that makes me cringe the most happens just after David Brent is fired. (In case you've never seen the show, this is the Ricky Gervais character.) Toward the end of the episode, David shows up at Wernham Hogg with his dog. His former coworkers greet him—or, if not him, the dog—with interest, until he asks everyone to meet him after work hours. He addresses the office as a whole: "Who wants to go for a drink tomorrow?"

Silence.

"Yeah? Anyone?"

. . .

"Short notice. What about the day after that, have a beer?"

. . .

"Thursday's good—for me. Anyone?"

. . .

"What's good for you?"

Finally someone breaks the silence. "No one wants to have a drink with you," the woman seated next to Tim (that's British for Jim) says. "You don't even work here."

This is the nature of work friendships: They're fragile. Many are too weak to stand on their own after the structure of the workplace is removed. "In some ways," Alison Green tells me, "this is the most awkward of awkward workplace situations, because it's so fraught—it's more personal." Out of curiosity, I did a simple search on Green's site to get a rough estimate of how often she recommends being honest or frank. The phrase "be straightforward" appears 370 times; the words "be direct" appear 818 times. It's true that sometimes letter writers may have included these phrases themselves, but still: My point is Green loves straightforwardness. Yet even she acknowledges that when it comes to work friendships, this is not always the best option.

Take the David Brent scene, for example. It's not painful to watch because he's an idiot. It's painful because he's you, and your easily wounded feelings.

He's also me. At a previous job, I got drinks with a colleague with whom I thought I'd shared a friends-at-first-sight moment. We met for drinks, and the night ended up feeling like a bad first date, with both of us clearly having conflicting motivations for being there. I'd thought this was a step toward actual friendship. We had so much in common! She was a runner, and so was I! She loved bar trivia, and so did I! And yet she kept turning the conversation back to work, at one point boring the hell out of me by taking out her phone to show me the redesign of the Web site we both worked for. At the end of the night, she let me know she was expensing our drinks, a signal I interpreted as a mark of our status. This was a meeting between work associates, not drinks with a friend.

It is good to have friends at work. I hardly think you need me to back that statement up with research, but I'll do it anyway, because there is tons of it. For instance, one does not expect to be charmed by something called the Gallup Q12 Employee Engagement Survey, a twelve-item questionnaire designed to measure the "health" of a workplace, but item 10 is surprisingly endearing: Do you have a best friend at work? If you do, then according to Gallup's research, you are more likely than those who don't to have been praised or recognized in some way for your performance over the last week. Maybe the compliments were from your bestie. They still count.

I adore my work best friends, all of them, past and present and future. You never have to go for coffee alone, your birthday never goes uncelebrated and your haircuts never go unnoticed. It's some-one you can trust with your most embarrassing asks. Do you have deodorant / floss / a tampon / an extra pair of flats because all I have are my gym shoes? For you, I do, work best friend. Once I somehow left my *wallet* on my desk overnight, and so the next morning I texted my work best friend to ask if she would bring it down for me so I could get in the building. She did, of course. Another time I quietly asked a different work best friend at a different job if the lanyard I wore displaying my building ID smelled like cat pee. It did, of course. If you think it might smell like cat pee, you already have your answer, her response gently reminded me.

A work best friend shields you from the gossip you don't need to know, the stuff that would only hurt your feelings, but gives you the intel you do need to hear. Even better: She'll also give you the details on the petty dramas she overhears about your other col-leagues, and for any and all venting needs, she is all ears (or, more likely, eyes, because in my experience all of this is often done on-line). This can backfire if done carelessly. At a long-ago internship, my work best friend sent me an angry instant message about our boss but accidentally sent it to . . . our boss. She apologized again and again, but the damage was done. Later that summer, I re-turned the favor by accidentally sending a bitchy text *about* her *to* her; I meant to send it to a mutual friend whom we knew from a previous workplace.

The lesson it seems like you should take from these mishaps is *stop talking shit*, but that seems implausible as well as unnecessary, because gossip serves the common good. Studies like "Gossip and Ostracism Promote Cooperation in Groups," published in *Psycho-*

logical Science in 2014, argue that people shape up after being gossiped about, behaving more cooperatively than they did before feeling ostracized. Shit talking works, kind of. Just maybe move the online bitching off Slack and to your private Gchat. On a related note, what an exciting moment that is. It is hard to overstate the importance of the first Gchat in the progression of a friendship.

All friendships are ambiguous by nature. Neither of you was forced into this relationship, and either of you can end it the moment you're no longer interested, which is why it's so precious when it works. And yet in *The Meaning of Friendship* the philosopher and writer Mark Vernon muses that work friendships are especially ambiguous because when it comes down to it, they are defined not by mutual liking but by their utility. It's an understanding that helps explain the many varieties of awkwardness that occur among work friends. The first office environment I was ever a part of was my college newspaper, and I noticed even then that the clique we student editors formed there wasn't based on status, exactly. We let younger staff writers hang out with us—*as long as they were good.* Vernon asks, "Why is it so easy to dislike a colleague who doesn't pull their weight, or someone who makes work for others, even when outside of work they may be perfectly likable people?" If relationships at work are based on what you can give me, and you're giving me garbage, then I am not going to reward you with my friendship.

It's also why running into a coworker outside work feels so weird. It doesn't matter how much I like the colleague I happen to see in the wild—my first impulse is always to hide, or to simply avert my eyes until we've passed each other. If we've unconsciously defined our relationship by its usefulness, how are we supposed to relate to each other when we're in a context where that usefulness has become useless? "The reason for the discomfort is that stripping work relationships of their utility, and the environment in which the relationship makes sense, simultaneously removes their *raison d'etre*," Vernon writes. "So outside work, people find it hard to know how to relate to one another." In one of his later books, *Frame Analysis*, Erving Goffman argues that the social world is a lot more organized than we think. To go back to his dramaturgical view of social life, seeing a colleague outside work would be like seeing Daenerys from *Game of Thrones* still in her full mother-of-dragons getup as an inmate on *Orange Is the New Black*. It's a jarring challenge to the way your brain has organized the world.

People are always promising to keep in touch after they leave a job, and yet isn't it strange how most of them don't? Even those we sincerely liked and really did mean to keep in touch with. In *Then We Came to the End*, a 2007 best seller by Joshua Ferris written almost entirely in the first person plural, employees at an ad agency are laid off one by one. In the final chapter, a character named Benny gets an e-mail from a former colleague, Hank Neary. "The name was familiar," Ferris writes, "he knew he should have known it, but the longer he stared at it the more it eluded him." He can't place it. How quickly we forget.

But even within the confines of the office, friendships can be tricky to navigate. Between messages about deadlines and projects, Kyle and his boss—two millennials at a San Francisco (where else?) start-up—would often joke around on Gchat or plan to meet up over the weekend for drinks. "At times we were so close that I didn't know whether he was speaking to me as the boss or as my friend," he told *MEL* magazine in 2016, "and it got to a point where they mixed together." When Kyle resigned, his boss clearly took it personally, resulting in several tense conversations that made Kyle regret ever blurring the lines between work and friendship to begin with.

Kyle and his boss are an example of what organizational psychologists have called "multiplex relationships," which the authors of a 2015 paper in *Personnel Psychology* defined as "multifaceted relationships that superimpose friendship with work-focused interactions." Their research adds nuance to the Gallup survey, getting at the ambivalence of workplace friendships.

For instance, this study did find that people who reported more "multiplex relationships" tended to be better overall performers. But employees who reported having the most work friends also "tended to report having difficulties maintaining their relationships"; they also reported higher levels of emotional exhaustion. It's harder to give a friend honest feedback about an idea or a project that just isn't working. You don't want to make her feel dumb, both because you care about her feelings and your friendship and because you know your criticism might change the way she sees you. You were a friend. Now you're kind of just a jerk.

Given the inherent complication of these relationships, it's tempting to side with the more cynical self-help takes about work friends, like this cheery 2011 headline from *Forbes:* "3 Reasons Workplace Friendships Are a Lie." Reason number one, for example, is this: "You can't be friends with someone you see as competition or who sees you as competition." Is that true, though? I can be competitive with my "real" friend too; it's possible to see competition as motivation and not a threat.

Green tells me that she has received hundreds of letters over the years about awkward work friendships, enough for her to loosely categorize them into four groups. Tons of these questions are about the complainers, the friends who always seems to have some new issue at work they need to vent about. Or there's the manipulators, who uses their friendship with you to their advantage by dumping their work on you.

Then there's the "I don't like you in that way" situation, where the other person really wants to be friends and you do not. Finally, on the flip side, there's the "Is everyone hanging out without me?" dilemma, when you watch your coworkers leave together for happy hour, and no one invited you.

"I don't think there's a flawless way to handle any of this," Green says. "It's about minimizing the amount of weirdness that you're each going to feel." She still believes in being direct, but in matters of workplace friendship, she advises starting with a lighter touch. For the first three categories—the complainer, the manipulator, and the "I don't like you in that way" coworker—you can turn people down, but gently. You can blame work, saying that you're too busy to listen to them complain or to do their work or to meet up for drinks after work. Most people will get the hint after you do this a few times.

For those who don't, try a little more clarity. You can say that complaining bums you out, and so do people who take advantage of you, though the colleague who comes on too strong in pursuing a friendship is trickier. "I think if you have any warmth or goodwill toward the person, it's a nice thing that you do just occasionally getting coffee with them," Green says. "Normally, I'm a proponent of being straightforward. But I'm a bigger proponent of getting the outcome you want with a minimum of hurt feelings on both sides."

As for the people who feel left out: It could just be that you're new, or maybe your role in the company keeps you isolated. Either way, there are ways to start making connections. Start slowly. Don't weird them out by inviting them to dinner if you've never hung out outside the office, but getting coffee to talk about a work project is a good way to start. Build from there, little by little. "You're going to get signals of whether stuff is clicking," Green said. "If you're getting good signals from that . . ." She pauses. "This totally sounds like you're asking someone out," she says. "But it's a lot of the same thing!" It's a little bit magical whenever you find another human you click with, whether romantically or platonically. Again, there are no set rules, except the one that applies when there are no rules: Keep in mind what you want. That should help you deal with some of the ambiguity.

The challenge of it is to find out whether you like each other beyond the relationship's transactional, utilitarian origin. But that's a good enough place to begin to form the foundation of a real friendship. While I was writing this, I happened to get an e-mail from the woman I had an awkward happy hour with, the one who expensed our drinks and kept turning the conversation away from the personal and back to the professional. She wants to get a drink. It doesn't mean we're friends. But it doesn't mean we're not.

I HEARD A STORY RECENTLY ABOUT AN ACQUAINTANCE'S former boss. When underlings would go into this person's office to discuss something like a pay raise or promotion, the boss had a habit of greeting their request with silence. Quiet, tense seconds ticked slowly by, and the joke among the staffers was that they'd often leave having instead volunteered to take a pay cut or demotion—anything to end the excruciating silence.

This anecdote has stuck with me, because it is not hard for me to imagine myself responding in the same way as these nervous employees. Sometimes I feel like I try to stomp out awkward silences by verbally tap-dancing on top of them. *Look at me, don't look at the fear and judgment and ambiguity that this conversational pause symbolizes, look at meee!* My uneasiness is no doubt at least partially cultural. If you'll recall the awkward-silence study mentioned in chapter 5, researchers found that Dutch and English speakers judged pauses to become uncomfortable around 4 seconds of silence. Contrast that with a study of Japanese speakers, who in one study let silences last as long as 8.2 seconds. English speakers, and perhaps especially we Americans, love our noisy chitchat.

It's an overgeneralization, but I'd wager that one reason Americans are uncomfortable with awkward silences is our individualistic natures, fostered by our culture. Here I'm going to call back once more to the notion of the irreconcilable gap. Perhaps we fill the uncertainty of an awkward silence with our own imaginations, guessing at what the pause might be causing the other person to think, and especially what they might be thinking about *us*. As noted in chapter 2, a negotiation will automatically throw you into this mode of thinking, because it's one of the few scenarios in life in which you have to explicitly say, "*This* is what I think I'm worth. Do you agree?"

The topic of salary negotiation tactics is a book-length subject, but I'd like to spend some time considering one discrete strategy that feels pertinent to my particular, peculiar interests, as it is rife with both uncertainty and social discomfort: the awkward silence. It's true what I said earlier in this chapter, that sometimes fear of ambiguity makes us freeze and say nothing. But this is one instance where "saying nothing" can be the best response, making it a secret weapon for the shy, the awkward, and the easily tongue-tied.

One thing Alison Green has recently chided her readers about when it comes to negotiations is that you will not always get a clear signal from your manager, or from a hiring manager, that unmistakably spells out: *Now it is time to begin negotiating.* "They *might* give you an opening to do it, but they might not," Green wrote to someone who had been offered an internal promotion, and though she did not perceive herself to have formally accepted the position, her bosses apparently did. "So you want to be ready to bring it up yourself."

Women in particular may be more likely to be bothered by this form of ambiguity. One 2012 Harvard Kennedy School study of 2,500 job applicants found that when a job listing did not specifically state that salary was negotiable, men were more likely than women to negotiate. But if a listing *did* say that salary was negotiable, the gender gap disappeared, and men and women were about equally likely to initiate salary talks. And by the way, if you're worried about coming off as overly aggressive, don't be. In one 2014 Columbia University experiment, 57 percent of mock negotiators who believed they were being assertive, or even overassertive, were seen by their negotiating partners as being *under*assertive. Yet another example of how hard it can be to see yourself clearly.

One way to manage uncertainty is to minimize it. The obvious advice here is to do your research and have in mind a range of figures suitable for your field, your role, and your experience. The not-obvious advice is what to then *do* with that information.

Katie Donovan, founder of the consultancy firm Equal Pay Negotiations, is a proponent of the awkward-silence negotiating technique. As she has phrased it, "The first step is to be silent, hush up, or SHUT UP!" If, for example, you are offered a starting salary of $40,000 when you know that the median salary for this position is $48,000, you can say something like this: "Thank you for the offer. I'm a little surprised about the salary, though. Based on my research I would have expected it to be in the $50,000 range."

It's a good start; there is no phrase more quietly lethal in the corporate world than "I'm a little surprised." But it only works if you say this and then say *nothing*. During this pause, Donovan explains, the hiring manager is likely trying to work out how serious you are and how much more to offer. "Remember," Donovan writes, "rarely is an initial job offer made at the maximum salary budgeted. The hiring manager most likely will have the authority to increase the salary during the meeting." They might not be able to reach the number you're asking for, but let *them* tell you that; don't undercut yourself by saying that for them.

Another way to use silence: Ask for a moment to think. A few years ago, I got to interview the researcher and best-selling author Brené Brown around the release of her 2015 book *Rising Strong*. I was struck by how often she did this. She would pause, often for several seconds at a time, in a way that seemed to signal that she was deeply considering her answer. Silence doesn't have to feel confrontational to be effective.

It's possible that the awkward-silence technique could backfire by resulting in the kind of awkwardness that reflects badly on *you*, making you seem shifty or socially inept. And it's also not the right strategy for every context. I recently came across a 2009 paper in the *Journal of Palliative Medicine* about how it can backfire when inexperienced therapists try to "use silence," because if the clinician is uncomfortable with the silence, the patient will likely be too.

Studies of the need-for-closure concept mentioned earlier in this chapter have found that there are some ways to manage your discomfort with uncertainty, which might help you hold your ground in a strategic awkward silence. In experiments researchers have found that people become more comfortable with uncertainty when they think they're going to have to explain or defend their decisions later. I started doing this a while ago, before I realized it had been given the blessing of psychological science. I make a decision, and then I make sure it's the best one by imagining how I would justify it to someone else. It helps.

There's a scene in the 1995 movie *Before Sunrise* in which Julie Delpy's character is having her palm read by a fortune-teller, who tells her, "You need to resign yourself to the awkwardness of life."

I like this quote, but I'd exchange the phrase "resign yourself" for something slightly more upbeat. You could spend your time and energy trying to avoid uncertainty in social or work situations, or you could "resign yourself" to it, accepting the ambiguity without enthusiasm. But I've started to think that in certain contexts, you could *use* it, maybe even transforming the awkwardness into a superpower, as my friend's former boss did with uncomfortable silences.

"My advice is that you should embrace it," Green said, "and find the humor in it." As we'll see in the next chapter, one of the best ways to get over your fear of the uncertainty is to remind yourself how *funny* all of this is. If you can't laugh at awkwardness, you are missing out on some of the best anecdotes in your own autobiography. "Awkwardness," Green reminds, "is not going to kill you."

CHAPTER 10

Laughing at Imaginary
Tumblers of Spilled Whiskey

"Don't you think people have too many clothes these days?" asks the man holding a pretend tumbler of whiskey.

"Oh, *no*," I reply, gesturing with my invisible glass of wine for emphasis. "Quite the opposite—I think people don't have nearly *enough* clothes. I collect them, myself."

This is the sort of quality comedic scene that you too can create, if you register for the free Monday-night improv class at the Magnet Theater in Midtown Manhattan. It's one of the first lines out of my mouth and already I've broken the only rule everyone knows about improv: "yes, *and*," the idea that you're supposed to accept the premise your partner has suggested and then build on it. Whoops.

The instructor has paired off the dozen or so of us who showed up, and my partner is a short young man in a stained orange T-shirt who has not let a receding hairline stop him from growing his stringy hair to his shoulders. We are pretending to be fancy people at a fancy cocktail party, and when the instructor points to us, we're to start chatting about the given subject, which is clothes. After the scintillating exchange between my partner and me, he motions to another duo to start, and then another, until it's our turn again. The man in the orange tee mimes spilling his drink onto his shirt, adding an imaginary stain to the very real ones.

"Oh, no," he says. He looks at me, eyebrows raised as if he's expecting something, for a long moment. When I look back blankly, he adds, "It's just—you said you had so many clothes. . . ."

And then I get it. He is trying to get me to take my shirt off and give it to him. This small man with the long hair and receding hairline is actually trying to get me to take my shirt off in a room full of strangers, in a free improv class on a Monday freaking night. The instructor seems to realize this in the same moment that I do and quickly interjects with a shaky laugh: "Aaaand *scene!*"

Everything about this is embarrassing. We do another exercise where we get into groups of three and are told to mirror one another, with one person starting the movements and the other two following along. I stare at the tightly wound man in glasses who has been elected our group leader; he widens his mouth and lifts his arms in the air, as if he's pretending to be a monster to scare a small child. Something about his wholehearted commitment and total lack of detached irony triggers such deep second-hand embarrassment in me that I feel my fight-or-flight response kick in and seriously consider leaving. After all: free class. But I stay, and I calm down, and it's the weirdest thing. On paper, everything we did in the class sounds like something I would've hated. Even remembering it now, it still *sounds* like something a rational person would find inane. After the mirroring activity, I give an impromptu speech about "why people who are always early are more annoying than people who are always late." (I was late to the class, so I picked that topic because it seemed like it would be funny. It wasn't.) At the end of the night, I have to jump in the middle of the circle of strangers and lead them in singing "Sweet Caroline."

And yet the most embarrassing thing about all of this turns out to be that *I loved it*. It felt something like awkwardness exposure therapy, where the point was to confront the *oh god oh god what do I say what do I do* feeling and figure out how to withstand it. I'm reminded once more of Erving Goffman's theory that social life is a performance. He thought that all of us largely stick to preestablished scripts, and largely we do, of course. But not here. With every silly improv exercise, I lightened up a little, even when things take a wrong turn. I lost my train of thought while giving a speech and had to stand in front of a disinterested audience for several moments of silence. A creep tried to get me to disrobe in front of the class. And still I was . . . fine?

It reminds me a little of the message at the heart of the 2015 book *Nonsense*, in which science journalist Jamie Holmes synthesizes the scientific literature on ambiguity intolerance. In it he argues that instead of organizing our lives so that we quash every instance of uncertainty, we should try to become more comfortable with the unknown. A good life "isn't so much about success or failure," he writes, "but whether we stay in learning mode, continue to seek out ambiguity, and view uncertainty as the doorway to invention." One way to look at awkwardness is that it's the uncomfortable feeling of social uncertainty, when you don't know whom to talk to at a party or you can't think of a single witty thing to say on a first date. But what if—this is corny, and I'm sorry about that, but I mean it—what if you could reconceptualize social uncertainty so that it started to feel more like "the doorway to invention"? At one point during the class, the instructor tells us, "Improv throws you in without a plan, and you figure out how to figure it out." If I could learn to roll with uncertainty in a classroom full of strangers, I hoped that would help me think better on my feet in my regular life too. Maybe there are times to throw out Goffman's social scripts, and maybe improv could help me figure out what to say or do instead.

Years ago I was on an overnight backpacking trip on the Olympic Peninsula with my friends Christie and Sara. The morning we left, we were struggling to make it through the steep hike out of the valley where we'd camped, and as we walked, Christie, instead of complaining, told me how she coaches herself through anything scary or uncomfortable. "I just tell myself that eventually I'll be back on my couch, watching TV," she said. In class, as the man I'm supposed to be mirroring contorts his face into monstrous expressions, I remind myself of Christie's advice, and instead of running out the door, I play along and make weird faces right back. At the end of the evening, a woman and I are paired together and tasked with creating a scene in which one of us got a part in the high school play and the other didn't. It feels like we're kids playing pretend, and I'm so surprised by how much fun I'm having.

A few days later, I am indeed back on my couch, watching TV.

The class was supposed to be only a funny little side note, something that, frankly, I only did as a stunt, all for the sake of adding a little *color* to this chapter you're reading. I'd write a few paragraphs making fun of it and then return to my regular life. The problem with this plan turns out to be that I didn't predict how much I would genuinely enjoy the experience. I pull my MacBook onto my lap and type "beginner improv nyc" into the Chrome search bar, quickly finding a class at a comedy school called the People's Improv Theater (PIT); this one meets once a week for four weeks and is $185. Before I can fully think it through, I fetch my credit card and in a few minutes receive a confirmation e-mail. It congratulates me because I had the courage, it says, to #followthefear.

I close out of Gmail and tell no one what I've just done.

IN EARLY 2017, THE SECOND CITY THEATER ANNOUNCED AN unusual partnership: It would be joining forces with the Center for Decision Research, a psychology lab focused on the study of decision making and judgment at the University of Chicago Booth School of Business. Second City would function as a "pop-up research lab," providing psychology researchers with a way to get out of the lab and into the real world, studying the ways improv comedy changes people—and, potentially, gathering the necessary evidence to challenge those who oversell its benefits.

"I don't think even five years ago that this conversation would've gone anywhere," said Kelly Leonard, executive vice president of Second City, on a January 2017 episode of the Second City podcast, recorded shortly after the announcement of the partnership with the University of Chicago. He noted that although improv is an art form that began in the 1950s, it's become much more popular in recent years. "I do apologize to the rest of America," he added, "because there's a lot of bad improv going on."

Among the key figures in this partnership is Nicholas Epley, the University of Chicago professor whose work on perspective taking I mentioned in chapters 3 and 4. "The critical overlap" between improv and psychological science, Epley told Leonard on the podcast, is that "what you're doing all the time is experimental manipulation," and that's essentially what improv is all about. With improv the participants are saying, "Let's try it this way. Let's try it that way," Epley continued. "And in an experiment, all we do is assign people to do it one way and then another or one way *or* another. So improv inherently has scientific methodology."

As I'm writing this, it's much too early to point to any conclusions from this pairing, but Epley and Leonard mused about the possibilities. After apologizing for the proliferation of bad improv, Leonard said, "I think the reason people do it is because it does feel good. And I think, in fact, one of the ways it feels good is because it is so others focused. A huge requirement of improvisers, and certainly a hallmark of experienced improvisers, is their ability to adopt the viewpoint of the person across from them."

Already people seem to be picking up on the notion that improv may have psychological benefits. On the first day of my class at the PIT, our instructor—whose name was Megan Baker and whom we all instantly adored—asked all eighteen of us to go around the room and say our names, along with what made us register for the class. Because this was improv, there was a goofy game attached to it as well: We had to pick an adjective that started with the same letter as our first name and do some kind of movement along with it. "I'm here because I can be pretty shy and introverted," said Eddie, a young man standing to my right, echoing the sentiments of about half the class. For his adjective Eddie picked "enthusiastic"; for his movement he clapped his hands. Throughout the night, anytime anyone said Eddie's name, the rest of us burst into wild applause, causing him to laugh, and blush a little.

In life it can be terrifyingly awkward when we don't know what to say or what to do, or when we *thought* someone wanted one thing from us when really they wanted something else. The bulk of Epley's work is centered on the ways that we read and misread people, and in their conversation Leonard pointed out that these kinds of misconceptions—when viewed with just the right attitude, in just the right light—are inherently kind of hilarious. "When you think about comedy—it's an expectation that's been subverted," Leonard said. "That's all jokes, but that's also any sort of comedic setup. You think it's going to go one way, but it goes another way. And usually the other way reveals some level of truth that you maybe hadn't thought about."

In 2013 University of Pennsylvania psychologist Gordon Bermant published a paper titled "Working With(out) a Net: Improvisational Theater and Enhanced Well-being" in the academic journal *Frontiers in Psychology*. In it he makes the case that improv is similar to several aspects of applied psychology, including psychotherapy. Improv's "yes, *and*" edict, for example, is comparable to the "unconditional positive regard" (UPR) relationship between client and therapist.

"It can be frightening to anticipate going on stage to make it up as you go along. This is the felt sense working without a net," he writes. "But there is a source of support in improv that can alleviate the fear of failure. It is the realization that my only obligation on stage is to my scene partner, whose only obligation is to me. In the terms already introduced, there is reciprocity of UPR and *Yes &* . . . in every exchange. If all play authentically to each other, fear of failure loses its sting."

TWO YOUNG WOMEN EXIT AN OFFICE BUILDING AND WALK onto the public sidewalk, one after the other. The first motions to the second to stand under a tree, near the street corner, and she does as suggested. Once she's in position, the second woman looks back to the first woman and points downward, as if to say, *Here?* The first nods in reply. And so the second, hands stuffed into her winter jacket, does what she came out there to do. She sings.

"Mary had a little lamb, little lamb, little lamb, Mary had a little lamb whose fleece was white as snow," she sings loudly as cars pass in the background. "Everywhere that Mary went, Mary went, Mary went, everywhere that Mary went the sheep was sure to go."

She takes a deep breath and begins the song over again. "Mary had a little lamb, little lamb, little lamb, Mary had a little lamb, whose fleece was white as snow," she continues, and as she does, a man in an overcoat carrying a to-go cup of coffee passes her. Still she keeps singing. "And everywhere that Mary went, Mary went, Mary went, everywhere that Mary went the sheep was sure to go."

During the third repetition of the song, a bicyclist rides close by the singer. Her voice shakes for a moment, but she doesn't stop. "Everywhere that Mary went, her sheep were sure to go," she sings, finally finished, as the first woman applauds.

The "Mary Had a Little Lamb" stunt seems like something that wouldn't be out of place on the hidden-camera show *Impractical Jokers*, in which a quartet of comedians dream up the silliest, most embarrassing things they could do in public and then do them. But this is an example of a "social mishap exposure," a real, clinical version of what I stumbled into with improv: exposure therapy for awkward moments. More specifically, this is intended for people with social anxiety, a condition that has been defined rather poetically as a "disorder of lost opportunities." Most people hate awkwardness. But people with social anxiety are so afraid of it that it actively makes their lives worse, as it causes them to avoid social situations for fear of embarrassing themselves. It's an extreme and often crippling version of what most of us experience, which suggests that what is helpful for them to overcome their severe fear could be helpful for the rest of us to keep in mind too.

People with social-anxiety disorder have extreme and often irrational fears about interacting with their fellow humans, Stefan Hofmann, director of the social anxiety program at Boston University's Center for Anxiety and Related Disorders, told me for a piece published on *Science of Us*. "They believe that there are these social standards that everybody's following, and social rules," he said. "And so they sort of live in this very tiny confine of their belief that overstepping these kinds of invisible social boundaries would lead to disastrous, long-lasting social consequences."

Hofmann takes his patients' concerns seriously, thinking deeply about the way they are imagining looking unintelligent or ridiculous in front of others. He listens to those fears. And then he makes his patients run headlong into them.

Hofmann and his fellow clinicians take their patients through a kind of exposure therapy, part of an overall twelve- to sixteen-session cognitive-behavioral therapy (CBT) approach to treating social anxiety. Think of the most embarrassing, most excruciatingly awkward thing you can imagine happening while you're out in public. Now imagine actually having to do that thing.

This is much like the approach for treating obsessive-compulsive disorder. As part of CBT, psychiatrists work with their patient on whatever obsession or compulsion is giving them trouble—perhaps it's that they can't leave the house without turning around and checking, again and again, whether they really unplugged their curling iron. Or maybe they can't stop focusing on their smartphone, checking again and again for text or social media messages. The CBT approach is this: Instead of going back to check on the curling iron situation—or instead of ignoring your partner and checking your Twitter mentions for the fourteenth time that evening—what if you just . . . didn't? What if you didn't check your phone for one hour? One night? One weekend? How long can you stand it?

Social mishap exposures work just like any kind of exposure therapy you've heard of before. "You present the stimulus or situation that people are afraid of, either repeatedly or for a prolonged period of time," Hofmann explained. "And the person, as a result— or the animal, or any organism—as you repeatedly present the feared stimulus over and over again, or for a prolonged period of time, the fear response eventually decreases." If, through repeated exposures, arachnophobes can get to the point where they can not only be in the same room as a tarantula but pick one up and hold it with their bare hands—well, he reasons, why shouldn't the same idea work for social phobia?

The exposures take all forms, as they are tailored around each individual's deepest social fears, but everyone starts with the same basic task: public speaking. Despite everything else there is to fear in the world, especially in the election year that was 2016, 25 percent of those surveyed in the 2016 version of Chapman University's annual survey of American fears still named "public speaking" among their top fears, reporting that they were either afraid or very afraid of public speaking. At the social-anxiety clinic, most of the patients work together in groups, providing a natural audience for one another. Each patient's speech is structured so that it addresses the specific things that person fears most. Are they afraid of looking dumb? Okay, then they have to talk about a subject they know very little about, with minimal time to prepare: a subject vast and unknowable, like black holes, or dating. Are they afraid of tripping over their own words or losing their train of thought? Great—that means they have to intentionally stutter or take a long pause right in the middle of their speech.

It gets more outrageous from there, because soon afterward, they enter the real world. Each patient works with a therapist to, again, specifically tailor the exercise to address that person's deepest social fears, things like looking silly, being the center of attention, causing a scene. The therapy isn't based on *Impractical Jokers*, but honestly, it's close enough. Hofmann told me that years ago he saw a similar series that got him thinking. It consisted of "people doing really awkward things in front of other people and observing how other people respond to that," he told me. "And I thought, *Oh, this is brilliant. I wonder if I can get my social-anxiety patients to do that. If they can do that, they can do anything.*"

Here's a list of some actual exposure scenarios patients at Hofmann's clinic have used:

- Going to a bookstore and saying to an employee, "Excuse me, I was looking for books about farting."
- Interrupting a group at a restaurant and asking them to serve as an audience for you so you can practice a maid-of-honor or best-man speech.
- Standing directly in front of Fenway Park (remember, this clinic is in Boston) and asking ten people whether they know where Fenway Park is.
- Calling a nearby five-star hotel to negotiate a vacation package, complete with tickets to a ball game, a horse-drawn carriage tour of the city, and rose petals strewn on the bed, then rejecting the offer—and making no apologies for doing so—because you've "changed your mind."
- Going to a crowded restaurant and sitting at the bar, then asking the person next to you if they've seen the movie *When Harry Met Sally* and if they know who the actors were.
- This one, sadly, is no longer relevant, but it is still hilarious: renting a DVD from Blockbuster, walking out, and then immediately walking back in and telling the same employee you

rented from, "I would like to return this because I just realized I don't have a DVD player."
- Asking a pharmacist for some condoms, then saying, "Is this the smallest size you have?"

The point of Hofmann's social-mishap exposures is not to terrify patients. The point is to get them to think carefully about what exactly it is they're so afraid of, and whether their fears are overblown. It's important, he tells me, to tailor each exposure so that it's not merely a game; it must address each person's particular anxiety in a way that conforms to cognitive-behavioral therapy. Before the exposure, he'll ask the patient to predict how others will respond, and afterward he asks them to recall how people actually did respond. "You target what they expect would happen—'If I do that, people would scream at me, or they would throw me out of the bookstore,'" he said. "And, by the way, in most of the cases, nothing bad happens. But even if an awkward situation happens, and it occasionally does, then it's even better. . . . Because then, what happens next?

"We create situations that don't lead to actual disastrous consequences—you won't be thrown into jail or get fired or get divorced," he continued. "We only pick situations that are still acceptable within the larger social norms but are awkward. And even if a person screams at you—well, so what? A person screamed at you, and you still survived." He claims a success rate of 70 to 80 percent at his clinic, meaning that after the twelve- or sixteen-week program, the patient no longer meets the diagnostic criteria for social-anxiety disorder. "Initially, we were pretty hesitant, because we thought, *Well, we might traumatize people*—or they might not even do it at all," he said. "But in fact once you do the first few exercises with them, they absolutely embrace and love it."

In a 2013 paper published in the journal *Cognitive and Behavioral Practices*, Hofmann and three Boston University coauthors present a relevant case study about a forty-one-year-old social phobic named Mary (not her real name). As I read about some of the things Mary had to do—including the maid-of-honor-speech scenario listed above—I couldn't help it: I laughed. And then I felt awful about laughing. I told Hofmann that, and he said that this is at least partially the point: to help people stop taking themselves quite so seriously. "We want them to develop a healthy sense of making fun, of keeping humor in your life and just being able to laugh about that," he said. "Because it happens to absolutely everybody."

Hofmann's program is a strictly designed cognitive-behavioral approach to helping people with social anxiety, which is a recognized mental disorder. For people with severe social anxiety, treatment by a mental health professional is key. Even so, those of us with a more typical fear of social situations could take a page out of Hofmann's playbook and *lighten up*. For more everyday cases of social awkwardness, you could design your own take on Hofmann's social-mishap exposures. What's the worst social situation you could possibly imagine? Okay. Now go try that.

Before I tried improv, the worst thing I could imagine was trying improv. And so, in the spirit of Hofmann's advice, I tried improv.

IT'S ASTONISHING WHAT A PERSON CAN GET USED TO. AT home after my third class at the PIT, I update Andrew on the class's progress. "We did three-line scenes this time," I brag. Someone calls out a theme—*School!* or maybe *Rocket ships!*—and in three lines we build a small world. The rules are that by the third sentence, we need to have established our relationship to one another and our location; this can be complicated to do so quickly, which often means we use a lot of lines like "Oh, hello, fellow rocket ship repairman" or "Hey, brother, what a nice day it is to be fishing on this lake." I expect Andrew to be impressed. Instead he's amused.

"I think you've developed an unusually high tolerance for awkwardness," he says. "You do realize you're talking about *amateur improv?* I don't think there's anything more awkward than amateur improv."

I consider this. The first two classes twisted my stomach in knots with nerves, and afterward I went home unable to forget some dumb thing I'd said or done in class. At the end of the second class, for instance, the instructor, Megan, had us gather around in a tight circle and told everyone they would have to jump in the middle and share an embarrassing story, after which the rest of the class would cheer and applaud. Most of these stories, as I should've predicted, began, "Once, in high school, I was so drunk . . ."

I didn't drink in high school. I didn't drink until just before my twenty-first birthday, because teenage me was a straitlaced rules follower, a personality trait adult me is sometimes embarrassed by. As one after another of my classmates told stories about teenage drunken antics, I thought it would be funny if *my* embarrassing story was about *not* drinking. Before thinking it through, I jumped in the circle and said, "I didn't drink until I was twenty-two!" It didn't really make sense, and it also wasn't even true, but everyone cheered and applauded wildly anyway, just as they had for everyone else. By this point, I'd already read the spotlight effect study multiple times, so I told myself that no one noticed, and if they did, no one cared. But that didn't stop the memory from bouncing around in my mind for days.

It's not that the activities we do in the third class have gotten any less awkward than that. We mime making a sandwich, we stand in front of the class and give one another (purposefully) bad advice, and it isn't as if the three-line scenes are brilliant either. At one point, Enthusiastic Eddie and I get the prompt "Thanksgiving," and so I open with "Hey, roomie, you should come to Thanksgiving with me at my parents' house." He takes a moment to think and comes up with "Yes, and . . . I'll bring a gift." I pause. "Yes, and . . . ," I say, stalling. "Yes, and they love wine." And yet somehow it *feels* less awkward, no doubt because I've absorbed a set of guidelines to withstand the discomfort, some of which are worth keeping in mind outside of improv too.

As I said earlier in this chapter, the rule of "yes, and" is well known even by those who've never taken an improv course. In the context of improv, it means that you agree to the concept your partner has introduced, and then you add to the scene by giving them something new to work with. In my (admittedly pathetic) scene with Eddie, my "yes, and" was accepting the fact that he would be bringing a gift to this imaginary Thanksgiving feast and adding the detail that it was a bottle of wine.

In everyday life, I think about this a little more metaphorically. The "yes" part is something like that nouveau cliché of "being present," in that you're accepting the reality of where you are. That can even mean accepting ambiguity for what it is. Just because something is unclear now doesn't necessarily mean it's going to turn out to be negative.

As for the "and," I've started to think that this could mean adding my own sincerity to the situation. In certain contexts, awkwardness can make me seem aloof or uncaring. I don't know what to say, so I don't say anything. For me, the meaning of that one little word—"and"—reminds me that I can add to a conversation by saying what I mean, even if I say it badly. In a way, it's a version of Alison Green's go-to advice: to meet awkward situations with straightforwardness.

Also: Listen! Spend more time listening to the person in front of you than you do frantically trying to think of what you're going to say next. In the context of improv, if you're not paying attention to the fact that your partner has suggested that the two of you are on a school bus, because you came up with a great joke that makes sense only if you're at a supermarket, so you spend the rest of the scene trying to drive the imaginary bus to a supermarket, this will be a boring, confusing scene for your audience.

In the context of real life, it's rude, first of all, but it's also making small talk harder than it has to be. People get so freaked out by having to make small talk, but it's so much easier if you just *listen*. It might help you find common ground that you can build upon, or it could help you pick up something interesting the other person said that you can ask about. Small talk can be so fascinating, if you learn how to do it right. In my early twenties, I went out on a Friday night with a bunch of the same people I went out with most Friday nights, but this time one of the guys had brought along his cousin. Most of the group wasn't willing to entertain her with small talk, but I was trapped next to her in a booth, so I gave it a go. She turned out to have the most unusual job I'd ever heard of: She traveled the world finding rare and unique varieties of flowers and then brought those flowers back to her lab to study. Who knew that was a job? I didn't.

And one more rule that I've stolen for myself: There are no mistakes; there are only opportunities. Tina Fey nods to this one briefly in *Bossypants*, in which she points out that "many of the world's greatest discoveries have been by accident. I mean, look at the Reese's Peanut Butter Cup, or Botox." Fey doesn't get much more into it than that, but this might be the idea that has meant the most to me after leaving this little class. Outside improv, it could mean accepting, and even expecting, imperfection and being happy to adapt.

As our last class ended, most of us hung around outside the building. I think if someone had suggested getting a drink all of us would've gone for it, but everyone was too shy, so after a few minutes of awkwardly standing around, we all headed on our way. I walked north on Sixth Avenue with two women from the class I'd grown to like a lot, Nijet and Bengs. They were both there for the same reason I was, not to become performers but to loosen up a little bit in everyday life. I think we were all also there to make friends.

Nijet asked us both if improv had "worked"—if we'd seen a difference in our lives outside the classroom. Bengs thought it had; she felt a little quicker on her feet at work. I agreed and added that the biggest surprise to me had been the reminder that trying to be funny rarely works. (Truthfully, I think the three of us were consciously yes-anding one another in the conversation, agreeing and adding a little bit more.) "How about you?" I asked Nijet. She smiled. "Yesterday at work, two of my coworkers were dancing and acting all crazy," she said. "Normally, I would've just ignored them. But I started dancing too." Little by little, she's started to feel a little less afraid of the scenes that come unscripted. And, I think, so have I.

———

A WOMAN ABOUT MY AGE WALKS INTO THE RESTAURANT alone and approaches the bar. Is she Jessica? She could be Jessica. She's looking around like she's meeting someone but doesn't see them. "Jessica?" I ask, giving a little wave from my perch at the end of the bar. She looks at me, frowns, and quickly shakes her head. She is not Jessica.

The summer after I completed the improv class, I was nearing the end of my awkwardness studies when I realized something: Nothing fazed me anymore. I could do things now that once would have mortified me. Hearing the sound of my own voice used to make me cringe, but now, as I mentioned at the end of chapter 2, I could listen back to interviews without flinching. (Well, mostly.)

At work I started meeting ambiguous situations head-on instead of avoiding them. Sometimes I still get cringe attacks, but now I know how to combat them so that they hurt a little less. I *took an improv class*, dammit, and I stuck with it all four weeks, which is more than I can say for about half of my classmates.

What *would* make me feel awkward at this point? And then an idea came to me. Why not try to find out?

Out of curiosity, I assigned myself an experiment: Seven Days of Awkward. The rules were lax, but I decided to blend Stefan Hofmann's guidelines and the improv rules I'd just learned. I would dream up social situations to put myself in over the next week, and whatever came to mind—no matter how strange—I had to "yes, and" myself, by which I meant that I had to agree to the idea *and* participate fully in it. No reluctance and no half-assing it.

And so here I am, at a wine bar in SoHo, waiting for Jessica. In January 2016, I had signed up for the confusingly named Hey! VINA, an app that is best described as being "like Tinder, but for friendship." It's for women's friendship, more specifically, and it really does work exactly like a dating app. You swipe left to reject someone or right to indicate that you're into them. When I first signed up for the app, I had fun swiping through the ladies but balked whenever someone suggested meeting up in real life. Now, because of my self-assigned awkward week, I was having the opposite problem.

"I'm free tonight! After work? Around 6:15?" I wrote to a woman named Daniella, who was not free that night.

"Any other day work for you?" she replied.

"Oh okay no prob!" I wrote. "I'm actually pretty free this week so whenever!" She never wrote back. This became a pattern.

Jessica, however, was as eager as I was. I got matched with her on a Monday, and by Wednesday we were at the wine bar, where she arrived just a minute or two after I mistook that other woman for my awkward friend date. When Jessica sat down and started looking at the wine list, I offered her a taste of my vermentino. She either didn't hear me or did and decided to ignore me, which is fair enough, because I realized the minute I said it how odd it was. Who *would* take a sip from the wineglass of someone they had known for all of thirty seconds?

"So," she said after placing her order. "This is a little weird, right?"

"It's *so* weird!" I said. "What made you try it?" She was somewhat new to the city, she told me, having moved to town from Pennsylvania not quite a year ago. Usually she made friends at work, but here all of her coworkers were at least a decade older than she was. Plus, she'd met her boyfriend through a dating app. Why not try meeting friends that way too? We had a nice time, chatting about work and our respective hair salons and how shamefully long it had been since either of us had visited our respective hair salons. The bartender came by. "You ladies want another round?"

"Do you want another?" I asked her. I would have gotten one. But she said no, and we left shortly afterward.

Later that night, I tried my next challenge: dining alone. It's something I've done before, but only at the bar, where there's usually at least one other solo diner. It seemed like it would feel sufficiently weird to make a reservation for one and then sit at a table for one in the middle of a busy restaurant, so that's exactly what I did. I chose Union Square Cafe, mostly because I'd recently read and enjoyed *Sweetbitter*, which the author wrote while she was a waitress there.

At my table, before my food comes, I survey the rest of the restaurant. It's a busy night, and every table is full. I am trying to resist the urge to busy myself with my phone, which seems like cheating, and yet it feels almost sociopathic to sit here *without* looking at my phone. I stare out at my fellow diners from my table in the corner. After a few minutes of this, I decide it's fair to make an exception for the phone if I can use it to further Awkward Week. I unearth it from my bag and pull up Facebook Messenger, where I write a note to Stacey. On my list of potentially cringe-worthy things I could do this week is "try to repair a friendship," and Stacey (which is not her real name) was one of my best friends from high school but stopped talking to me shortly after we grad-uated. She deleted me from MySpace back then, but she's recently added me on Facebook, so . . . Let's see how this goes. "It's nice to have reconnected!" I write. "How have you been?"

I'm still mulling over the message when the server, a young guy with floppy brown hair and kind eyes framed by wire-rimmed glasses, arrives with bread and butter, plus a little dish of olives. "So, where are you coming from tonight?" he asks. Something about his tone makes me think he's expecting an interesting an-swer, like I'm visiting from out of town, which would explain why I'm here alone.

"Uh. Just—work," I say. "Long day!" Normally I am better at

conversing with servers than this. But after I sort of admit to *not* being from out of town, I swear I read pity in his eyes, although I understand that the neuroscientist Lisa Feldman Barrett from chapter 3 would tell me I am just guessing at what his facial expression means. He leaves, I hit "send" on the note to Stacey, and soon afterward my appetizer arrives. It turns out dining alone is awkward only until your meal comes, and then it is pretty great. All that food on the table, just for you. I spread a demure amount of butter onto my bread, then realize there is no one at the table I have to share the butter with and glop on some more.

I check my phone again while waiting for the bill and find that Stacey has already written back. "I'm headed into class," she said, "but I'm going to write as soon as I get out!" The last time I saw her, I realize, happened to also be at a restaurant. We went to the same college, but she distanced herself from me just a few weeks into our freshman year. Now, looking back, I get it. Most people want to reinvent themselves after high school, and she probably didn't want me hanging around reminding her of her younger self. It was a big school, an easy place to lose someone if that's what you wanted to do. The fall of our junior year, I saw her at a restaurant near campus, but we pretended not to notice each other. And now here she is again, in my phone.

Over the next couple of days, I see a movie alone on a weekend night. I strike up two conversations with strangers on the subway, both of which go nowhere, which I might've expected. To a guy waiting to board the train with a bike, I say, "Is it ever hard to find room on the train when you have your bike?" He mumbles something inaudible in response, and I wonder now if he thought I was passive-aggressively telling him how annoying it is when people get on the train with their bikes. Maybe I subconsciously was? Either way, in the moment, I don't push it. To a different guy, on a different day, who sits down next to me while trying to juggle a large camera bag, a tripod, and a Nalgene full of what looks like Gatorade, I say, "That's a lot of stuff!" He grunts in reply.

I also make myself do some networking, meeting with an editor for no reason at all except that I like the site she runs and want to hear about it. I try another Hey! VINA meet-up at another wine bar, this time with a woman named Sophie who lives just two blocks away from me. She has just moved from Montana, and her personality could be best described as a smile that has assumed human form.

"I figure every new person you meet," she tells me, "you can learn something from, even if you don't click with them." From Sophie I learn that awkward silences don't have to be so awkward. "Let's see, what else, what else," she says when we hit a conversational dead end, and it works. We move on, finding something else to chat about. Somewhere in the middle of my second glass of wine, I tell her about Awkward Week, and she gets a kick out of it. By the end of the night, we've exchanged numbers, and we hug good-bye. It wasn't awkward at all. None of this, in fact, has been more than moderately awkward. All the things that used to make me cringe have lost much of their potency. I feel invincible.

THE NEXT MORNING I GET A QUICK COFFEE WITH MY FRIEND Meena, who physically recoils when I tell her everything I've been up to all week. Her reaction is a welcome gut check, confirming that Awkward Week *has* been sufficiently awkward; it's me that's not. "I think I've de-awkwarded myself," I say. She doesn't know, until I tell her, that she is part of my experiment too. We're having coffee in the cafeteria at her work, which used to be my work too. I thought it might feel strange to be in the building again, where at any moment I could run into a former coworker, who would be understandably weirded out that I'm in the building. And I do see a few old coworkers, and they are a little weirded out. But still. It's mildly awkward at best.

"I used to be afraid of flying," Meena is saying. "But then one year I had to fly a lot for work, and now"—she shrugs—"it doesn't bother me anymore. Maybe it's like that."

She might be right, I think. But I have one last idea.

Every couple of months, it seems, some journalist decides to write a first-person piece about professional cuddlers, who offer "nonsexual cuddle sessions" that they describe as therapeutic, connecting people to the psychological and physiological benefits of human touch. Typically name-checked in these stories is a site called Cuddlist.com, which connects people with "certified professional cuddlers." Most of these stories also contain several references to how awkward the experience is. Perfect. I fill out a questionnaire and book a session with Emma, for the afternoon after my coffee with Meena.

On the subway ride up, I start writing in my head this section you're reading now. "It was sometime during my hour of spooning with a stranger that I realized: I had lost the ability to feel awkward," it will begin. I'm getting a little nostalgic for the once-familiar feeling. It still shows up, but it's more muted now. This is overall a great improvement, because it means I can hold my own against challenges that once would've flattened me. After a reorganization at work, I realized I wasn't sure anymore who my boss was. This is a ridiculous thing to have to admit, and in the past I would've said nothing, preferring to wait for context clues to figure it out on my own. Instead I simply asked. It was indeed a little awkward, but also, who cares? It was something I needed to do.

And yet the closer I get to my cuddling appointment, the less self-assured I start to feel.

Emma (whose name has been changed) offered a discount if cuddling clients came to her place instead of her going to theirs, and I start cursing my cheapness as I enter her apartment. It's a lovely space, decorated in warm yellow tones, but the fact is that I am in a stranger's apartment, which is making me increasingly uncomfortable. There is fear of awkwardness, and then there is fear of being murdered in an unfamiliar apartment. I ask to use her bathroom, where I stare at myself in the mirror for several long minutes. *You could leave*, a quiet voice in my head says.

But I don't. I place my shoes by the front door and head down the long, narrow hallway to Emma's living room. She gives me her spiel about the importance of consent, which I nod through (this was covered in all the other journalists' write-ups) and then she tells me that she likes to hold cuddling sessions in her room.

You could leave, the voice says again.

Out loud I say, "Sure," and follow Emma into her room, where she invites me to get comfortable on her bed. I lie down on my back, instantly feel self-conscious about having sprawled out on a strange woman's bed, and then tense up my torso so that I'm doing a kind of half sit-up, with my head slightly lifted from the pillow. "How would you like to start?" she asks.

I have no idea how to answer this beyond nervous laughter. So I do that, and then say, "I guess I'll just take the usual! What is a typical session like?"

She frowns. "There is no such thing as a typical session," she says. "Everything is tailored to the client. We could start with lying down next to each other, or we could spoon, or even simply have a long hug, or I could give you a back rub. . . ." She trails off.

"Um," I say. "How about the second one?" She blinks at me. (*You could leave you could leave you could leave.*)

"Well, I don't remember what the second one was," she says, and I although I do, I also don't want to remind her that it was spooning. "Are you always so nervous about touch?" she asks, gesturing to my body and the pseudocrunch into which it has frozen itself. "What about when you go on dates?" I consider waving my left hand, and the engagement ring attached to it, in her face, but I resist.

"I mean, dates have social norms to follow, you know? This doesn't," I say. I try to explain my cover story for being there. The week before, I'd watched the eclipse of August 21, 2017, with some coworkers, and when I went up to the group, one of them greeted me with a side hug over the shoulders. It was so sweet. But it startled me, and I froze. It was only for a split second, after which I recovered enough to return the hug, but I think she noticed, because she quickly removed her arm. I told Emma that I am a little awkward around unexpected physical contact and that I booked this session as a kind of exposure therapy. It's only a partial truth, but it is still a truth. As I chatter through all of this, the voice grows louder (*You can leave!*) and louder (*YOU CAN LEAVE!!!*) and then, in a flash, I decide to listen to it.

"Sorry—sorry, I've got to go. I'll pay you, of course," I say in a rush. I leave the bed, find my purse, and dig the $80 fee out of my wallet, and then practically *sprint* down the hall, where I shove my feet in my flip-flops and then keep running, out the door and down three flights of stairs. I don't stop until I've exited her building and rounded the corner, when I have to pause to remind myself how to get back to the subway.

And then I start laughing, hysterically, loudly, and all alone. I can think of only a handful of times in my life when I've laughed harder than I did that afternoon. The whole hourlong subway ride home, brief bursts of laughter keep escaping my mouth as if it's some kind of involuntary physiological response, like the hiccups. It's relief, obviously, because I am so, so glad to have escaped such intense awkwardness, but it's also relief over the fact that my awkwardness radar is still functioning. It's not that I've eradicated the feeling. It's still there, though it's lost its power over me in some of the more mundane situations that used to summon it. Maybe I really have reconceptualized awkwardness for myself.

In particular, ambiguity isn't necessarily such a bad thing. The early stages of a relationship are stressful because everything is uncertain, but isn't that also what makes it so thrilling? Texting with someone new is such a thrill precisely *because* you don't know what this person is going to say, or where the two of you are going, or whether you're headed there together. My little weeklong experiment reminded me that so many of the situations we call *awkward* are often also filled with opportunity. Take the weirdness of the Tinder-for-friends app: Maybe we'd meet up and suffer through awkward silences because we had nothing to say to each other. Or maybe we'd click and disprove the idea, put forth in countless trend stories, that it's impossible to make new friends as an adult. You could think of it like the anxiety-reappraisal research from chapter 3, which suggests that you'll be better off if you learn to reframe your nerves as excitement. In the same way, social uncertainty can be understood as nerve-racking, but it can be so exciting too. Anything could happen, which means that *anything* could happen.

On the train home, my phone buzzes, and I see that I've gotten two texts. One is from Emma, recommending that I try a male cuddler instead. The other, sent just two minutes earlier, is from Sophie. Fun to meet up yesterday! she wrote. Good luck with your awkward project.

CHAPTER 11

The Awkward Age, Part 2

John Dorcic is backstage, one hand holding a yellow can of Montauk Brewing Company ale, the other parting the velvet curtains so he can see through to the stage. "Oh, man," he says, shaking his head and laughing softly. He turns to me and the woman I'm standing next to. "You guys have to come see this."

It's the evening after my audition for *Mortified*, the show mentioned at the start of this book in which brave souls take the stage to share the weird things they created when they were teenagers with "three hundred of their closest strangers," as Dorcic, who hosts the show in Brooklyn each month, likes to put it. Tonight is a performance night, and a woman named Abby is currently onstage; I've been listening to her piece with Dorcic and another performer, a woman in her midthirties named Jamie. It's hard to know what's happening without seeing it, but from what I can tell, there's something on the projection screen behind Abby, something that has caused the audience to burst into the biggest laughs

I've heard so far tonight. At Dorcic's invitation, Jamie steps forward and silently moves the curtains aside so she can see.

Her eyes widen, and she turns back to me. "Oh my god," she whispers. "I did that!"

When Jamie arrived in the green room earlier that night, the producers greeted her with hugs and warm hellos to welcome her back. It's her third time performing at *Mortified*, and tonight she took the stage first, reading the fan fiction her seventeen-year-old self wrote about Jamie Kennedy, an actor who can generously be described as medium famous for a few years in the 1990s and early 2000s. Before the show, I try to place him.

"Wasn't he in *Can't Hardly Wait*?" I ask her.

Jamie sighs a little. "No, that was Seth Green," she says, and I get the feeling she's been correcting people on this point for twenty years.

The piece she reads is a short story she wrote in high school, starring herself and Kennedy, who meet and fall in love. A central point of tension is the two of them trying to figure out what will happen when they get married and how to deal with the problem of their names: After she takes his last name, they'll *both* be Jamie Kennedy.

"I know! You'll be boy Jamie, and I'll be girl Jamie," a grown-up girl Jamie read onstage earlier that night. I can't relate to the specifics—clearly, as I'm not even entirely sure who Jamie Kennedy is. But I know that feeling of harboring deep affection for someone no one else seems to *get* and, underneath that, feeling ashamed and isolated—and underneath *that*, also feeling a little smug about how unique it makes you. I only met Jamie an hour ago, and I have to keep reminding myself that I don't actually know her very well. But I related so closely to this piece of her teenage self she just shared that it *feels* like I know her, even just a little bit.

Backstage, she moves aside so I can look through the curtains. On the projection screen behind Abby there are two hand-drawn figures on a sheet of notebook paper. One is her body prepuberty, a straight-up-and-down stick figure. The other is her body post-puberty, with bulges and lumps, along with little arrows labeling the things that especially displeased teenage Abby about her new body. My mind flashes back to my fourteen-year-old self scrawling two self-portraits in my own journal, one of the way I saw myself at the time and the other of how I would look after I lost weight. It's not exactly the same as Abby's, but it's similar enough to make me cringe in self-recognition at her drawing.

"Oh my god," I say quietly back to Jamie. "*I did that.*"

A few minutes later, Abby finishes her piece and pops back through the curtains, leaving behind her thunderous, appreciative applause from the audience. Her face is flushed, and she wears an un-self-consciously wide grin, which she flashes at those of us clustered by the stage as we each high-five her.

"That was *so* fun," she keeps saying. The next performer takes the stage, and I want to watch, because I know his will be weird even by *Mortified* standards—he'll be playing a narrated, video-taped tour of his extensive clock collection, which he made when he was ten—but instead I follow Abby back to the green room. Jamie trails behind us both.

Abby sits on one of the couches, still beaming and still gripping her journal, a regular notebook her teenage self had covered in stickers. When you're a kid scribbling down your hurt feelings, she says, "you feel so awkward and alone." This reminds me of what was, when I first heard about it, most mystifying to me about *Mortified* and its many participants; revisiting something I wrote in earnest even last *year* is often enough to make me want to hide in shame forever. Last week I was prepping for my *Mortified* audition alone at home, reading my old journals and losing myself in the hallways of Granger Middle School. I felt awkward and alone while writing these words, and reading them again brought the feeling right back. The spell was broken when I heard the lock jiggle and Andrew entered the apartment. I shoved the journals underneath the coffee table in a panicked rush, like he'd caught me looking at porn, though honestly that might've been less embarrassing.

But being up there onstage, Abby continues, and sharing your embarrassment with others gives fresh perspective to those lonely hours of pouring your heart out onto the page. "All these people are on your side," she says. It puts the words from your past into new context: your present. You felt alone then, but if that was true, then how do we explain the warmth and recognition coming from the crowd tonight? It speaks to the value of revisiting your past self. You couldn't see then what you can see now. Looking back, it's easier to take a third-person perspective of yourself, with an assist from the natural distance of time. You could think of it as a way of dissolving the irreconcilable gap entirely.

Given the vantage point of the future, it becomes easier to see your past self both more clearly and in proper context. "Sharing the shame," as *Mortified* advertisements phrase it, reminds you that you weren't really alone then, and you aren't alone now either. In the green room, Jamie and I tell Abby that we both did the post-puberty drawings of our bodies too, or at least something very similar. Abby looks amazed.

"Really?" she asks. Yeah, really, we tell her. She smiles. "This is why I love *Mortified*."

IN 2001 A TWENTYSOMETHING DAVE NADELBERG WAS IN his childhood bedroom, taking it in almost the way you might look at a former partner. It was familiar and strange and comforting and unsettling all at the same time. He was home to visit his mother, who was sick, and her illness, combined with his compli-cated feelings about being back in his hometown, had given him a kind of weary nostalgia. Also, he'd kept in touch with almost no one who still lived there, so he was a little bored too. He started exploring his old bedroom, opening drawers and peering into closets with the distanced curiosity of an archaeologist.

Eventually he came across a box of his teenage writings, in-cluding a love letter he'd written when he was about sixteen. "I had forgotten that the letter existed," he told me, "but as soon as I found it, it was like a flood of memories rushed back into my brain." The letter was written to a girl named Leslie whom he'd never actually met. "First off," he writes, "let me introduce myself . . . my name is Dave. (Yep, that way cool guy who gave you this letter!)"

The letter was so personal, so idiosyncratic, and yet, Nadel-berg believed, not at all unique. Surely other people had hung onto similar ghosts of their past awkward selves. Skip ahead about a decade and a half, and this instinct appears to have been right. The stage show exists today in twenty-one cities both nationwide and across the world, with international chapters in places like London, Paris, and Oslo. You can find the 2013 documentary *Mortified Nation* on Netflix, and in 2015 the Public Radio Exchange launched *The Mortified Podcast*. Teenage awkwardness assumes many forms.

And yet for a long time while I was researching awkwardness, I avoided *Mortified*. It sounded so mean-spirited, especially when I heard it was billed as a comedy show. Teenagers are so afraid of being laughed at, a fear that never completely goes away but is at its most extreme in adolescence. I hated the idea of an event designed around laughing at the earnestness scrawled in teenage journals, no doubt because when I was in middle and high school, my journals were my lifeline. All day at school, I was a quiet, well-behaved, good Christian A student, but in those pages I could silently scream the things I would never say out loud. The thought of reading those achingly sincere words out loud made me feel sick, even if twenty years separated me and the girl who wrote them. It sounded so cruel, like it would be fueled by that same contempt cringe I sensed in the audience when I saw *Tinder Live*.

In a funny coincidence, *Tinder Live* and *Mortified* even take place at the same venue, something that came to highlight their differences. The former taps into the discomfort of cringing in order to isolate the person causing the awkwardness. The latter, I soon learned, uses that same feeling, but in a very different way. Cringing at *Mortified* is so steeped in compassion that it ends up uniting the audience and the performer *and* the performer's awkward teenage self. "This is the only comedy show where the audience *starts* on your side," Dorcic likes to tell newbies. A stand-up comic, for example, has to begin a set by winning the audience over, but that's not necessary at *Mortified*. The crowd is right there with every performer, from the moment he or she steps onstage.

I caught my first *Mortified* show in the late summer of 2016 and attended shows obsessively after that. After every show, I left feeling a little smaller, but the good kind of small, the kind that felt like self-indifference: *You're not that big a deal, and isn't that great?* Each one reminded me that my problems weren't all that unique, and my weirdness wasn't all that weird.

I was taken aback by how warmhearted it is, but I was equally surprised at how *funny* it is. At one show, a woman did a little show-and-tell about her "Lovin' Leo" GeoCities page, one of the first fan sites for Leonardo DiCaprio, which she built and maintained as a lovestruck middle schooler in 1997. At another, a guy played guitar and sang the excessively dirty songs he wrote while he was a horny teenage boy sent away to a strict sleepaway religious camp. There's a show I attend on the Thursday of that chaotic, confusing week after the 2016 election, and the laughs are especially huge that night, both because we need it and because of the performers. One of them is a guy who kept a detailed journal throughout high school, and at one point the projector displays a two-column list he kept at the back of the notebook. One column is labeled "Girls I've Kissed," and underneath there are about a half dozen or so names. The other is labeled "Girls I've Had Sex With." There are zero names on this list.

"The specific is universal," creative-writing teachers like to tell their students, and I've never felt the truth of that statement to the degree that I do at *Mortified*. In the "Lovin' Leo" woman I see my absurdly intense love of all things Hanson at that age. In the religious-camp guy, I see my own struggles to reconcile my faith with my longing to just be a regular teenager. And even though I never kept a list of people I'd hooked up with, I see in the list maker my own compulsion to record everything that felt important. It turns out we were all deeply strange kids, and not only that, "we were all [the] *same* strange kid," Nadelberg has written of *Mortified*. And who are we kidding? That teenage weirdo still exists, somewhere inside all of us.

***

"WHAT DOES THIS CHARACTER WANT? AND DOES SHE GET IT?"

A few weeks after hanging out backstage at *Mortified*, I am FaceTiming with Stephen Chupaska, who is producing the piece I'll be performing in just a few short weeks. He's asked me a version of the question nearly every *Mortified* participant hears at some point in the process, though it's more often phrased like this: "Tell me about the kid who wrote this diary."

It's something Nadelberg has been doing since the earliest days of *Mortified*, to help people get over the extreme weirdness of exposing their teenage hearts in front of total strangers. "I do think of our past selves like—we *are* that kid who wrote that love letter or that diary entry or that song lyric when we were fourteen," he said. "But there's [also] been so much personal growth in that time, both physical and mental."

Mortified producers have found over the years that subtly encouraging that feeling of separation many of us have from our past selves helps people get a clearer look at who they were when they were younger. Chupaska, for instance, is encouraging me to think of this surreal exercise as a writing project and of myself at thirteen as the main character, as we edit one hundred pages of junior high angst into a linear narrative. "Rather than saying, 'Tell me about yourself when you were thirteen,' I usually will say something like 'Tell me about the girl who wrote that diary,'" Nadelberg told me. "People are much more comfortable talking about someone who they don't recognize as being themselves."

He pauses. "Even though that person is *one hundred percent* them."

Through his work with *Mortified*, Nadelberg has come to the same conclusion as many of the psychology researchers who study the tenuous relationship between the past and present selves. Past You often feels so distant that it may as well be somebody else entirely. Sometimes it's worth taking advantage of that feeling of separation. In the mid-2000s, psychologists at Cornell recruited a few dozen undergrads and asked them to take a little survey ranking their high school awkwardness, from minus five (extremely awkward) to plus five (not at all awkward, the type to be celebrated on the homecoming court). Those in the bottom third, who ranked themselves at a one or below, were invited to a second round of questioning centered specifically on their social ineptitude as teenagers.

From here the experiment is similar to those discussed in chapter 8 about self-clarity. The former awkward teenagers in this study were to write about "a specific social interaction [during high school] in which they were, or felt as if they were, socially awkward." How to choose? Should it be the time your best friend dashed out of class and onto the quad—where you were milling about during a free period—to wrap a cardigan around your waist, because you'd apparently gotten your period and it had seeped through your school-uniform khakis? It was an incredibly kind thing to do, but good god, if *she* saw the stain from inside a classroom window—who else did?! Or perhaps you should pick the time you and a teammate on the swim team were on your way to a meet, and you were giggling hysterically at the thought of someone falling off the block before a race—and then, not a half hour later, you actually *did* fall off the block before a race?

So many options. Regardless, the Cornell students were told to choose one and write about it. About half of them were asked to take a first-person perspective when writing about their embarrassing memory, and the other half were told to tell their story in the third person, like the disembodied voice of Ron Howard narrating *Arrested Development*. Afterward they filled out a questionnaire rating how awkward they still felt they were now, in comparison with their high school selves; they also rated their own social skills in comparison to those of their peers at Cornell. There was also one extra twist: Seated nearby was an incognito experimenter who, unbeknownst to the formerly awkward Cornell students, was quietly judging the students' social skills. The secret experimenter never initiated conversation but would pleasantly reply when the student did, a decent enough way to measure a person's sociability.

When analyzing their results, the researchers noticed a difference in the survey responses between those two groups. Those who'd been prompted to recall their high school memory from a third-person perspective tended to think of their current selves as less awkward than they had been in high school, compared with those who'd been told to write from the first-person perspective. The outside perspective takers also rated their social skills higher in comparison with those of their Cornell peers—and they *also* passed with flying colors the test they didn't even know they were taking, tending to initiate conversation with the covert experimenter more than the inside perspective takers did.

This self-distancing strategy is helpful for *Mortified* performers, including me. I knew Chupaska's question about the piece's "main character" was just a bit of writing advice to help us shape the story into a tight ten minutes, but I couldn't help seeing it as a metaphor. There are benefits to taking a third-person perspective on yourself, gains that extend beyond disassociating from middle-school awkwardness.

Studies on so-called self-talk, for instance, have found that people who took a distanced perspective when motivating themselves (by saying, "You can do this," or even using their own name, as in, "Melissa can do this") reported less anxiety than people who used the first person ("I can do this"). Those who took that outsider view of themselves also performed better in a subsequent task than those who stayed inside their own point of view.

Other research has shown that taking a third-person perspective on your own life can lead to better decisions. You know how it's always easier to solve a friend's problem than your own? It's the same principle. "As an outsider, it's relatively easy for you to advise them through that problem," Ethan Kross, a University of Michigan psychologist, told the *New York Times* about his and others' work on self-distancing. "One of the key reasons why we're so able to advise others on a problem is because we're not sucked into those problems. We can think more clearly because we have distance from the experience."

It's a handy mental strategy, this notion of creating your own personal irreconcilable gap, and I've used it when running half marathons, to coax myself to pick up the pace even though I'm so tired; I've also used it when making big decisions, like whether or not to leave a job. What advice would I give a friend? It's also an interesting, alternative route toward self-awareness. Your actions are all other people have to go on when they're forming their opinion of you. What is your behavior saying about you?

Still, it doesn't feel entirely accurate to me as Chupaska and I start to edit down my journal entries. I'd love to look at these words I wrote years ago and dismiss them by telling myself, *That's not me anymore*. And that's true; people can and do change, and I'm no exception. But at the same time, some part of my mind quietly counters, *Of* course *it's still you.*

I bring this up to Nadelberg, and he agrees. "People do grow from who they were as a kid. And I think where maybe *Mortified* finds success is in the fact that the reality is this confusing in-between," he tells me. "The reality is you're not that kid you were! But you're still *totally* that kid you were. You're not that weird, insecure girl in the back of math class . . . but yet *you are completely still that person*," a fact, he adds, that is "both comforting and completely depressing."

WHAT'S THE DEAL WITH JAZZ?

Writer Amy Rose Spiegel wondered as much in a *BuzzFeed* article published in February 2013. That was her headline: "What's the Deal with Jazz?" *BuzzFeed* has done some impressive journalism over the years, but this is the kind of post most people still imagine when they think of a typical *BuzzFeed* article. It's cluttered with GIFs and embedded videos and insights such as "Jazz Guys account for, like, 74 percent of all fedora wearers, which basically makes them criminals in the rest of the world's eyes."

Journalists seized on Spiegel's story on Twitter. "Congrats this is fucking idiotic," wrote Nathaniel Friedman, now a writer at *GQ* and elsewhere. "This post is bad and you should feel bad," wrote Jared Keller, now an editor at the military-focused publication *Task & Purpose*.

It was not a great post, but such is often the way of online journalism. The exhausting thing about this line of work is that the Internet—and your boss—just keeps wanting more, more, more, and so you keep pumping out #content, even when you have no good ideas or, maybe worse, when you have a decent idea but not enough time to research it properly. This is especially a problem for young writers, who are just trying to do what their bosses are asking for, only realizing later that their words might come back to haunt them one day.

When Spiegel hit "publish" on the jazz post, she was just twenty-two, barely a month out of college. She later told *Slate*'s Will Oremus that the idea for the post sprang from an idle comment she'd made to her editor about not loving jazz. "My editor was like, 'You should really write about "What's the deal with jazz?"' I was like, 'No, I don't want to do that,'" Spiegel told Oremus. "He sort of pushed me into it, and so finally I wrote the post and didn't think it would be a big deal."

But even the things you're initially proud of can sometimes embarrass you when you read them later. Science writer Bethany Brookshire has said that she often recalls with fondness a seriously bizarre 2011 study in which scientists created tiny pants for their rat study subjects. "Every so often I go back to the study on rats in pants," Brookshire wrote recently on Twitter. "The study remains fabulous. The writing makes me CRINGE." Another science writer—the *New Yorker*'s Maria Konnikova—said in response, "I [feel] that way about most of my old pieces!" Brookshire wrote back, "My GOD I was terrible! I almost want to rewrite it entirely as it should have been done." Novelist Roger Rosenblatt also wrote as much for the *New York Times* in 2016. "We find mistakes. We find things that make us cringe," he wrote. "And the whole process kills whatever momentum we may be feeling."

I can relate. A few years ago, I was commuting home and listening to a favorite podcast, *Call Your Girlfriend*, which is cohosted by a writer I admired, Ann Friedman. I was only half listening, but then Friedman started reading aloud from a blog post she'd seen earlier that week, doing a voice as she read that was clearly meant to highlight the post's inanity. She didn't name the blogger, and she didn't name the publication, but she didn't have to. *I'd* written that post.

If it weren't emphatically agreed upon among journalists that it's unethical to unpublish stories, except in very specific circumstances, I think I would've deleted the post the moment I got home. And so I can't fault Spiegel for responding the way she did to the reaction on Twitter to her post. Five months later she deleted it.

"I was really ashamed at having my name on it," she told Oremus. "I'm sorry I did it. It was the ultimate, like, Amiri Baraka 'Jazz and the White Critic' kind of thing. I was so sorry about having done it, and I didn't want it in the world, and I also didn't feel like I should be taking full responsibility for it because I had been bullied into doing it after saying no. So I deleted it, and I knew that was against BuzzFeed's editorial policy, but I didn't care."

Journalistic ethics are their own animal. But I've been interested to watch in recent years the changing attitude overall toward deleting embarrassing relics from your past online self. Snapchat is the common example here, because its central feature is its ephemeral nature; the snaps and chats disappear. Instagram recently and blatantly copied this Snapchat feature with its introduction of "stories," photos that disappear after twenty-four hours. It seems to be a nod to the way teenagers are using social media. "There are only 25 photos on her page because she deletes most of what she posts," notes a 2016 *Washington Post* article about the social media habits of today's thirteen-year-olds. "The ones that don't get enough likes, don't have good enough lighting or don't show the coolest moments in her life must be deleted."

It's become a cliché among those of us in our late twenties and early thirties to say how thankful we are that social media didn't exist when we were teenagers. There are many things we mean when we say this. We're grateful to have narrowly avoided the intensity of Facebook- or Instagram-fueled cyberbullying, and while it was one thing to worry that everyone was hanging out without you, with social media, *you'd know*. But another thing we mean when we say this is *Thank god my embarrassing teenage self isn't permanently hanging out online.* "Silly music tastes, less-informed political statements, embarrassing photos of the 15-year-old you: digital dirt from long ago would threaten to debase today's impeccably curated identity project," the sociologist Nathan Jurgenson wrote in 2012. *You* know that you've changed since those photos were taken or that post was published or that tweet was tweeted. You can see it now the way others must have seen it then, how ridiculous you were. Why didn't anyone tell you?

Perhaps eventually, and especially as those who are teenagers now enter and graduate from college, the Internet will become a more impermanent place. It's possible to imagine that one day, nothing will exist online that could undermine the version of yourself you've painstakingly curated. People grow; they change their views and cringe at the person they used to be. Consider Glenn Beck in these past few years, for god's sake: He has been publicly acknowledging his role in creating division in the United States. "We have to start believing the best in each other instead of expecting the worst," he told Krista Tippett on a 2017 episode of her public radio show *On Being*. "And I'm guilty—I hate to say that because I can't imagine how many people in your audience just rolled their eyes and went, 'You've got to be—coming from

Glenn Beck?'" Maybe, some have argued, the Internet should acknowledge that people change and let them shake off the remnants of the person they used to be.

But to believe that is to believe in identity stasis, the idea that *now* you've arrived and have become your true self. Past You was embarrassing. Current You has it figured out. But Current You will soon enough become Past You, and the cycle will begin all over again. Writing this book has been an everyday exercise in this, in that sometimes I would read in horror chapters I'd written months earlier. Who *was* that person? If you ever want to do any kind of creative work, you have to learn to appreciate Past You's best efforts. Future You probably will find parts of it cringeworthy, but this seems like her problem.

Besides, every person you meet changes you a little bit. You're a different you depending on whom you're with. "The self is part of social reality," writes Lisa Feldman Barrett in *How Emotions Are Made*. "It's not exactly a fiction, but neither is it objectively real in nature like a neutron. It depends on other people. In scientific terms, your predictions in the moment, and your actions that derive from them, depend to some extent on the way that others treat you." Maybe it's best, then, to accept the fleeting nature of your selves and hold the different versions of you in mind at once.

Even the embarrassing versions. Because of his extraordinary autobiographical memory, Nima Veiseh (whom we met in chapter 8) operates this way naturally. All of his past selves are at his fingertips, so to speak, and he thinks this might also be why he's not easily embarrassed. "Everything I do is a reflection of my entire data set," he tells me. "I couldn't have done any better, given the data set I had."

Past You was doing her best, and it's important to acknowledge that. But at the same time, good for you if she makes you cringe. She should! Anyone who doesn't regularly cringe over their past selves is probably not evolving. "There's so much in my first special that makes me cringe, but I'm not ashamed of it," the comedian Sarah Silverman told *Fast Company* in 2017. "You have to be accountable. And if you don't look back at your old shit and cringe, you're not growing."

In 2016 Amy Rose Spiegel published *Action*, a well-received book of essays about sex. In it she advises her readers not to be ashamed of sexual mishaps like premature ejaculation, farts, queefs, or other risks of having a human body. It's a smart, sharp book, and it's often very funny too, and though it's written about sexual mishaps, it's hard not to read into Spiegel's encouragement to her readers to be patient with themselves and learn from their personal disasters instead of trying to hide from them. "Fucking up," she writes at one point, "is how you go pro."

———

THE LIGHTS ARE BRIGHTER THAN YOU'D THINK, MUCH brighter than they've ever seemed from the audience. But this is fine. This is preferable, actually, because this means I don't even really see the three-hundred-ish people, mostly strangers, crowded before me as I stand onstage at Littlefield. Every seat is filled, and toward the back people have even plopped right down on the floor, as if we were gathered in someone's living room. But I see that only later, during intermission, when I nudge my way through the mass of hipsterish bodies to find Andrew and the rest of my friends. From the stage, all I can see are the lights.

It's my turn onstage at *Mortified*, and moments ago the little purple diary and I passed together through the curtains and toward the microphone. About ten days ago, I sent out a mass e-mail inviting people to the show. I hoped a few would come, maybe a half dozen if I was lucky. But in the days before the performance, I got one terrifying RSVP after another. In the end, more than twenty of my friends and colleagues come out.

Erving Goffman may have believed that all of social life is a performance, but something tells me he would've been weirded out by what I'm about to do. It's his dramaturgical theory made literal, though the metaphors are all mixed up. Normally I enact the part of Present Me as if she were an entirely separate entity from Teenage Me; I take care to play down the aspects of myself that still reflect her eagerness, her naïveté, her neediness. During my audition and subsequent FaceTime rehearsals with Chupaska, I've been encouraged to think of her this way, as an entity separate from myself. But onstage tonight I need to do the opposite, knitting the two of us back together.

Earlier in the evening, before Littlefield's doors opened to the audience, Dorcic gathered all of the performers onstage to stare out at the empty theater so we could feel a little more comfortable with the venue. At this point, I already felt like I'd been there for hours. I *had* been there for hours, or at least I'd been in the neighborhood for that long; I'd been so afraid of being late that I'd accidentally arrived eighty-five minutes early. I bought dinner at a nearby café and slowly ate a vegetarian sandwich, forcing myself to linger at the table until enough time had passed to ensure that I would arrive at the venue a very cool and casual ten minutes late.

Even still, I was the first to arrive. I introduced myself to my fellow performers as they came into the green room, desperate for someone who was as uncomfortable in the spotlight as I am. No luck. Almost all of them were professional storytellers and comedians; the woman who performed directly before me read the poop jokes her seven-year-old self scrawled in her older sister's journal. They were annoyingly clever for an elementary schooler, and also—poop jokes? I'm supposed to follow something as comedically foolproof as poop jokes? There was one other nonprofessional, but he hardly counted, as he was a *Mortified* veteran, having first performed in the show more than ten years ago. I felt alone in my nerves.

About an hour before the audience started to arrive, Dorcic encouraged us to pace around the stage, familiarizing ourselves with what it felt like up there. Something small I noticed when I started regularly attending these shows is that every performer, even the ones who were clearly not professionals, could confidently raise and lower the mic stand. An uncooperative mic stand is a great way to throw someone off when they're in the spotlight, like Stephan Aarstol's malfunctioning slideshow from chapter 6. But unlike those *Shark Tank* producers, who pressed the remote into Aarstol's hand and left him to figure it out, Dorcic made sure every last one of us knew how to operate the microphone situation. As the only true newbie here tonight, I was especially touched by this gesture. I was also so tightly wound with nerves I felt like I was going to explode. One thing or the other led to an ache in my jaw that I knew meant I was about to cry. But I held it back so I could take in Dorcic's pep talk.

"This is the only comedy show where the audience *starts* on your side," he said, and if you feel like you've heard that before, you have, and so had I. He gives a version of the same speech before every show.

"And that means," he continued, "that they will turn on anyone who hates you—including you."

Any show falls apart if an audience senses insincerity, which happens when the performer doesn't fully commit to the role. This is true in our everyday social performances too, Goffman would've argued, and it helps explain a wide range of things that make my skin crawl, as noted in chapter 2. (See: running into a coworker at the grocery store.) Things get awkward when you try to play multiple roles at once, and the same is true here tonight.

Years ago, Dorcic told us, a performer in the show read his piece in an exaggerated tone, doing a vocal caricature of a teenage boy. It was a way of distancing himself from his own words and broadcasting to the audience, *I get it. This is totally stupid. This isn't who I am anymore.* The approach doesn't work for a simple reason: It isn't funny. That night, Dorcic said, "the audience turned on him." The longer he went on that way, the fewer laughs he got. *Mortified* used to be a twice-a-night show, and this was the early one. Later that night, he read the piece without affectation, the way Dorcic encouraged the rest of us to do. He killed.

And yet onstage, under the blinding lights, I don't need this reminder; I quickly return to my teenage self.

"School started today," I begin. "Everybody (well, *almost* everybody) was really nice. But I *HATE* it!" Something about that last line, the fervor in the capitalized *HATE*, is what does it: I feel like I'm channeling the girl who wrote this.

Before tonight, I've been thinking a lot about what Jamie, whom you will remember as the author of the Jamie Kennedy fan fiction mentioned earlier in this chapter, told me when I hung out with her backstage at *Mortified*. By reading publicly the stories her seventeen-year-old self wrote in private, she said she sometimes wondered, *Am I honoring her? Or am I making fun of her?*

It's a question I wrestled with too, but I've come to believe it's the former. In a strange twist from your actual adolescent years, when you're onstage at *Mortified*, you desperately *want* people to laugh at you. That's the whole point. In chapter 1, back when I first encountered this show, I couldn't figure out what *Mortified* performers were seeking from the experience. But I think it's the audience's laughter or, more pointedly, what the laughter symbolizes. If it's funny, then it's relatable, and if it's relatable, then it means your teenage self could've relaxed a little bit. The secrets you kept weren't that shameful after all.

And so this is why I'm tense when I begin my piece. What if no one laughs? I know this isn't a tough crowd, as Dorcic likes to remind performers, but what if all I get are weak, pity laughs? That might be worse than crickets.

The first entry functions as exposition; that's how I wrote it too, back then. In the journal it's five and a half pages of bubbly handwriting, providing an hour-by-hour breakdown of my first day at my new middle school, to which I transferred in the middle of seventh grade. They're necessary details to set the "plot," as it were, in motion, but it's pretty dull too, and it's one of the longer entries in the piece. I fear I'm losing the audience, and it's making me feel protective of thirteen-year-old me, and a little guilty too. She's only here because I dragged her forward twenty years.

I make it through and move on to the second entry. "I just can't *believe* I don't live in Nashville anymore," I say as a mournful teenage me. Without even meaning to, when I speak, my voice is coming out in a slightly higher pitch than usual, and I'm doing the thing where I make everything sound like a question. "People here are okay, but I loved *everyone* there. Everyone *there*?" Slight, strategic pause before what I hope will be a laugh line. "Loved *Hanson!*"

It works! Oh my god, it works. Everyone's cracking up.

Meanwhile, I'm remembering the absurd but very real anguish this caused me back then. I have a fuzzy memory of putting up a picture of Hanson in my locker in those first few days at my new school, only to have another kid make fun of it. Just the teasing is blurry in this memory; I remember the picture vividly. (It was the one on the back of their 1997 album, if you want to know.) I took it so hard when I learned how much my classmates disdained my favorite band; at that point I'd incorporated them so deep within my self-concept that it was like I believed my classmates' rejection of Hanson was a rejection of *me*.

I mean, are you kidding me? All of that is so *funny*. This comedy gold had been hiding in my past, and I didn't know it until this moment onstage, when the line gets a huge laugh. And as they laugh, I feel a little less tense. Dorcic promised that after you get your first laugh, it's smooth sailing from there, and he's right. My time onstage starts to fly by. Soon I'm on the May 11 entry. My favorite part.

"I *actually wrote* some graffiti today," I say as thirteen-year-old me, and it's almost like she's here, confiding her darkest sin to the audience. "I was in the bathroom, and someone had written 'I hate Granger,' and someone else had written 'I do too.' So then *I* wrote . . . '*Ditto*.'" The crowd loses it. I knew this part would be hilarious, and it is.

"I disguised my handwriting," I continue as her. "Even if someone *does* find out I did it, I don't care. I *meant it*."

In the journal I scrawled a replica of this "graffiti," because I was so proud of my rebellion. At this point, the projector behind me is supposed to be displaying the sketch, so I turn to look at it—and am greeted instead by a picture of my younger self. I sent Christina Galante, the show's lead producer, several options last week, and of course she picked the dorkiest one. In it I'm wearing big plastic glasses, and I'm sprawled out on the floor, lying on my side with my left hand on my hip and my head propped up by my right hand. *Oh, hey, Past Me.* I'm surprised to see her, but then again, she's been here all night, speaking through me, and also kind of speaking *to* me. After years of shushing her, it feels like I'm finally listening to what she had to say.

And then, all of a sudden, it's over. In a daze, I exit the stage (my play-off music is "MMMBop," as I could've guessed), accept the proffered high fives, and then lock myself in the tiny bathroom for a few moments to compose myself. Before the show, the producers teased me for being so uptight at my audition. It was only about eight weeks ago, but it feels like ages. That day I wondered of the people who volunteer to perform in this show, *What do they know that the rest of us don't?* I guess I'm one of them now, so let me try to answer that.

We know that the only way to stop cringing over your past awkward self is to share your shame with a compassionate audience. Sometimes I think the stranger the things are that make you cringe, the more likely they are to hit home with a big crowd. We don't all know the specifics, but we all know that feeling. The memories recorded in that little diary of mine look so different now, all shiny and appealing and ready for prime time. I think it was the crowd's laughter that did that, and the only way I know how to describe that laughter is that it felt like light. These goofy stories and overwrought teenage feelings from my past that were hidden away in the shadows are now out in the open, and I get to see them clearly again. There's that cliché people use about embracing their imperfections: *Own it!* It's the kind of thing that gets repeated so often that it hardly seems to mean anything anymore, but it's something I started thinking about shortly after the show. What do we mean when we say that?

Months later I'm talking to Martha Rynberg, W. Kamau Bell's close friend, whom we met in chapter 4. Rynberg writes and performs in a San Francisco show called *Lady Parts*, in which she relives onstage some of the most awkward moments from her past. It's not exactly like *Mortified*, in that she writes herself a script based on her memories (and then plays every part), but it draws on the same cringeworthy feeling.

In a recent one, she told a story about a date with her partner, in which they decided to visit a trampoline park, purely for the sake of doing something whimsical and fun. ("I chronically have trouble with fun," Rynberg tells me.) As they're bouncing around, Rynberg realizes in horror that she's wetting her pants with every jump. "And not just a little," she tells me. "Every time I jumped, there was this golden spurt, over and over and over. And I went to the bathroom several times—I didn't know where the pee was coming from!" Eventually, she says, "I had to give in to it and just have this urine date."

The natural urge in moments like this is to push the awkwardness away from ourselves. *That's not really me; that's not who I am.* It hurts to cut yourself into pieces like that. I'd rather find a way to bring that awkward part back in, and in *Mortified* I've hit on the same insight that Rynberg has in her work: The best way to be comfortable with that part of yourself again is to share the awkwardness with someone else. It's the choice between contemptuous cringing and compassionate cringing, but directed toward yourself. You bring back the pushed-away piece of you.

Most of my friends who saw me perform that night tell me variations on the same thing: *You're so brave.* Some of them tell me they have their own teenage journals lying around, and maybe they'll do the show too. I hope they do. Joan Didion once said that it's worth staying on nodding terms with the people we used to be, and for me, *Mortified* was one way to achieve that. "Instead of feeling, like, shoulders slumped, and like a wilted person, I can be like, 'Everybody look at this! Take a look at how silly this is,'" Rynberg says. "And then I get to own that part again, instead of pushing it away."

Talk about silly: Shortly after the show, I get to experience a small, strange benefit of uniting my past embarrassments with my present self. Two months later, Hanson releases their first new single in years. I would've missed this entirely if it weren't for several friends who were at *Mortified* that night, who each send me the same write-up from NPR's Web site: "Hanson's Got a New Song, and Guess What? It's Fantastic." Guess what? *It's true*. I did not expect to bring *this* piece of my past back to the present.

But, more important, I'm also a little more comfortable now with the other parts of teenage me that are still hanging around. It's not so bad to be enthusiastic about stuff, and if I still come off as a goody-goody at times, well, now I know that the psychological literature would call that trait *conscientiousness*. You might try taking another look at the pieces of your personality you've shoved away somewhere. I bet they're not so bad. I bet they're kind of funny.

Once you can laugh at yourself, you're home free. When I started this project, I was hoping that by the end I would've figured out how to construct a sturdy barrier between me and all the things that make me cringe. But now I'm so grateful for this odd little emotion and the power it has to connect us—me, you, Past Me, Past You—through mutual human ridiculousness. There will always be awkwardness, and the only way to keep it from isolating us is if we start cringing together.

ACKNOWLEDGMENTS

I wrote this in my head long before I finished writing *Cringe-worthy*. There are so many people to thank! To Eric Nelson, thank you for guiding the first steps of this process and believing in the idea from the start. And to Merry Sun, a great big caps-lock THANK YOU for being such a dream of an editor. You could see what I was trying to say even when I did a questionable job of saying it; it felt sort of like the way I will blab a lot of nonsense to the gal who cuts my hair, and she somehow understands what I meant and gives me the exact haircut I was envisioning (only better). To Mackenzie Brady Watson, thank you for helping me shape my vague idea into something booklike. And to Joanna Volpe, thank you for being so dependable—your taste and your experience have been invaluable resources to me throughout this process.

So many sources were so helpful as I reported and wrote this book, but I want to give a special acknowledgement to Sören Krach and Frieder Paulas. Your work inspired me when I first encountered it years ago, and it continues to do so today. (Also, you guys are terrific hosts—thank you for being great tour guides in Berlin and Lübeck!) Likewise, I owe so much to all my pals at *Mortified*: Dave Nadelberg, Christina Galante, John Dorcic, and Stephen Chupaska. Thank you for being so generous with your time!

Thanks to Alice Robb, Chris Bonanos, and Carolyn Murnick for always being around whenever I was in the middle of a book-related meltdown; I hope I was even half as helpful to each of you as you have been to me. And thank you to Linda Dahlstrom, not only for reading an early version of the manuscript, but for teaching me practically everything I know in the first place about health/science writing.

To my family: Mom, Dad, and Tyler. You are just the best. I love you.

And to Andrew: Writing this book not only upended my world for the better part of two years, but yours too. And yet you never complained, and were always supportive. I'm so lucky to have you in my life. ENH.

NOTES

CHAPTER 1: THE AWKWARD AGE, PART 1

9 **de Botton has written:** Alain De Botton, *The Course of Love* (New York: Simon & Schuster, 2016).

10 **his "dramaturgical" theory:** Erving Goffman, *The Presentation of Self in Everyday Life* (New York: Random House, 1959), xi.

11 **and be your true self:** Goffman, *The Presentation of Self in Everyday Life*, 112.

11 **In an episode of his podcast:** Pete Holmes, "You Made It Weird #357: Mike Birbiglia #4," *Nerdist* (audio blog), March 8, 2017, http://nerdist.com/you-made-it-weird-357-mike-birbiglia-4 (accessed September 8, 2017).

12 **heard of the reminiscence bump:** Jonathan Koppel and David C. Rubin, "Recent Advances in Understanding the Reminiscence Bump: The Importance of Cues in Guiding Recall from Autobiographical Memory," *Current Directions in Psychological Science* 25, no. 2 (April 1, 2016), doi:10.1177/0963721416631955.

13 **linked to our self-concept:** Joseph M. Fitzgerald, "The Distribution of Self-Narrative Memories in Younger and Older Adults: Elaborating the Self-Narrative Hypothesis," *Aging, Neuropsychology, and Cognition* 3, no. 3 (1996), doi:http://dx.doi.org/10.1080/13825589608256626.

14 **"trait" and "state":** Alycia Chin et al., "Bored in the USA: Experience

Sampling and Boredom in Everyday Life," *Emotion* 17, no. 2 (2017), doi:10.1037/emo0000232.

14 **The philosopher Adam Kotsko:** Adam Kotsko, *Awkwardness: An Essay* (Winchester, UK: O-Books, 2010), 26.

15 **"There's no such thing":** "Oprah Winfrey, Part 2: A Vision for Success," *What It Takes* (audio blog), September 7, 2015, https://itunes.apple.com/us /podcast/what-it-takes/id1025864075?mt=2 (accessed September 8, 2017).

CHAPTER 2: THE TRIBAL TERROR OF SELF-AWARENESS

21 **In 1969 anthropologist:** William Grimes, "Edmund Carpenter, Restless Scholar, Dies at 88," *New York Times*, July 10, 2011, www.nytimes.com/2011 /07/08/arts/edmund-carpenter-archaelogist-and-anthropologist-dies-at-88 .html; Edmund Carpenter, "The Tribal Terror of Self-Awareness," in *Principles of Visual Anthropology*, 3rd ed. (New York: Mouton de Gruyter), 481–91.

21–22 **"10,000 years of media history" . . . "tribesmen responded alike":** Carpenter, "The Tribal Terror of Self-Awareness," 481–82.

22–23 **"The tape-recorder startled them" . . . "When mirrors become":** Ibid., 483–84.

23 **some anthropologists are skeptical:** Mark Pendergrast, *Mirror Mirror* (New York: Basic Books, 2003), 368.

24 **the "FaceTime Facelift":** Austin Considine, "Video Close-Ups: Not for the Vain," *New York Times*, April 17, 2012, www.nytimes.com/2012/04/19 /fashion/ready-for-my-video-chat-close-up.html.

24 **"What they'll say is":** Austin-Weston, The Center for Cosmetic Surgery, "Facetime Facelift—Dr. Robert Sigal." February 22, 2012, www.youtube .com/watch?v=W0ABfj0ydPA (accessed September 8, 2017).

24 **with one important exception:** Austin-Weston, The Center for Cosmetic Surgery, "What Is the Facetime Facelift?—Dr. Robert Sigal," February 22, 2012, www.youtube.com/watch?v=zSgW3YxERKU (accessed September 8, 2017).

24 **"a mirror on steroids":** Considine, "Video Close-Ups: Not for the Vain."

25 **Rochat calls "the irreconcilable gap":** Philippe Rochat, *Others in Mind: Social Origins of Self-Consciousness* (New York: Cambridge University Press, 2010).

25 **In 1964 Bell Labs:** Jeff Hecht, "Heard, but Not Seen," *New Scientist*, December 17, 2016.

26 **$200 in today's dollars:** Coinnews Media Group, US Inflation Calculator, www.usinflationcalculator.com (accessed September 8, 2017).

26 **"it wasn't entirely clear":** Lisa Guernsey, "Cautionary Tale; The Perpet-

ual Next Big Thing," *New York Times*, April 13, 2000, www.nytimes.com /2000/04/13/technology/cautionary-tale-the-perpetual-next-big-thing.html.

26 **According to a recent Google:** Edward C. Baig, "Knock Knock, Who's There? Google Duo Voice Calling," *USA Today*, August 16, 2016, www .usatoday.com/story/tech/columnist/baig/2016/08/16/knock-knock -whos-there-google-duo-voice-calling/8867305.

26 **publications ranging from:** Michael Hsu, "A Simple Trick for Looking Your Best on Skype, FaceTime or Other Video Chat," *Wall Street Journal*, June 23, 2016, www.wsj.com/articles/a-simple-trick-for-looking-your-best -on-skype-facetime-or-other-video-chat-1466696159; Alexandra Samuel, "How to Look Pretty on Video Chat," *SELF*, May 24, 2013, www.self .com/story/beauty-look-pretty-video-chat.

27 **"if you were at all vain":** David Foster Wallace, *Infinite Jest* (New York: Back Bay Books, 2009), 147.

27 **"They created mayhem"** . . . **"behavior of these women":** Rochat, *Others in Mind*, 26.

29 **Some psychologists who study embarrassment:** At the University of Louisville's Conference on Neglected Emotions, which I attended in April 2017, some of the researchers—including Michelle Mason of the University of Minnesota and Jennifer Cole Wright of the College of Charleston— mused about this.

30 **Ellen DeGeneres used to have:** "Ellen DeGeneres: Here and Now," HBO, June 25, 2003.

31 **social life is a stage:** Erving Goffman, *The Presentation of Self in Everyday Life* (New York: Random House, 1956).

31 **the "information game":** Goffman, *The Presentation of Self in Everyday Life*, 8.

33 **Contemporary social science:** Julianne Holt-Lunstad et al., "Loneliness and Social Isolation as Risk Factors for Mortality: A Meta-analytic Review," *Perspectives on Psychological Science* 10, no. 2 (March 11, 2015), doi:10.1177/1745691614568352.

36 **If you show people:** Theodore H. Mita, Marshall Dermer, and Jeffrey Knight, "Reversed Facial Images and the Mere-Exposure Hypothesis," *Journal of Personality and Social Psychology* 35, no. 8 (August 1977): 597–601, http://psycnet.apa.org/buy/1979-31008-001.

36 **White recently published:** David White, Clare A. M. Sutherland, and Amy L. Burton, "Choosing Face: The Curse of Self in Profile Image Selection," *Cognitive Research: Principles and Implications* 2, no. 23 (April 14, 2017), doi:https://doi.org/10.1186/s41235-017-0058-3.

NOTES

37 **One recent review:** Erika N. Carlson and David A. Kenny, "Meta-accuracy: Do We Know How Others See Us?" in *Handbook of Self-Knowledge*, ed. Simine Vazire and Timothy D. Wilson (New York: Guilford Press, 2012), 242–57.

37 **In one relevant experiment:** D. A. Kenny and B. M. DePaulo, "Do People Know How Others View Them? An Empirical and Theoretical Account," *Psychological Bulletin* 114, no. 1 (July 1993): 145–61, www.ncbi.nlm.nih.gov/pubmed/8346325.

38 **A 2013 study explored:** Anne-Marie B. Gallrein et al., "You Spy with Your Little Eye: People Are 'Blind' to Some of the Ways in Which They Are Consensually Seen by Others," *Journal of Research in Personality* 47 (April 9, 2013), doi:http://dx.doi.org/10.1016/j.jrp.2013.04.001.

40 **Jean Piaget once wrote:** Jean Piaget, *Play, Dreams and Imitation in Childhood* (New York: W. W. Norton, 1963), 224.

40 **More recently the developmental:** Daniel J. Povinelli, "The Self: Elevated in Consciousness and Extended in Time," in *The Self in Time: Developmental Perspectives*, ed. Chris Moore and Karen Lemmon (Mahwah, NJ: Lawrence Erlbaum Associates, 2001), 75–95.

41 **in 2015 the salary-comparison:** Hannah Morgan, "How to Ask for a Raise—and Actually Get It," *U.S. News & World Report*, January 14, 2015, https://money.usnews.com/money/blogs/outside-voices-careers/2015/01/14/how-to-ask-for-a-raise-and-actually-get-it.

42 **It "just happened":** Wendy D. Manning and Pamela J. Smock, "Measuring and Modeling Cohabitation: New Perspectives from Qualitative Data," *Journal of Marriage and Family* 67, no. 4 (November 2005), doi:10.1111/j.1741-3737.2005.00189.x.

42 **A 2013 study probed:** Jesse Owen, Galena K. Rhoades, and Scott M. Stanley, "Sliding Versus Deciding in Relationships: Associations with Relationship Quality, Commitment, and Infidelity," *Journal of Couple & Relationship Therapy* 12, no. 2 (April 2013), doi:10.1080/15332691.2013.779097.

43 **the "backstage" action:** Goffman, *The Presentation of Self in Everyday Life*, 111–34.

45 **by "unfulfilled expectations":** Erving Goffman, "Embarrassment and Social Organization," *American Journal of Sociology*, 62, no. 3 (November 1956): 264–71, www.d.umn.edu/cla/faculty/jhamlin/4111/Readings/GoffmanEmbarrassment.pdf.

46 **In 2016 the NPD Group:** NPD Group, "52 Percent of Millennial Smartphone Owners Use their Device for Video Calling, According to the NPD Group," news release, March 29, 2016, www.npd.com/wps/portal/npd/us

/news/press-releases/2016/52-percent-of-millennial-smartphone-owners
-use-their-device-for-video-calling-according-to-the-npd-group (accessed
September 9, 2017).

CHAPTER 3: MAKING FACES AT EMOTIONALLY INTELLIGENT MACHINES

48 **"I think that, ten years":** Raffi Khatchadourian, "We Know How You
Feel," *New Yorker*, January 19, 2015, www.newyorker.com/magazine/2015
/01/19/know-feel.

49 **According to an internal study:** David Talbot, "Startup Gets Computers
to Read Faces, Seeks Purpose Beyond Ads," *MIT Technology Review*, October 28, 2013, www.technologyreview.com/s/519656/startup-gets-computers
-to-read-faces-seeks-purpose-beyond-ads.

50 **Apple bought Emotient:** Rolfe Winkler, Daisuke Wakabayashi, and
Elizabeth Dwoskin, "Apple Buys Artificial-Intelligence Startup Emotient," *Wall Street Journal*, January 7, 2016, www.wsj.com/articles/apple
-buys-artificial-intelligence-startup-emotient-1452188715.

51 **Researchers at MIT recently:** Adam Conner-Simons, Rachel Gordon,
and CSAIL, "Wearable AI System Can Detect a Conversation's Tone,"
MIT News, February 1, 2017, http://news.mit.edu/2017/wearable-ai-can
-detect-tone-conversation-0201 (accessed September 9, 2017).

51 **Disney has just filed:** Clarisse Loughrey, "Disney Wants to Make
Theme Park Rides Controlled by Your Emotions," *Independent*, February
1, 2017, www.independent.co.uk/arts-entertainment/films/news/disney
-theme-parks-rides-disneyland-controlled-by-emotions-patent
-a7556646.html.

53 **feelings don't have fingerprints:** Lisa Feldman Barrett, *How Emotions
Are Made* (Boston: Houghton Mifflin Harcourt, 2017).

54 **Right now Affectiva's technology:** Affectiva, https://developer.affectiva
.com/metrics (accessed September 9, 2017).

54 **Since the 1960s, researchers:** Paul Ekman, E. Richard Sorenson, and
Wallace V. Friesen, "Pan-cultural Elements in Facial Displays of Emotion,"
Science 164, no. 3875 (April 4, 1969): 86–88, www.ncbi.nlm.nih.gov/pubmed
/5773719.

55 **social intelligence hypothesis:** Edward L. Thorndike, "Intelligence and
Its Uses," *Harper's*, January 1920.

55 **"not because of our":** Nicholas Epley, *Mindwise* (New York: Vintage
Books, 2014).

56 **recounts an experiment designed:** W. B. Swann Jr. and M. J. Gill, "Confidence and Accuracy in Person Perception: Do We Know What We

Think We Know About Our Relationship Partners?" *Journal of Personality and Social Psychology* 73, no. 4 (October 1997): 747–57, www.ncbi.nlm.nih .gov/pubmed/9325592.

57 **"communication hacks for the socially":** Kristin Bock, "7 Communication Hacks for the Socially Awkward," *Science of People*, November 2015, www.scienceofpeople.com/2015/11/7-communication-hacks-for-the -socially-awkward (accessed September 9, 2017).

57 **our feelings "leak":** Paul Ekman Group, "Micro Expressions," no date, www.paulekman.com/micro-expressions (accessed September 9, 2017).

58 **seven basic emotions:** Ibid.

58 **Malcolm Gladwell helped popularize:** Malcolm Gladwell, "The Naked Face," *New Yorker*, August 5, 2002, www.newyorker.com/magazine/2002 /08/05/the-naked-face.

59 **these studies have failed:** John T. Cacioppo et al., "The Psychophysiology of Emotion," in *The Handbook of Emotion*, 2nd ed., ed. Michael Lewis and Jeannette M. Haviland-Jones (New York: Guilford Press, 2000), 173–91.

59 **One study looked:** Linda A. Camras et al., "Do Infants Show Distinct Negative Facial Expressions for Fear and Anger? Emotional Expression in 11-Month-Old European American, Chinese, and Japanese Infants," *Infancy* 11, no. 2 (March 1, 2007), doi:10.1111/j.1532-7078.2007.tb00219.x.

59 **points to four meta-analyses:** Cacioppo et al., "The Psychophysiology of Emotion"; Gerhard Stemmler, "Physiological Processes During Emotion," in *The Regulation of Emotion*, ed. Pierre Philippot and Robert S. Feldman (Mahwah, NJ: Lawrence Erlbaum, 2004), 33–70; Heather C. Lench, Sarah A. Flores, and Shane W. Bench, "Discrete Emotions Predict Changes in Cognition, Judgment, Experience, Behavior, and Physiology: A Meta-analysis of Experimental Emotion Elicitations," *Psychological Bulletin* 137, no. 5 (2011): 834–55; E. H. Siegel et al., "Emotion Fingerprints or Emotion Populations? A Meta-analytic Investigation of Autonomic Features of Emotion Categories," under review.

59 **"contained the fingerprint for":** Lisa Feldman Barrett, *How Emotions Are Made*, 22.

62 **In Barrett's view, for example:** Ibid., 72.

63 **"At the earliest stage":** Angela Chen, "Neuroscientist Lisa Feldman Barrett Explains How Emotions Are Made," *Verge*, April 10, 2017, www.the verge.com/2017/4/10/15245690/how-emotions-are-made-neuroscience -lisa-feldman-barrett (accessed September 9, 2017).

64 **This is known as:** Lisa Feldman Barrett, "Emotional Intelligence Needs

a Rewrite," *Nautilus*, August 3, 2017, http://nautil.us/issue/51/limits/emo
tional-intelligence-needs-a-rewrite.

64 **In a small 2016 study:** Yasemin Erbas et al., "Feeling Me, Feeling You:
The Relation Between Emotion Differentiation and Empathic Accuracy,"
Social Psychological and Personality Science 7, no. 3 (April 1, 2016), doi:10
.1177/1948550616633504.

64 **"Even though your brain":** Barrett, "Emotional Intelligence Needs a Rewrite."

65 **One of the most useful:** Alison Wood Brooks, "Get Excited: Reapprais-
ing Pre-performance Anxiety as Excitement," *Journal of Experimental Psychology: General* 143, no. 3 (June 2014), doi:10.1037/a0035325.

66 **"You realize that if":** Chen, "Neuroscientist Lisa Feldman Barrett Explains."

CHAPTER 4: YOUR GROWING EDGE

69 **In the mid-2000s, W. Kamau Bell:** "W. Kamau Bell—Obama," *Premium
Blend*, Comedy Central, December 23, 2005, www.cc.com/video-clips
/mdnldv/stand-up-w-kamau-bell—obama (accessed September 9, 2017).

69 **very first Obama joke:** Party Ben, "The First Obama Joke on Comedy
Central, Circa 2005," *Mother Jones*, January 15, 2009, www.motherjones
.com/politics/2009/01/first-obama-joke-comedy-central-circa-2005.

70 **"That Barack Obama joke":** "W. Kamau Bell's 'Awkward Thoughts' on
Racism and Black Comedy," *Fresh Air*, WHYY, May 1, 2017.

70 **"It used to be that":** "W. Kamau Bell—Obama."

71 **"Condoleezza Rice looks"** . . . **"like your daughter":** "W. Kamau Bell's
'Awkward Thoughts.'"

71 **"You don't like Bush's":** W. Kamau Bell, *The Awkward Thoughts of W. Kamau Bell* (New York: Dutton, 2017), 175.

72 ***And* as a black man":** "W. Kamau Bell's 'Awkward Thoughts.'"

72 **During a question-and-answer:** "#10: Anna Sale, Alicia Garza & Jessi
Klein," *Kamau Right Now!*, KALW, October 28, 2016.

73 **"It got super awkward":** "W. Kamau Bell's 'Awkward Thoughts.'"

77 **PISAB has been around:** People's Institute for Survival and Beyond,
"Who We Are," www.pisab.org/who-we-are (accessed September 9, 2017).

81 **In a 2011 paper:** Robin DiAngelo, "White Fragility," *International Journal
of Critical Pedagogy* 3, no. 3 (2011): 54–70, http://www.overcomingracism
.org/resources/White-Fragility.pdf (accessed September 10, 2017).

83 **"Durably Reducing Transphobia":** David Broockman and Joshua Kalla,

"Durably Reducing Transphobia: A Field Experiment on Door-to-Door Canvassing," *Science* 352, no. 6282 (April 8, 2016), doi:10.1126/science .aad9713.

86 **called System 2 thinking:** Daniel Kahneman, *Thinking, Fast and Slow* (New York: Farrar, Straus and Giroux, 2011).

CHAPTER 5: THE AWKWARDNESS VORTEX

98 **"End the Awkward" campaign launched:** "What Not to Do . . . In a Job Interview—Scope," YouTube, September 4, 2015, www.youtube.com /watch?v=xLRM0tQmmC8 (accessed September 9, 2017).

98 **launched in 2014:** Richard Hawkes, "Let's End the Awkward," *Scope*, May 8, 2014, https://blog.scope.org.uk/2014/05/08/end-the-awkward (accessed September 9, 2017).

98 **According to Scope's own:** Hardeep Aiden and Andrea McCarthy, "Current Attitudes Towards Disabled People," research report, May 2014, www.scope.org.uk/Scope/media/Images/Publication%20Directory /Current-attitudes-towards-disabled-people.pdf?ext=.pdf (accessed September 9, 2017).

99 **named Emily Ladau:** *Words I Wheel By*, http://wordsiwheelby.com/emily -ladau-bio (accessed September 9, 2017).

101 **"Effects of Focus of Attention":** S. R. Woody, "Effects of Focus of Attention on Anxiety Levels and Social Performance of Individuals with Social Phobia," *Journal of Abnormal Psychology* 105, no. 1 (February 1996): 61–69, www.ncbi.nlm.nih.gov/pubmed/8666712.

101 **"Anxious and Egocentric":** A. R. Todd et al., "Anxious and Egocentric: How Specific Emotions Influence Perspective Taking," *Journal of Experimental Psychology: General* 144, no. 2 (April 2015): 374–91, www.ncbi.nlm .nih.gov/pubmed/25602753.

102 **A team of behavioral scientists:** Mark L. Knapp et al., "The Rhetoric of Goodbye: Verbal and Nonverbal Correlates of Human Leave-Taking," *Speech Monographs* 40, no. 3 (1973), doi:http://dx.doi.org/10.1080/036377 57309375796.

102 **A similar study in 1978:** Stuart Albert and Suzanne Kessler, "Ending Social Encounters," *Journal of Experimental Social Psychology* 14 (November 1978), doi:https://doi.org/10.1016/0022-1031(78)90048-3.

103 *Co. Design* **under the headline:** Eric Jaffe, "The Science of Politely Ending a Conversation," *Co. Design*, November 25, 2014, www.fastcodesign.com /3038950/the-science-of-politely-ending-a-conversation (accessed September 9, 2017).

NOTES

104 **One I did a while:** Science of Us, "Time Yourself: When Does Silence in a Conversation Get Awkward?" *New York*, May 13, 2014, http://nymag .com/scienceofus/2014/05/awkward-timer.html (accessed September 9, 2017).

104 **a 2011 study published:** Namkje Koudenburg, Tom Postmes, and Ernestine H. Gordijin, "Disrupting the Flow: How Brief Silences in Group Conversations Affect Social Needs," *Journal of Experimental Social Psychology* no. 2 (March 2011), doi:10.1016/j.jesp.2010.12.006.

104 **Another popular post:** Jesse Singal, "How to Deal with the Eye-Contact Awkwardness of Walking Down a Long Hallway or Street Toward Someone You Barely Know," *New York*, June 2, 2016, http://nymag.com/science ofus/2016/06/how-to-deal-with-the-eye-contact-awkwardness-of-long -hallways-and-streets.html.

105 **statements like these:** Rich Masters and Jon Maxwell, "The theory of reinvestment," *International Review of Sport and Exercise Psychology* 1, no. 2 (September 9, 2008), doi:http://dx.doi.org/10.1080/17509840802287218.

106 **too much self-focus can:** S. Beilock and R. Gray. "Why do athletes 'choke' under pressure?" in *Handbook of Sport Psychology*, 3rd ed., ed. Gershon Tenenbaum and Robert C. Eklund (Hoboken, NJ: John Wiley & Sons, 2007), 425–44.

106 **"a talk that will sound":** Erving Goffman, *The Presentation of Self in Everyday Life* (New York: Random House, 1956), 32–33.

107 **"trying to suppress your worries":** Sian Beilock, *Choke* (New York: Free Press, 2010), 184.

108 **"Just Say Hi" is an ad:** Cerebral Palsy Foundation, "'Just Say Hi' Videos," http://yourcpf.org/just-say-hi (accessed September 9, 2017).

108 **"No one's ever created":** Emily Ladau, "#JustActNormally—A Response to Cerebral Palsy Foundation's #JustSayHi Campaign," *Words I Wheel By*, October 22, 2015, http://wordsiwheelby.com/2015/10/just-act -normally (accessed September 9, 2017).

109 **Galinsky and his colleagues:** Todd et al., "Anxious and Egocentric."

109 **"When you get anxious":** Melissa Dahl, "You're Kind of Self-Centered When You're Nervous," *New York*, May 6, 2015, http://nymag.com/science ofus/2015/05/youre-kind-of-self-centered-when-youre-nervous.html (accessed September 9, 2017).

111 **If you take a group:** Robin C. Jackson, Kelly J. Ashford, and Glen Norsworthy, "Attentional Focus, Dispositional Reinvestment, and Skilled Motor Performance Under Pressure," *Journal of Sport & Exercise Psychology* 28, no. 1 (March 2006), doi:https://doi.org/10.1123/jsep.28.1.49.

CHAPTER 6: DANCE LIKE NO ONE'S WATCHING, BECAUSE NO ONE IS! EXCEPT WHEN THEY ARE

115 **six million viewers:** "Complete List of 2011–12 Season TV Show Viewership: 'Sunday Night Football' Tops, Followed by 'American Idol,' 'NCIS' & 'Dancing with the Stars,'" *TV by the Numbers*, May 24, 2012, http://tv bythenumbers.zap2it.com/1/complete-list-of-2011-12-season-tv-show -viewership-sunday-night-football-tops-followed-by-american-idol-ncis -dancing-with-the-stars/135785 (accessed September 9, 2017).

117 **"Man Freezes Up During":** WiredsetLLC, "Man Freezes Up During Pitch on ABC's *Shark Tank*," YouTube, March 15, 2012, www.youtube .com/watch?v=fcRuxfKH7zI.

117 **offered him $150,000:** Katherine P. Harvey, "Q&A: Tower Paddle Boards After 'Shark Tank,'" *San Diego Union-Tribune*, January 27, 2014, www .sandiegouniontribune.com/sdut-qa-tower-paddle-boards-after-shark -tank-2014jan27-htmlstory.html.

118 **$25 million in revenue:** Stephan Aarstol, *The Five Hour Work Day* (Austin, TX: Lioncrest, 2016), Kindle location 380.

118 **"He's killing it":** TowerPaddleBoards, "Mark Cuban and Howard Stern Talk About Tower," YouTube, March 19, 2013, www.youtube.com/watch ?v=HQ7GoKP_10A.

118 **called the spotlight effect:** Thomas Gilovich, Victoria Husted Medvec, and Kenneth Savitsky, "The Spotlight Effect in Social Judgment: An Egocentric Bias in Estimates of the Salience of One's Own Actions and Appearance," *Journal of Personality and Social Psychology* 78, no. 2 (2000), doi:10.1037//0022-3514.78.2.211.

118 **Writing about this research:** Paul Bloom, "Stop Being So Self-Conscious," *Atlantic*, December 17, 2015.

121 **Some newer research:** Erica J. Boothby, Margaret S. Clark, and John A. Bargh, "The Invisibility Cloak Illusion: People (Incorrectly) Believe They Observe Others More Than Others Observe Them," *Journal of Personality and Social Psychology* 112, no. 4 (2017), doi:http://dx.doi.org /10.1037/pspi0000082.

123 **"Although people surreptitiously":** Erica J. Boothby, "You're Too Focused on What You're Focused On," *New York Times*, April 29, 2017.

123 **in his doctoral dissertation:** Kenneth Knappe Savitsky, "Perceived Transparency and the Leakage of Emotional States: Do We Know How Little We Show?" (PhD diss., Cornell University, 1997).

123 **In another, related experiment:** Thomas Gilovich, Kenneth Savitsky,

and Victoria Husted Medvec, "The Illusion of Transparency: Biased Assessments of Others' Ability to Read One's Emotional States," *Journal of Personality and Social Psychology* 75, no. 2 (August 1998), www.ncbi.nlm .nih.gov/pubmed/9731312.

125 **"If you're an expert physicist":** Kevin Berger, "Ingenious: Nicholas Epley," *Nautilus*, August 27, 2015, http://nautil.us/issue/27/dark-matter /ingenious-nicholas-epley.

126 **detailed in a later paper:** Thomas Gilovich, Justin Kruger, and Victoria Husted Medvec, "The Spotlight Effect Revisited: Overestimating the Manifest Variability of Our Actions and Appearance," *Journal of Experimental Social Psychology* 38, no. 1 (2002), doi:10.1006/jesp.2001.1490.

127 **According to research conducted:** Thomas Gilovich and Victoria Husted Medvec, "The Experience of Regret: What, When, and Why," *Psychological Review* 102, no. 2 (1995), www.ncbi.nlm.nih.gov/pubmed/7740094.

128 **the subreddit /r/cringe:** "Man Freezes Up During Pitch on ABC's Shark Tank," Reddit.com, August 30, 2014, www.reddit.com/r/cringe /comments/2eyt7x/man_freezes_up_during_pitch_on_abcs_shark _tank (accessed September 9, 2017).

CHAPTER 7: YOUR FLAWS ARE MY PAIN

130 *New York Times* **story:** Jason Zinoman, "She Swipes Right on Tinder, and Everyone's In on the Joke," *New York Times*, June 21, 2017, www.nytimes .com/2017/06/21/arts/tinder-live-lane-moore-dating-app.html.

132 **begging a silent crowd:** Jonathan Martin and Ashley Parker, "Jeb Bush, an Also-Ran in Iowa, May Be Pivotal in New Hampshire," *New York Times*, February 3, 2016, www.nytimes.com/2016/02/04/us/politics/jeb -bush-an-also-ran-in-iowa-may-be-pivotal-in-new-hampshire.html.

133 **favorite psychology papers:** Sören Krach et al., "Your Flaws Are My Pain: Linking Empathy to Vicarious Embarrassment," *PLOS ONE*, April 13, 2011, doi:https://doi.org/10.1371/journal.pone.0018675.

139 **Some psychologists account:** Natalie Sest and Evita March, "Constructing the Cyber-troll: Psychopathy, Sadism, and Empathy," *Personality and Individual Differences* 119 (December 1, 2017), doi:https://doi.org/10.1016/j .paid.2017.06.038.

140 **cognitive empathy can be:** "Preventing Burnout with Cognitive Empathy," *Federal Practitioner* 31, no. 5 (May 2014): e1, www.mdedge.com/fed prac/article/81980/preventing-burnout-cognitive-empathy.

140 **A recent study tested:** Sest and March, "Constructing the Cyber-troll."

141 **confirmed in a follow-up study:** Laura Müller-Pinzler et al., "When

Your Friends Make You Cringe: Social Closeness Modulates Vicarious Embarrassment-Related Neural Activity," *Social Cognitive and Affective Neuroscience* 11, no. 3 (March 2016), doi:10.1093/scan/nsv130.

141 **When I read a piece published:** Hayley Phelan, "When You Love Your Friend But Hate Her Social-Media Presence," *The Cut*, May 17, 2017, www.thecut.com/2017/05/social-media-friendship-impact.html (accessed September 9, 2017).

141 **in a 1950 essay:** A. A. Phillips, *A.A. Phillips on the Cultural Cringe* (Melbourne, Australia: Melbourne University Publishing, 2006).

142 **"and so all too often":** Jenna Guillaume, "How I Realised I'm a Bogan, and Why You Probably Are Too," *BuzzFeed*, January 26, 2017, www.buzzfeed.com/jennaguillaume/australian-culture-does-exist-and-its-bogan?utm_term=.mf2e13PgGg#.hmKpMdrPgP (accessed September 9, 2017).

142 **weeks after Trump's inauguration:** Jeffrey Frank, "The Embarrassment of President Trump," *New Yorker*, February 14, 2017, www.newyorker.com/news/daily-comment/the-embarrassment-of-president-trump.

142 **businesses a "national embarrassment":** Emily Jane Fox, "Donald Trump's Plan to Keep His Businesses Is a National Embarrassment," *Vanity Fair*, January 11, 2017, www.vanityfair.com/news/2017/01/donald-trumps-plan-to-keep-his-businesses-is-a-national-embarrassment.

142 *Paste* **magazine published:** Jacob Weindling, "The 8 Most Embarrassing Moments from Trump's *ONE DAY* at NATO," *Paste*, May 26, 2017, www.pastemagazine.com/articles/2017/05/donald-trumps-8-most-embarrassing-moments-from-his.html.

142 **the *Nation* used that:** Joshua Holland, "Our Embarrassment in Chief's International Trip Is No Laughing Matter," *The Nation*, May 23, 2017, www.thenation.com/article/embarrassment-chiefs-international-trip-no-laughing-matter.

142 **a poll from the McClatchy:** Marist Poll, "2/23: Trump Approval Rating at 41% . . . Nearly Six in Ten Call Trump's Conduct 'Embarrassing,'" news release, February 23, 2017, http://maristpoll.marist.edu/223-trump-approval-rating-at-41-nearly-six-in-ten-call-trumps-conduct-embarrassing (accessed September 9, 2017).

143 **psychologist John Gottman:** Ellie Lisitsa, "The Four Horsemen: Contempt," Gottman Institute, May 13, 2013, www.gottman.com/blog/the-four-horsemen-contempt (accessed September 9, 2017).

143 **Krach sends me the latest paper:** D. Laneri et al., "Mindfulness Meditation Regulates Anterior Insula Activity During Empathy for Social Pain," *Human Brain Mapping* 38, no. 8 (August 2017), doi:10.1002/hbm.23646.

143 **the sociologist Neil Gross:** Neil Gross, "Does Trump Embarrass You?" *New York Times,* June 16, 2017, www.nytimes.com/2017/06/16/opinion /sunday/does-trump-embarrass-you.html.

145 **Philippe Rochat has theorized:** Philippe Rochat, *Others in Mind: Social Origins of Self-Consciousness* (New York: Cambridge University Press, 2010), 114.

146 **report on "teen werewolves":** Fernando Alfonso III, "The Dark Side of Reddit's Cringe Culture," *Daily Dot,* March 3, 2014, www.dailydot.com /irl/reddit-cringe-cringepics-bullying (accessed September 9, 2017).

147 **wrote on a post titled:** "Taylor Swift Fans Have a Message for Her as She Walks In," Reddit, February 8, 2015, www.reddit.com/r/cringe /comments/2v6gev/taylor_swift_fans_have_a_message_for_her_as_she (accessed September 9, 2017).

148 **"telling a bad joke":** "I Believe That r/cringe and r/cringepics Does Nothing but Perpetuate Cyberbullying. CMV," Reddit, May 20, 2013, www.reddit.com/r/changemyview/comments/1ep88w/i_believe_that _rcringe_and_rcringepics_does (accessed September 9, 2017).

148 **"Imagine having to be":** "What Makes You Beautiful Screamo," Reddit, February 25, 2014, www.reddit.com/r/cringe/comments/1yxqcu/what_makes _you_beautiful_screamo (accessed September 10, 2017).

148 **"You look . . . like Beavis":** Alfonso, "The Dark Side of Reddit's Cringe Culture."

149 **"I know exactly how":** "Boom Goes the Dynamite," Reddit, September 1, 2017, www.reddit.com/r/cringe/comments/6xe771/boom_goes_the _dynamite/?limit=500 (accessed September 10, 2017).

149 **"Having social anxiety":** "The Original Cringe. It Hurts Bad," Reddit, March 19, 2013, www.reddit.com/r/cringe/comments/1amd99/the_original _cringe_it_hurts_bad/?limit=500 (accessed September 10, 2017).

150 **a children's tennis instructor:** "'That's Great! He's Real!'" Reddit, January 29, 2017, www.reddit.com/r/cringe/comments/5qw7qy/thats_great _hes_real (accessed September 10, 2017).

CHAPTER 8: CRINGE ATTACKS

153 **actual dictionary definition:** *Merriam-Webster's Collegiate Dictionary,* 11th ed., s.v. "cringe," www.merriam-webster.com/dictionary/cringe.

155 **sixty or so people:** Linda Rodriguez McRobbie, "Total Recall: The People Who Never Forget," *Guardian,* February 8, 2017, www.theguardian .com/science/2017/feb/08/total-recall-the-people-who-never-forget.

155 **a condition discovered in 2006:** E. S. Parker, L. Cahill, and J. L.

McGaugh, "A Case of Unusual Autobiographical Remembering," *Neurocase* 12, no. 1 (February 2006), doi:10.1080/13554790500473680.

156 **example of "persistence":** Dean Burnett, *Your Brain Is an Idiot* (New York: W. W. Norton, 2016).

156 **"You might be wandering":** Ibid., 62.

157 **"computer that kept opening":** Ibid., 34.

157 **she calls "mind pops":** Ferris Jabr, "Mind-Pops: Psychologists Begin to Study an Unusual Form of Proustian Memory," *Scientific American*, May 23, 2012, www.scientificamerican.com/article/mind-pops.

157 **Kvavilashvili and her colleagues:** L. Kvavilashvili and S. Schlagman, "Eliciting Involuntary Autobiographical Memories in the Laboratory: Developing a New Method of Investigation," lecture, International Conference of the Society of Applied Research on Memory and Cognition, University of Aberdeen, July 2003.

159 **Studies have shown that self-defining:** Joseph M. Fitzgerald, "The Distribution of Self-Narrative Memories in Younger and Older Adults: Elaborating the Self-Narrative Hypothesis," *Aging, Neuropsychology, and Cognition* 3, no. 3 (1996), doi:http://dx.doi.org/10.1080/13825589608256626.

161 **In a 2015 study:** Ekaterina Denkova, Sanda Dolcos, and Florin Dolcos, "Neural Correlates of 'Distracting' from Emotion During Autobiographical Recollection," *Social Cognitive and Affective Neuroscience* 10, no. 2 (February 1, 2015), doi:https://doi.org/10.1093/scan/nsu039.

161 **"Sometimes we dwell on":** Beckman Institute, "New Study Suggests a Better Way to Deal with Bad Memories," news release, April 18, 2014, https://beckman.illinois.edu/news/2014/04/emotion-regulation-strategy (accessed September 10, 2017).

163 **"Some people roll":** Mark R. Leary et al., "Self-Compassion and Reactions to Unpleasant Self-Relevant Events: The Implications of Treating Oneself Kindly," *Personality Processes and Individual Differences* 92, no. 5 (2007), doi:10.1037/0022-3514.92.5.887.

163 **Since about 2003:** Kristin D. Neff, "Self-Compassion: An Alternative Conceptualization of a Healthy Attitude Toward Oneself," *Self and Identity* 2, no. 2 (2003) doi:http://dx.doi.org/10.1080/15298860309032.

164 **Neff's research suggests:** Kristin D. Neff, Ya-Ping Hsieh, and Kullaya Dijitterat, "Self-Compassion, Achievement Goals, and Coping with Academic Failure," *Self and Identity* 4, no. 3 (2005), doi:10.1080/13576500444000317.

164 **In one relevant study, Neff:** Ibid.

165 **In a weirder study:** Leary et al., "Self-Compassion and Reactions to Unpleasant Self-Relevant Events."

167 **In her 2011 book:** Kristin Neff, *Self-Compassion: The Proven Power of Being Kind to Yourself* (New York: William Morrow, 2011).

168 **"a full seven seconds":** Leah Beckmann, "Just Give It 7 Seconds," *Jezebel*, June 5, 2017, https://jezebel.com/just-give-it-7-seconds-1795766407.

169 **This three-questions advice:** Leary et al., "Self-Compassion and Reactions to Unpleasant Self-Relevant Events."

169 **"when we fail, it's not":** Olga Khazan, "Why Self-Compassion Works Better Than Self-Esteem," *The Atlantic*, May 6, 2016, www.theatlantic.com/health/archive/2016/05/why-self-compassion-works-better-than-self-esteem/481473.

171 **"he is nobody.":** C. S. Lewis, *Mere Christianity* (New York: HarperCollins, 2009), 128.

171 **Humility is a misunderstood:** Wright spoke about this at a talk I attended at the University of Louisville's Conference on Neglected Emotions in April 2017.

171 **"occupy a rightful space":** Alan Morinis, *Everyday Holiness* (Boulder, CO: Shambhala, 2008), 45.

172 **"This is not to say":** Thomas Nadelhoffer et al., "Some Varieties of Humility Worth Wanting," *Journal of Moral Philosophy* 14, no. 2 (2016), doi:10.1163/17455243-46810056.

172 **research on intellectual humility:** Cindy Lamothe, "How 'Intellectual Humility' Can Make You a Better Person," *New York*, February 3, 2017, http://nymag.com/scienceofus/2017/02/how-intellectual-humility-can-make-you-a-better-person.html (accessed September 10, 2017).

172 **"humility is a corrective":** Jennifer Cole Wright et al., "The Psychological Significance of Humility," *Journal of Positive Psychology* 12, no. 1 (April 22, 2016), doi:http://dx.doi.org/10.1080/17439760.2016.1167940.

173 **among bar patrons:** RIM Dunbar, Anna Marriott, and NDC Duncan, "Human Conversational Behavior," *Human Nature*, 8, no. 3 (September 1997): 231–46, doi:https://doi.org/10.1007/BF02912493.

174 **the more questions you ask:** K. Huang et al., "It Doesn't Hurt to Ask: Question-Asking Increases Liking," *Journal of Personality and Social Psychology* 113, no. 3 (September 2017), doi:10.1037/pspi0000097.

CHAPTER 9: AWKWARD SILENCES AT THE OFFICE

177 **On this particular day:** Alison Green, "My Coworkers Heard My Roommates Having Sex While I Was on a Conference Call," *Ask a Manager*, March 31, 2014, www.askamanager.org/2014/03/my-coworkers-heard-my -roommates-having-sex-while-i-was-on-a-conference-call.html (accessed September 10, 2017).

178 **Since 2007 Green:** Melissa Dahl, "If You Have an Awkward Work Problem, This Is the Person to Ask About It," *New York*, May 18, 2016, http:// nymag.com/scienceofus/2016/05/if-you-have-an-awkward-work -problem-this-is-the-person-to-ask-about-it.html (accessed September 10, 2017).

181 **Consider a classic 1960s:** Julie Beck, "How Uncertainty Fuels Anxiety," *Atlantic*, March 15, 2017.

181 **Other research has suggested:** David J. Linden, *Touch: The Science of the Hand, Heart, and Mind* (New York: Penguin Books, 2015).

182 **called a "need-for-closure" scale:** Donna M. Webster and Arie W. Kruglanski, "Individual Differences in Need for Cognitive Closure," *Journal of Personality and Social Psychology* 67, no. 6 (December 1994): 1049–62, http:// psycnet.apa.org/doiLanding?doi=10.1037%2F0022-3514.67.6.1049.

182 **But other, related research:** Jamie Holmes, *Nonsense: The Power of Not Knowing* (New York: Crown, 2015).

184 **Green's advice worked:** Alison Green, "Update: My Coworkers Heard My Roommates Having Sex While I Was on a Conference Call," *Ask a Manager*, April 2, 2014, www.askamanager.org/2014/04/update-my-coworkers-heard -my-roommates-having-sex-while-i-was-on-a-conference-call.html (accessed September 10, 2017).

187 **Gallup Q12 Employee Engagement:** James K. Harter et al., "Q12 Meta-Analysis," Gallup Consulting, 2008, https://strengths.gallup.com/private /resources/q12meta-analysis_flyer_gen_08%2008_bp.pdf (accessed September 10, 2017).

188 **"Gossip and Ostracism Promote":** Matthew Feinberg, Robb Willer, and Michael Schultz, "Gossip and Ostracism Promote Cooperation in Groups," *Psychological Science* 25, no. 3 (January 24, 2014): 656–64, http://journals .sagepub.com/doi/abs/10.1177/0956797613510184.

189 **work friendships are especially:** Mark Vernon, *The Meaning of Friendship* (New York: Palgrave Macmillan, 2010), 15.

190 **In one of his later:** Erving Goffman, *Frame Analysis* (Boston: Northeastern University Press, 1986), 20.

NOTES

190 **"The name was familiar"**: Joshua Ferris, *Then We Came to the End* (New York: Little, Brown and Company, 2007), 358.

190 **"At times we were so"**: Peter Kiefer, "Your Boss Is Not Your Friend," *MEL*, June 10, 2016, https://melmagazine.com/your-boss-is-not-your-friend -9831421dfe93.

191 **"multifaceted relationships that superimpose"**: Jessica R. Methot et al., "Are Workplace Friendships a Mixed Blessing? Exploring Tradeoffs of Multiplex Relationships and Their Associations with Job Performance," *Personnel Psychology* 69, no. 2 (November 5, 2015), doi:10.1111 /peps.12109.

191 **headline from *Forbes***: J. Maureen Henderson, "3 Reasons Workplace Friendships Are a Lie," *Forbes*, May 20, 2011, www.forbes.com/sites/jmaureen henderson/2011/05/20/3-reasons-workplace-friendships-are-a-lie /#206ad43558c.

194 **awkward-silence study mentioned**: Namkje Koudenburg, Tom Postmes, and Ernestine H. Gordijin, "Disrupting the Flow: How Brief Silences in Group Conversations Affect Social Needs," *Journal of Experimental Social Psychology* 47, no. 2 (2011), doi:10.1016/j.jesp.2010.12.006.

194 **study of Japanese speakers**: Haru Yamada, "Yappari, as I Thought: Listener Talk in Japanese Communication," *Global Advances in Business and Communication Conference & Journal* 4, no. 1 (2015), article 3, http://commons .emich.edu/cgi/viewcontent.cgi?article=1052&context=gabc.

195 **"give you an opening"**: Alison Green, "When No One Gives You an Opening to Negotiate Salary," *Ask a Manager*, March 13, 2017, www.aska manager.org/2017/03/when-no-one-gives-you-an-opening-to-negotiate -salary.html.

195 **One 2012 Harvard Kennedy**: Andreas Leibbrandt and John A. List, "Do Women Avoid Salary Negotiations? Evidence from a Large Scale Natural Field Experiment," NBER working paper no. 18511, Harvard Kennedy School, 2012, www.nber.org/papers/w18511.

196 **In one 2014 Columbia**: Daniel R. Ames and Abbie S. Wazlawek, "Pushing in the Dark: Causes and Consequences of Limited Self-Awareness for Interpersonal Assertiveness," *Personality and Social Psychology Bulletin* 40, no. 6 (2014), doi:10.1177/0146167214525474.

196 **"The first step is to be"**: Katie Donovan, "Tactic: Silence Is Golden When Negotiating," Equal Pay Negotiations, 2011, https://equalpaynegotiations .com/2011/04/19/tactic-silence-is-golden-when-negotiating (accessed September 10, 2017).

197 **try to "use silence"**: Anthony L. Back et al., "Compassionate Silence in

the Patient-Clinician Encounter: A Contemplative Approach," *Journal of Palliative Medicine* 12, no. 12 (December 2009), doi:10.1089/jpm.2009.0175.

197 **In experiments researchers:** Holmes, *Nonsense*, 54.

CHAPTER 10: LAUGHING AT IMAGINARY TUMBLERS OF SPILLED WHISKEY

201 **journalist Jamie Holmes:** Jamie Holmes, *Nonsense: The Power of Not Knowing* (New York: Crown, 2015), 174.

203 **In early 2017, the Second City:** University of Chicago Booth School of Business, "New Partnership with Second City Works and the University of Chicago Booth School of Business to Study How Improvisation Can Promote Better Workplace Dynamics," news release, January 31, 2017, https://newschicagobooth.uchicago.edu/newsroom/new-partnership-second-city-works-and-university-chicago-booth-school-business-study-how (accessed September 10, 2017).

203 **"I don't think even five":** "Nicholas Epley, the Center for Decision Research—Behavioral Science Meets Improvisation," *Getting to Yes, And,* January 31, 2017, http://secondcityworks.com/nicholas-epley-center-decision-research-behavioral-science-meets-improvisation (accessed September 10, 2017).

205 **In 2013 University of Pennsylvania:** Gordon Bermant, "Working With(out) a Net: Improvisational Theater and Enhanced Well-being," *Frontiers in Psychology* 4 (2013), doi:10.3389/fpsyg.2013.00929.

206 **Two young women exit:** PERBLU, "In Vivo Exposure," YouTube, February 8, 2012, www.youtube.com/watch?v=90xMSaNqjEw&feature=youtube.

207 **a "disorder of lost opportunities":** Murray B. Stein and Jack M. Gorman, "Unmasking Social Anxiety Disorder," *Journal of Psychiatry & Neuroscience* 26, no. 3 (May 2001): 185–89, www.ncbi.nlm.nih.gov/pmc/articles/PMC1408304.

207 **"there are these social standards":** Melissa Dahl, "The Best Way to Get Over Social Anxiety Is by Embarrassing Yourself in Public," *New York,* November 14, 2016, http://nymag.com/scienceofus/2016/11/how-to-get-over-social-anxiety.html (accessed September 10, 2017). (This section has been adapted, with permission, from that *New York* article.)

209 **25 percent of those:** Chapman University, "America's Top Fears 2016: Chapman University Survey of American Fears," October 11, 2016, https://blogs.chapman.edu/wilkinson/2016/10/11/americas-top-fears-2016 (accessed September 10, 2017).

212 **In a 2013 paper:** Angela Fang et al., "Social Mishap Exposures for Social

Anxiety Disorder: An Important Treatment Ingredient," *Cognitive and Behavioral Practices* 20, no. 2 (May 1, 2013), doi:10.1016/j.cbpra.2012.05.003.

216 **"the world's greatest discoveries"**: Tina Fey, *Bossypants* (New York: Little, Brown and Company, 2011), 82–83.

CHAPTER 11: THE AWKWARD AGE, PART 2

232 **"my name is Dave"**: David Nadelberg, *Mortified: Real Words. Real People. Real Pathetic.* (New York: Gallery Books, 2006), 273.

236 **In the mid-2000s, psychologists:** L. K. Libby, R. P. Eibach, and T. Gilovich, "Here's Looking at Me: The Effect of Memory Perspective on Assessments of Personal Change," *Journal of Personality and Social Psychology* 88, no. 1 (2005), doi:10.1037/0022-3514.88.1.50.

238 **Studies on so-called:** E. Kross et al., "Self-Talk as a Regulatory Mechanism: How You Do It Matters," *Journal of Personality and Social Psychology* 106, no. 2 (February 2014), doi:10.1037/a0035173.

238 **"As an outsider, it's relatively"**: Kristin Wong, "The Benefits of Talking to Yourself," *New York Times*, June 8, 2017, www.nytimes.com/2017/06/08/smarter-living/benefits-of-talking-to-yourself-self-talk.html.

240 **"Jazz Guys account for"**: Amy Rose Spiegel, "What's the Deal with Jazz?" *BuzzFeed*, February 14, 2013, www.buzzfeed.com/verymuchso/whats-the-deal-with-jazz?utm_term=.xsnq4qYdQd#.vujX9XwO6O.

241 **"My editor was like"**: Will Oremus, "Why a Young Writer Secretly Deleted Her Own BuzzFeed Post," *Slate*, August 15, 2014, www.slate.com/blogs/future_tense/2014/08/15/what_s_the_deal_with_jazz_why_a_buzzfeed_writer_secretly_deleted_her_post.html (accessed September 10, 2017).

241 **"rats in pants"**: Sci Curious (@scicurious), "Every so often I go back to the study on rats in pants. http://ow.ly/eCsR3043zih The study remains fabulous. The writing makes me CRINGE," Twitter, September 9, 2016, 4:30 a.m., https://twitter.com/scicurious/status/774253651342856193.

241 **"We find mistakes"**: Roger Rosenblatt, "To a Writer, a Body of Work Is a Taunt," *New York Times*, July 25, 2016, www.nytimes.com/2016/07/31/books/review/to-a-writer-a-body-of-work-is-a-taunt.html.

242 **"There are only 25"**: Jessica Contrera, "13, Right Now," *Washington Post*, May 25, 2016, www.washingtonpost.com/sf/style/2016/05/25/13-right-now-this-is-what-its-like-to-grow-up-in-the-age-of-likes-lols-and-longing/?utm_term=.596d2bded31e.

243 **"Silly music tastes"**: Nathan Jurgenson, "'Glad I Didn't Have Facebook

in High School!'" *Cyborgology*, November 26, 2012, https://thesociety pages.org/cyborgology/2012/11/26/glad-i-didnt-have-facebook-in-high -school.

243 **"We have to start believing"**: "Glenn Beck: What You Do Will Be a Pivot Point," *On Being*, Public Radio Exchange, May 11, 2017.

244 **"part of social reality"**: Lisa Feldman Barrett, *How Emotions Are Made* (Boston: Houghton Mifflin Harcourt, 2017), 190–191.

245 **"There's so much in"**: Joe Berkowitz, "Sarah Silverman: 'If You Don't Look at Your Old Sh*t and Cringe, You're Not Growing,'" *Fast Company*, May 31, 2017, www.fastcompany.com/40425332/sarah-silverman-if-you -dont-look-at-your-old-sht-and-cringe-youre-not-growing.

245 **"how you go pro"**: Amy Rose Spiegel, *Action: A Book about Sex* (New York: Grand Central Publishing, 2016), 182.

INDEX

INDEX

INDEX

INDEX

INDEX

INDEX